Fodor's 94 Santa Fe, Taos, Albuquerque

Ron Butler

To my daughter, Alexandra.
They'll love you in Santa Fe.

Fodor's Travel Publications, Inc.
New York • Toronto • London • Sydney • Auckland

Copyright © 1994
by Fodor's Travel Publications, Inc.

Fodor's is a trademark of Fodor's Travel Publications, Inc.

All rights reserved under International and Pan-American Copyright Conventions. Published in the United States by Fodor's Travel Publications, Inc., a subsidiary of Random House, Inc., New York, and simultaneously in Canada by Random House of Canada Limited, Toronto. Distributed by Random House, Inc., New York.

No maps, illustrations, or other portions of this book may be reproduced in any form without written permission from the publisher.

ISBN 0-679-02547-2

"New Mexico" is taken from *Phoenix: The Posthumous Papers of D. H. Lawrence* by D. H. Lawrence and edited by Edward McDonald. Copyright © 1936 by Frieda Lawrence, renewed © 1964 by The Estate of Frieda Lawrence Ravagli. Used by permission of Viking Penguin, a division of Penguin Books USA Inc. and Laurence Pollinger Ltd.

Fodor's Santa Fe, Taos, Albuquerque

Editor: Craig Seligman
Editorial Contributors: Valerie Martone, Marcy Pritchard
Creative Director: Fabrizio LaRocca
Cartographer: David Lindroth
Illustrator: Karl Tanner
Cover Photograph: Scott Lynn Riley

Design: Vignelli Associates

About the Author

Ron Butler, who is based in Tucson, Arizona, has held editorial staff positions on *Esquire*, *True*, and *Penthouse* magazines. His articles have appeared in such publications as *Travel & Leisure*, *Travel Holiday*, and *Ladies' Home Journal*, and his books include *Esquire's Guide to Modern Etiquette* (Lippincott) and *The Best of the Old West* (Texas Monthly Press).

Special Sales

Fodor's Travel Publications are available at special discounts for bulk purchases (100 copies or more) for sales promotions or premiums. Special editions, including personalized covers, excerpts of existing guides, and corporate imprints, can be created in large quantities for special needs. For more information, write to Special Marketing, Fodor's Travel Publications, 201 E. 50th Street, New York, NY 10022, or call 1–800–800–3246. Inquiries from the United Kingdom should be sent to Fodor's Travel Publications, 20 Vauxhall Bridge Road, London, England SW1V 2SA.

MANUFACTURED IN THE UNITED STATES OF AMERICA
10 9 8 7 6 5 4 3 2 1

Contents

Maps

Foreword

Travel writers never truly appreciate the diligence and support of regional state and city tourist offices and others they meet along the way until they've returned from the trail, so to speak, and in hindsight recall all the help and assistance they've received. So I wish particularly to thank Sharon Maloof and Mike Pitel of the New Mexico Department of Tourism; Judy Framan, vice-president of the New Mexico Bed & Breakfast Association, and her husband, Elliot; Charlotte Silva, managing director of the Inn of the Governors in Santa Fe; John Meigs of Fort Meigs in San Patricio; and Saki Karavas, owner and genial host of the historic, legendary Hotel La Fonda de Taos—only a few of the many friendly people of New Mexico who help make the West such a warm place.

While every care has been taken to ensure the accuracy of the information in this guide, the passage of time will always bring change, and consequently the publisher cannot accept responsibility for errors that may occur.

All prices and opening times quoted here are based on information supplied to us at press time. Hours and admission fees may change, however, and the prudent traveler will avoid inconvenience by calling ahead.

Fodor's wants to hear about your travel experiences, both pleasant and unpleasant. When a hotel or restaurant fails to live up to its billing, let us know and we will investigate the complaint and revise our entries where the facts warrant it.

Send your letters to the editors of Fodor's Travel Publications, 201 E. 50th Street, New York, NY 10022.

Highlights '94 and Fodor's Choice

Highlights '94

Talk about trendy. Santa Fe was just named in an extensive reader survey conducted by *Condé Nast Traveler* as the *best* city in the world, outshining such longtime stalwarts as Venice, Paris, London, and San Francisco. Amazingly, Santa Fe wasn't even listed among the selected candidate cities; it was a write-in choice. "A soul-enchanting landscape, a well-endowed cultural life, elegant hotels, and some of the country's finest restaurants have made Santa Fe a mecca for the discriminating traveler. It represents Southwest sophistication at its best," said editor-in-chief Thomas Wallace in making the announcement. The resulting publicity, including wire service stories, has brought even more new visitors to the "City Different." All the attention has its down side as well, though. The median price of a single-family home in Santa Fe has climbed to $135,000—37% above the national average. Real estate taxes are soaring. Many people born in the former Spanish colonial capital can no longer afford to live there. Such is the price of success.

Accolades for New Mexico are coming from everywhere. The **Mabel Dodge Luhan House,** now a bed-and-breakfast inn in Taos, was just named a National Historic Landmark by the U.S. Department of the Interior. Mabel Dodge Luhan was an heiress and longtime Taos resident, a collector of famous artists and writers. It was she who brought D. H. Lawrence to Taos with his wife, Frieda. Lawrence lived there for 22 months over a three-year period, writing several important works during that time, and although Taos has long attracted artists and writers, none has had a more profound impact on the community.

"I won't say we can't keep them on the shelves," says Susanna Tvede, manager of the **Taos Book Shop,** the oldest bookstore in New Mexico, "but Lawrence has always been a big seller here. We move hundreds of copies each year—*Lady Chatterly's Lover, The Virgin and the Gypsy, The Plumed Serpent,* and of course the short stories. The out-of-print books are in particularly big demand—*Mornings in Mexico,* for instance, which he wrote here."

Last year the 1,000-year-old **Taos Pueblo** was designated a World Heritage Site—the United Nations' equivalent of a National Historic Landmark. It is New Mexico's second (the other is **Chaco Canyon**), and one of only 17 in the entire United States. The news delights opponents of the long-discussed and much-disputed plan to build a commercial airport in Taos. Jets landing and taking off in proximity to the Taos Pueblo would surely rattle its fragile adobe walls into a pile of rubble. No airport.

Meanwhile, a U.S. Department of Commerce study ranked both Albuquerque and Santa Fe second nationally (behind Philadelphia) as historical, cultural, and minority centers, praising them for "capitalizing on their Hispanic and Native American heritage by devising events that enhance their appeal."

Ottmar Liebert, whose classical guitar is flavored with jazz and pop influences, sold over half a million copies of his *Nouveau Flamenco,* much of its appeal riding on the popularity of his song "Santa Fe." Born in Cologne, Germany, to a Chinese-German father and a Hungarian mother, Liebert is a longtime Santa Fe resident who has often appeared in local clubs. **R.C. Gorman,** the globe-trotting Navajo artist who lives in Taos—he virtually commutes between there and Japan, where his work is in big demand—continues as a larger-than-life goodwill ambassador for New Mexico. **Allan Houser,** a Chiricahua Apache and one of America's premier sculptors, was honored last August with the opening of the **Allan Houser Sculpture Garden,** part of the new Museum of the Institute of American Indian Arts, just east of the Santa Fe Plaza in the renovated former Federal Post Office.

Good food remains another strong incentive for visiting New Mexico. Santa Fe's trendy **Coyote Cafe** has won numerous accolades, the most recent of them being the James Beard Awards nomination as the Best Southwestern Restaurant. At the same time, owner-chef Mark Miller was inducted into the prestigious Fine Dining Hall of Fame during the National Restaurant Association Convention in Chicago. Success breeds success. Miller has opened a Coyote Cafe clone called the Red Sage in Washington, D.C. In Taos, the **Villa Fontana** was named one of the 10 "best of the best" Italian restaurants in the U.S. by Italian food critic Luigi Veronelli in his *I Ristoranti di Veronelli U.S.A.* guide. The just-published *Rancho de Chimayo Cookbook* (Harvard Common Press, Boston), written by Santa Fe authors Cheryl Alters Jamison and Bill Jamison, sold out its first printing within weeks of its release, and the presses are rolling again. The book celebrates the popular Rancho de Chimayo restaurant, which is considered the best in the state for authentic New Mexican cuisine, using recipes over 300 years old. Meanwhile, **Woolworth's** exercised its final five-year renewal option on the lease of its store on the Santa Fe Plaza, ensuring **Frito Pies** for hungry customers at least through 1998.

Fodor's Choice

No two people will agree on what makes a perfect vacation, but it can be fun and helpful to know what others think. We hope you'll have a chance to experience some of Fodor's Choices yourself while visiting New Mexico. For detailed information on individual entries, see the relevant sections of this guidebook.

Lodging

Inn of the Anasazi, Santa Fe (*Very Expensive*)

Inn of the Governors, Santa Fe (*Expensive*)

Inn of the Animal Tracks, Santa Fe (*Moderate*)

Taos Inn, Taos (*Expensive*)

American Artists Gallery House, Taos (*Moderate*)

Hotel La Fonda de Taos, Taos (*Moderate*)

Hyatt Regency Albuquerque, Albuquerque (*Expensive*)

Elaine's, A Bed and Breakfast, Albuquerque (*Moderate*)

La Posada de Albuquerque, Albuquerque (*Moderate*)

Inn of the Mountain Gods, Mescalero (*Expensive*)

Scenic Drives

The High Road to Taos (the old road linking Santa Fe and Taos)

The Enchanted Circle (90-mile loop from Taos through canyon and alpine country, with a few colorful mining towns thrown in)

Route 66, America's most nostalgic highway, which includes a colorful stretch that now constitutes Albuquerque's Central Avenue

Turquoise Trail (the old route between Albuquerque and Santa Fe)

Historic Buildings

Museum of Fine Arts, Santa Fe

Palace of the Governors, Santa Fe

Santuario de Chimayo, Chimayo

San Francisco de Asis Church, Ranchos de Taos

Taos Pueblo, Taos

Ernie Pyle Memorial Library, Albuquerque

Romantic Sites

Any spot beside the road under a cottonwood tree during chile-harvesting season (August–September), where enterprising farmers have set up tumble dryer–like roasting machines to roast bagfuls of freshly picked chiles for sale to passing motorists.

Santa Fe at Christmastime, with *farolitos* (tiny lanterns) glowing everywhere

Taos Book Shop, Taos (many serious romances, as in books, have begun in bookstores)

Courtyard in the Millicent Rogers Museum (Taos) with the Native American maiden statue by R. C. Gorman

Outdoor hot tubs at Ten Thousand Waves, Santa Fe

Puye Cliff Dwellings, Santa Clara Pueblo, near Santa Fe

Taste Treats

Hatch chiles

Sopapillas, the light, fluffy pastry bread served warm with honey during spicy Mexican meals to help neutralize the hotness

Indian fry bread (American cousin of sopaipillas, available at the pueblos and wherever Native American food is featured)

Chilaquilese con chorizo (warm cheese dip with bits of Mexican sausage and chile)

Blue corn tortillas

Red chile burritos

Green chile salsa

Restaurants

The Compound, Santa Fe (*Expensive*)

La Tertulia, Santa Fe (*Moderate*)

Rancho de Chimayo, Chimayo (*Moderate*)

El Patio de Taos, Taos (*Expensive*)

Chile Connection, Taos (*Moderate*)

Antiquity Restaurant, Albuquerque (*Moderate*)

Casa Vieja, Albuquerque (*Moderate*)

New Mexico

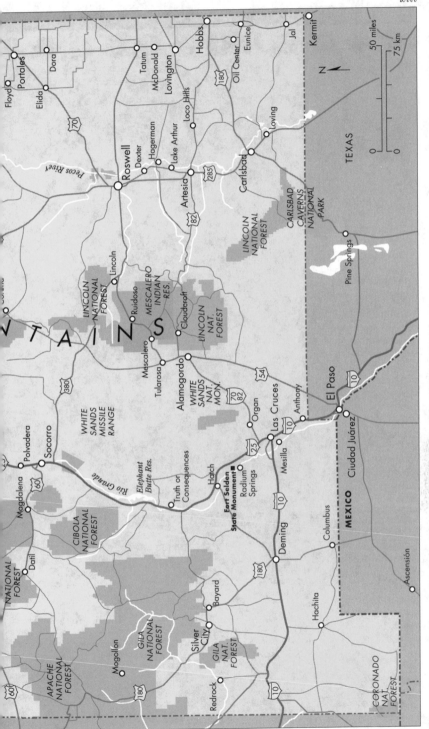

N

50 miles
75 km
0
0

TEXAS

Kermit

Jal

Eunice

Oil Center

Hobbs

Lovington

McDonald

Tatum

Floyd

Portales

Dora

Elida

70

Pine Springs

Loving

Carlsbad

CARLSBAD CAVERNS NATIONAL PARK

LINCOLN NATIONAL FOREST

Loco Hills

180

Hagerman

Lake Arthur

Dexter

Roswell

Pecos River

Artesia

285

82

Lincoln

LINCOLN NATIONAL FOREST

Ruidoso

MESCALERO INDIAN RES.

Cloudcroft

LINCOLN NAT. FOREST

NTAINS

Mescalero

Tularosa

Alamogordo

WHITE SANDS NAT. MON.

70 82

Organ

54

El Paso

10

Ciudad Juárez

MEXICO

Anthony

Las Cruces

380

WHITE SANDS MISSILE RANGE

Polvadera

Socorro

60

Magdalena

Datil

NATIONAL FOREST

CIBOLA NATIONAL FOREST

Rio Grande

Elephant Butte Res.

Truth or Consequences

Hatch

25

Mesilla

10

Fort Selden State Monument

Radium Springs

10

Columbus

Ascensión

Deming

180

Hachita

Bayard

Silver City

GILA NAT. FOREST

GILA NATIONAL FOREST

Mogollon

60

APACHE NATIONAL FOREST

180

Redrock

10

CORONADO NAT. FOREST

World Time Zones

Numbers below vertical bands relate each zone to Greenwich Mean Time (0 hrs.).
Local times frequently differ from these general indications,
as indicated by light-face numbers on map.

Algiers, **29**

Anchorage, **3**

Athens, **41**

Auckland, **1**

Baghdad, **46**

Bangkok, **50**

Beijing, **54**

Berlin, **34**

Bogotá, **19**

Budapest, **37**

Buenos Aires, **24**

Caracas, **22**

Chicago, **9**

Copenhagen, **33**

Dallas, **10**

Delhi, **48**

Denver, **8**

Djakarta, **53**

Dublin, **26**

Edmonton, **7**

Hong Kong, **56**

Honolulu, **2**

Istanbul, **40**

Jerusalem, **42**

Johannesburg, **44**

Lima, **20**

Lisbon, **28**

London (Greenwich), **27**

Los Angeles, **6**

Madrid, **38**

Manila, **57**

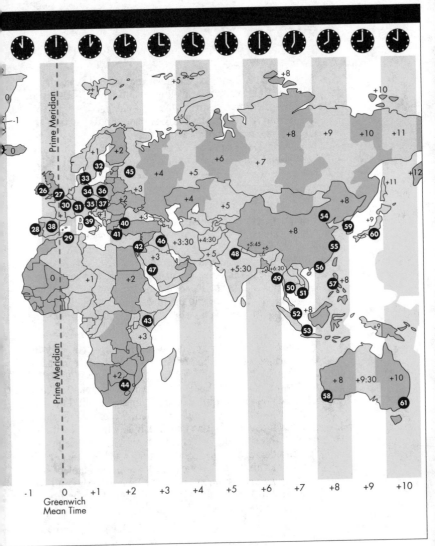

Introduction

I t was winter, a good 25 years ago, when I first visited New Mexico. I was traveling with Gerta, the beautiful young German woman who was not yet my wife. We headed out from Tucson with the famous Southwestern artist Ted DeGrazia and his wife, Marion, in DeGrazia's big Mercedes. DeGrazia wanted to sketch and paint Christmas ceremonial dances at the various pueblos. A fanatic about color, he was also looking for a red blanket of a certain shade. He'd been searching for months and he was sure he'd find it in New Mexico.

I don't recall where we stayed in Santa Fe, our first stop, but I remember being surprised at how shocked DeGrazia was when he learned that Gerta and I would be sharing the same room, even though we weren't married. I guess it just wasn't done in those days. I also recall that we shopped under the portales at the Palace of the Governors on the Santa Fe Plaza; I still have the inlaid turquoise and silver cuff links I bought there. I understand cuff links are coming back.

We went on to Taos, where we paid a perhaps-too-early-in-the-morning visit to the writer Frank Waters, a friend of DeGrazia's. I had a copy of Waters's *The Man Who Killed the Deer* that I was hoping to have autographed. Unannounced visits are quite common in the West, but ours couldn't have been more badly timed. Waters was just sitting down to breakfast and obviously having a tiff with his wife at the time (he has since remarried). Our arrival—"paying homage to the great writer" was his wife's ironic phrase, I think—set her off. A plate of scrambled eggs went flying across the kitchen, smashing into the wall. We could still hear the shouting as we got into the car. I never did get the book signed.

On Christmas Eve, we headed out to the services at Taos Pueblo. There was a huge crowd and no room to sit; we squeezed into the church balcony. A tall, powerfully built Indian standing next to me lit a cigarette. I told him he shouldn't smoke in church. He told me we were in an "Indian place" and he'd smoke if he wanted to. I wasn't about to argue. After the priest said Mass, two Indian Deer dancers, bedecked in deerskins and antlers, came thumping down the center of the church aisle, rattles shaking, chanting; they were followed by others and then by a Buffalo dancer. DeGrazia sketched away.

At Nambe Pueblo, where we went next, we were surprised to discover the same priest celebrating Mass. In fact, this priest was at every pueblo we visited that night, eventually saying "midnight" Mass at 2 in the morning at Santa Clara.

Somewhere along the way we got arrested. Driving down a long dirt road to one of the pueblos, we picked up an Indian who was going in the same direction. He was quite young and quite drunk, and it was the latter condition that found all four of us being led to the office of the tribal governor—who was apparently also a judge.

It was a serious offense, we were told, bringing alcohol into the pueblo. We hadn't, but because the intoxicated Indian was with us, it was assumed that we had contributed to his condition. For a while it looked as though we were going to spend Christmas Eve in jail, but then DeGrazia had a brainstorm. He opened his wallet and slowly laid out a string of credit cards, all gleaming plastic and bright colors. The governor-judge picked up each card and studied it carefully, running his finger over the embossed lettering. What message they transmitted, we don't know, but they did the trick. The cards were returned, and we were promptly released.

It was late and everyone was exhausted, but DeGrazia wanted to press on. An impressionist artist, he painted Indians with stylistic brilliance in a dazzling palette of colors. For the moment, however, he was making only quick pencil sketches. The more tired he was, he explained, the more blurred everything became, and only the most important details stood out. He worked best in that dreamlike state.

Before visiting the pueblos, Gerta and I had noticed a blanket in the window of the local J. C. Penney's. It was red, a terrible color red, a red that reminded us a bit of Campbell's tomato soup. We bought it, had it gift wrapped, and gave it to DeGrazia on Christmas morning. He seemed touched when he opened the box; it was just the color he was looking for, he said, trying to keep a straight face. How did we ever find it?

DeGrazia died in 1982. He had planned to move to Santa Fe and build a studio there in the foothills of the Sangre de Cristo Mountains, but that never came to pass. The city has expanded since that first visit and has changed, as have we all. Yet, like DeGrazia, I find New Mexico's spiritual pull at times overwhelming. And the impressions it leaves—especially after I go too long without sleep—are the most vivid of anywhere I've been.

Recently I was driving north from Carlsbad, alone, when I pulled up in front of the Inn of the Mountain Gods, centerpiece of the sprawling Mescalero Indian Reservation in the southern part of the state. Midway between Alamogordo and Roswell in Lincoln County, the reservation is home to more than 2,500 Mescalero Apaches, and the inn is Apache-owned and -run. The idea of vacationing for a few days on a Native American reservation appealed to me. I wanted to read, write, and relax away from it all. In the back of my mind were thoughts of hogans, tepees, and lazy curls of smoke rising from smoldering campfires.

These visions dissipated when a pleasant young man in jeans and a white shirt said, "Good morning, sir," as he unloaded my bags and then drove my car to an adjacent parking lot. Valet parking? I could have been in Beverly Hills.

But once inside, I knew I had come to the right place. The canyon-size lobby was dominated by a three-story-high copper-sheathed fireplace. Beyond, the glass-paneled walls looked out onto Mescalero Lake, and beyond the lake, the slender tips of ponderosa pine speared a bank of low-hanging clouds, all framed by a wall of jagged mountains. Indian paintings, artifacts, and wall hangings were displayed throughout the lobby. Even before I signed in I found myself pricing turquoise jewelry at a display case.

Three miles northeast is the town of Ruidoso, home of the Ruidoso Downs Racetrack. On Labor Day, the track's All-American Quarter Horse Futurity offers as much as $3 million in prize money; it's billed as the nation's richest purse. The town itself is small, one of those places where people still give directions by the number of bumps in the road. In addition to its shops and antiques stores, downtown Ruidoso has a number of saloons where the racetrack grooms, stable boys, and tipsters congregate. I stopped into one of these bars one night wearing a suit, and the bartender asked me if I was a doctor.

On the north, east, and west, Ruidoso is bordered by Lincoln National Forest. In 1950, after a devastating forest fire was brought under control in the Capitan Mountains, 30 miles northeast, firefighters found a badly burned bear cub clinging to a tree. Nursed back to health, the cub was later flown to the Washington, D.C., zoo. He was named Smokey, and became the symbol for the nation's campaign to prevent forest fires.

When I checked out of the hotel several days later, loaded down with Native American rugs, bracelets, pottery, images of another way of life, I felt ready once again to face the rigors of city, traffic, and deadlines.

Extolling the glories of an area of which one is particularly fond invariably leaves one with a sense of misgiving. I can't help but wonder to what extent I'm contributing to changing the things that I value. With a statewide population of about 1½ million, New Mexico isn't exactly being overrun. But I just heard that the Inn of the Mountain Gods was installing a hundred slot machines in its lobby. "I don't know why I paint Indians," DeGrazia once wrote to me. "Maybe I'm afraid that the Indians are going to vanish and I want to be around them to fill my eyes."

1 Essential Information

Before You Go

Visitor Information

New Mexico Department of Tourism (Lamy Bldg., 491 Old Santa Fe Trail, Santa Fe 87503, tel. 505/827–7400 or 800/545–2040). **USDA Forest Service, Southwestern Region** (Public Affairs Office, 517 Gold Ave., SW, Albuquerque 87102, tel. 505/842–3292). **Indian Pueblo Cultural Center** (2401 12th St., NW, Albuquerque 87102, tel. 505/843–7270).

Tours and Packages

Should you buy your travel arrangements to New Mexico packaged or do it yourself? There are advantages either way. Buying packaged arrangements saves you money, particularly if can find a program that includes exactly the features you want. You also get a pretty good idea of what your trip will cost from the outset. Generally, you have two options: fully escorted tours and independendent packages. Escorted tours are most often via motorcoach, with a tour director in charge. They're ideal if you don't mind having limited free time and traveling with strangers. Your baggage is handled, your time rigorously scheduled, and most meals planned. Escorted tours are therefore the most hassle-free way to see a destination, as well as generally the least expensive. Independent packages allow plenty of flexibility. They generally include airline travel and hotels, with certain options available, such as sightseeing, car rental, and excursions. Independent packages are usually more expensive than escorted tours, but your time is your own.

While you can book directly through tour operators, you will pay no more to go through a travel agent, who will be able to tell you about tours and packages from a number of operators. Whatever program you ultimately choose, be sure to find out exactly what is included: taxes, tips, transfers, meals, baggage handling, ground transportation, entertainment, excursions, sports or recreation (and rental equipment if necessary). Ask about the level of hotel used, its location, the size of its rooms, the kind of beds, and its amenities, such as pool, room service, or programs for children, if they're important to you. Find out the operator's cancellation penalties. Nearly everyone charges them, and the only way to avoid them is to buy trip-cancellation insurance (*see* Trip Insurance, *below*). Also ask about the single supplement, a surcharge assessed to solo travelers. Some operators do not make you pay it if you agree to be matched up with a roommate of the same sex, even if one is not found by departure time. Remember that a program that has features you won't use, whether for rental sporting equipment or discounted museum admissions, may not be the most cost-wise choice for you. Don't buy a Rolls-Royce, even at a reduced price, if all you want is a Chevy.

Fully Escorted Tours Escorted tours are usually sold in three categories: deluxe, first-class, and tourist or budget class. The most important differences are the price, of course, and the level of accommodations. Some operators specialize in one category, while others offer a range.

Contact **Maupintour** (Box 807, Lawrence, KS 66044, tel. 800/255–4266 or 913/843–1211) and **Tauck Tours** (11 Wilton Rd., Westport, CT 06881, tel. 800/468–2825 or 203/226–6911) in the deluxe category; **Caravan Tours** (401 N. Michigan Ave., Chicago, IL 60611, tel. 800/227–2826 or 312/321–9800), **Domenico Tours** (751 Broadway, Bayonne, NJ 07002, tel. 800/554-8687 or 201/823-8687), and **Globus-Gateway** (95–25 Queens Blvd., Rego Park, NY 11374, tel 800/221–0090 or 718/268–7000) in the first-class category. **Cosmos,** a sister company of Globus (at the same number), offers packages in the budget category.

Most itineraries are jam-packed with sightseeing, so you see a lot in a short amount of time (usually one place per day). To judge just how fast-paced the tour is, review the itinerary carefully. If you are in a different hotel each night, you will be getting up early each day to head out, travel to your next destination, do some sightseeing, have dinner, and go to bed, then you'll start all over again. If you want some free time, make sure it's mentioned in the tour brochure; if you want to be escorted to every meal, confirm that any tour you consider does that. Also, when comparing programs, be sure to find out if the motorcoach is air-conditioned and has a restroom on board. Make your selection based on price and stops on the itinerary.

Independent Packages Independent packages are offered by airlines, tour operators who may also do escorted programs, and any number of other companies from large, established firms to small, new entrepreneurs.

Contact **American Airlines' Fly AAway Vacations** (tel. 800/321–2121), **Continental Airlines' Grand Destinations** (tel. 800/634–5555), **Delta Dream Vacations** (tel. 800/872–7786), and **United Airlines' Vacation Planning Center** (tel. 800/328–6877).

Their programs come in a wide range of prices based on levels of luxury and options—in addition to hotel and airfare, sightseeing, car rental, transfers, admission to local attractions, and other extras. Note that when pricing different packages, it sometimes pays to purchase the same arrangements separately, as when a rock-bottom promotional airfare is being offered, for example. Again, base your choice on what's available at your budget for the destinations you want to visit.

Special-interest Special-interest programs may be fully escorted or inde-
Travel pendent. Some require a certain amount of expertise, but
most are for the average traveler with an interest and are
usually hosted by experts in the subject matter. When the
program is escorted, it enjoys the advantages and disad-
vantages of all escorted programs; because your fellow
travelers are apt to be passionate or knowledgeable about
the subject, they can prove as enjoyable a part of your travel experience as the destination itself. The price range is
wide, but the cost is usually higher—sometimes a lot higher—than for ordinary escorted tours and packages, because of the expert guiding and special activities.

Biking **Backroads** (1516 5th St., Suite Q333, Berkeley, CA 94710-
1740, tel. 800/245–3874 or 510/527–1555) has an inn-to-inn
bike trip through northern New Mexico, including Santa
Fe, with stops at Indian pueblos, Spanish colonial villages,
art galleries, and fine craft studios. The tour also includes a
river rafting trip on the Rio Grande.

Archaeology **The Archaeological Conservancy** (415 Orchard Dr., Santa
Fe 87501, tel. 505/982–3278) offers archaeologist-guided
tours of pre-historic sites and contemporary Indian villages
in New Mexico.

Nature and **Earthwatch** (680 Mount Auburn, Box 403N, Watertown,
Ecology MA 02272, tel. 607/926–8200) sponsors scientific expeditions to various areas of the country. New Mexico is not always included in its schedule each year, so call to see what's
offered.

National Audubon Society (950 Third Ave., New York, NY
10022, tel. 212/546–9140) also runs programs to New Mexico on occasion.

Victor Emanual Nature Tours (Box 33008, Austin, TX
78764, tel. 512/328–5221) specializes in birdwatching and
natural history trips.

River Sports **Whitewater Information and Reservations** (100 E. San
Francisco St., Santa Fe 87501, tel. 800/338–6877 or 505/
983–6565) offers overnight rafting trips on the Rio Grande
and the Rio Charma.

New Wave Rafting Company (Rte 5, Box 302A, Santa Fe
87501, tel.505/984–1444 or 505/455–2633) offers overnight
rafting expeditions that depart daily from Santa Fe Plaza.

Tips for British Travelers

Tourist Contact the **United States Travel and Tourism Administra-**
Information **tion** (Box 1EN, London W1A 1EN, tel. 071/495–4466).

Passports British citizens need a valid 10-year passport.
and Visas
A visa is not necessary unless (1) you are planning to stay
more than 90 days; (2) your trip is for purposes other than
vacation; (3) you have at some time been refused a visa, or

refused admission to the United States, or have been required to leave by the U.S. Immigration and Naturalization Service; or (4) you do not have a return or onward ticket. You will need to fill out the Visa Waiver Form, 1–94W, supplied by the airline.

To apply for a visa or for more information, call the U.S. Embassy's Visa Information Line (tel. 0891/200–290; calls cost 48p per minute or 36p per minute cheap rate). If you qualify for visa-free travel but want a visa anyway, you must apply in writing, enclosing an SAE, to the U.S. Embassy's Visa Branch (5 Upper Grosvenor St., London W1A 2JB), or, for residents of Northern Ireland, to the U.S. Consulate General (Queen's House, Queen St., Belfast BT1 6EO). Submit a completed Nonimmigrant Visa Application (Form 156), a valid passport, a photograph, and evidence of your intended departure from the United States after a temporary visit. If you require a visa, call 0891/234–224 to schedule an interview.

Customs British visitors aged 21 or over may import the following into the United States: 200 cigarettes or 50 cigars or 2 kilograms of tobacco; one U.S. liter of alcohol; gifts to the value of $100. Restricted items include meat products, seeds, plants, and fruits. Never carry illegal drugs.

Insurance Most tour operators, travel agents, and insurance agents sell specialized policies covering accident, medical expenses, personal liability, trip cancellation, and loss or theft of personal property. Some policies include coverage for delayed departure and legal expenses, winter-sports, accidents, or motoring abroad. You can also purchase an annual travel-insurance policy valid for every trip you make during the year in which it's purchased (usually only trips of less than 90 days). Before you leave, make sure you will be covered if you have a preexisting medical condition or are pregnant; your insurers may not pay for routine or continuing treatment, or may require a note from your doctor certifying your fitness to travel.

The **Association of British Insurers,** a trade association representing 450 insurance companies, advises extra medical coverage for visitors to the United States.

For advice by phone or a free booklet, "Holiday Insurance," that sets out what to expect from a holiday-insurance policy and gives price guidelines, contact the Association of British Insurers (51 Gresham St., London EC2V 7HQ, tel. 071/600–3333; 30 Gordon St., Glasgow G1 3PU, tel. 041/226–3905; Scottish Provincial Bldg., Donegall Sq. W, Belfast BT1 6JE, tel. 0232/249176; call for other locations).

Tour Operators Several companies, such as **British Airways Holidays** (Atlantic House, Hazelwick Ave., Crawley, W. Sussex RH10 1NP, tel. 0293/518022) and **Jetsave** (Sussex House, London Rd., East Grinstead, W. Sussex RH19 1LD, tel. 0342/312033), can arrange fly/drive tours of the region.

Hints for Travelers with Disabilities Main information sources include the **Royal Association for Disability and Rehabilitation** (RADAR, 25 Mortimer St., London W1N 8AB, tel. 071/637–5400), which publishes travel information for the disabled in Britain, and **Mobility International** (228 Borough High St., London SE1 1JX, tel. 071/403–5688), the headquarters of an international membership organization that serves as a clearinghouse of travel information for people with disabilities.

When to Go

The best time to go to New Mexico is a matter of personal preference. If you're interested in a particular sport, activity, or special event, go when that's available and don't worry too much about the weather. Most ceremonial dances at the Native American pueblos occur in the summer, early fall, and at Christmas and Easter. The majority of other major events are geared to the traditionally heavy tourist season of July and August: The Santa Fe Opera, Chamber Music Festival, and Native American and Spanish markets all take place during those two months. The Santa Fe Fiesta and New Mexico State Fair in Albuquerque are held in September, and the Albuquerque International Balloon Fiesta is in October.

The relatively cool climates of Santa Fe and Taos are a lure in summer, as is the skiing in the Taos area in winter. Christmas is a wonderful time to be in New Mexico because of Native American ceremonials as well as the Spanish religious folk plays, special foods, and musical events. Hotel rates are generally highest during the peak summer season but fluctuate less than those in most major resort areas. If you plan to come in July or August, be sure to make reservations in advance. You can avoid most of the tourist crowds by coming during spring or fall. Spring weather is unpredictable; sudden storms may erupt. October is one of the best months to visit: The air is crisp, colors are brilliant, and whole mountainsides become tumbling cascades of red and gold.

Climate What follows are average daily maximum and minimum temperatures for Santa Fe and Albuquerque.

Santa Fe	Jan.	39F	4C	**May**	68F	20C	**Sept.**	73F	23C
		19	− 7		42	6		48	9
	Feb.	42F	6C	**June**	78F	26C	**Oct.**	62F	17C
		23	− 5		51	11		37	3
	Mar.	51F	11C	**July**	80F	27C	**Nov.**	50F	10C
		28	− 2		57	14		28	− 2
	Apr.	59F	15C	**Aug.**	78F	26C	**Dec.**	39F	4C
		35	2		55	13		19	− 7

Albuquerque	Jan.	46F	8C	**May**	78F	26C	**Sept.**	84F	29C
		24	– 4		51	11		57	14
	Feb.	53F	12C	**June**	89F	32C	**Oct.**	71F	22C
		28	– 2		60	16		44	7
	Mar.	60F	16C	**July**	91F	33C	**Nov.**	57F	14C
		33	1		64	18		32	0
	Apr.	69F	21C	**Aug.**	89F	32C	**Dec.**	48F	9C
		42	6		64	18		26	– 3

Information For current weather conditions for cities in the United
Sources States and abroad, plus the local time and helpful travel
tips, call the **Weather Channel Connection** (tel. 900/
WEATHER; 95¢ per minute) from a touch-tone phone.

Festivals and Seasonal Events

January **Native American New Year's Celebrations,** all pueblos.
Comanche, Deer, and other traditional dances, including
the Turtle dance (the men's traditional animal dance), are
performed at the Taos Pueblo. Tel. 505/758–8626.

February **Winterfestival,** Santa Fe. This celebration of winter takes
place during four days in late February, both in town and on
the slopes of the Santa Fe Ski Area. Events include snow-
sculpture competitions, downhill racing, hot-air ballooning, music, and drama. Tel. 505/983–5615.

March **Living History Weekend,** Columbus. The town of Columbus
sits on the border of Mexico, where a reenactment of the
1916 clash between American forces and Pancho Villa's
Mexican soldiers takes place at Pancho Villa State Park.
There are tactical demonstrations, field-camp drills, authentic equipment and uniforms, all lots of fun. Tel. 505/
928–2996.

April **Albuquerque Founder's Day,** Albuquerque. This event commemorates the April 23, 1706, founding of Albuquerque by
Governor Francisco Cuervo y Valdés, whose costumed per-
sona presides over the event. The celebration takes place at
the Old Town Plaza. Tel. 505/243–3696.

May **Buzzard Days,** Carrizozo. Rattlesnake races and horseshoe
competitions are held here during the second weekend in
May. Tel. 505/648–2472.

Spring Festival of the Arts, Santa Fe. This 10-day spring
arts festival consists of citywide exhibits, demonstrations,
lectures, tours, open studios, music, dance, and theater
performances. Contact Santa Fe Festival Foundation (1524
Paseo de Peralta, Santa Fe 87501, tel. 505/988–3924).

June **New Mexico Arts and Crafts Fair,** Albuquerque. On the last
weekend in June, the New Mexico State Fairgrounds hosts
this crafts spectacular that brings together more than 200
artists and craftspeople to display their talents. Spanish,
Native American, and other North American cultures are

represented, and there's plenty of food and entertainment. Tel. 505/884–9043.

July **Rodeo de Santa Fe,** Santa Fe. A taste of the Old West comes to Santa Fe in mid-July, with calf roping, bull riding, and a traditional rodeo parade. World-champion rodeo participants come from all parts of the United States and Canada to this event, held since 1959. Tel. 505/982–4659 or 505/471–4300.

Spanish Market, Santa Fe. Held on Santa Fe Plaza, this festive gathering features Spanish arts, crafts, and good things to eat. You can smell the green-corn tamales and chocolate mole from blocks around. Many exhibitors are from remote villages, where outstanding handicrafts are produced. Contact the Spanish Colonial Arts Society (Box 1611, Santa Fe 87501, tel. 505/983–4038).

August **Banjo and Fiddle Mini-Festival,** Santa Fe. This annual toe-tapping, banjo, fiddle, guitar, mandolin, old-time band, and bluegrass mountain-music festival takes place for two days in late August, attracting big-name folk musicians and thousands of loyal fans to the Santa Fe Rodeo Grounds. Contact the Banjo and Fiddle Contest (Rte. 7, Box 115-BK, Santa Fe 87505, tel. 505/983–8315 or 505/982–9848).

Bat Flight Breakfast, Carlsbad. On the second Thursday of August, early risers gather at the entrance to Carlsbad Cavern to eat breakfast and watch tens of thousands of bats, who've been out for the night feeding on insects, fly back into the cave. Tel. 505/785–2232).

Indian Market, Santa Fe. Native American arts, pottery, jewelry, blankets, and rugs are displayed and sold at the Indian Market on the Plaza in mid-August. Many of the town's 150 art galleries feature special shows of leading Native American artists. At least 800 artists and craftspeople are expected to attend the market. Contact Southwestern Association of Indian Affairs (SWAIA, Box 1964, Santa Fe 87501, tel. 505/983–5220).

September **Las Fiestas de Santa Fe,** Santa Fe. The city's biggest celebration begins the first Friday after Labor Day and commemorates the reconquest of Santa Fe from the San Juan Indians by Don Diego de Vargas in 1692. Parades, dancing, pageantry, ethnic foods, arts and crafts, fireworks, and the burning of *Zozobra* (Old Man Gloom) are all part of the fun. Contact Las Fiestas de Santa Fe (Box 4516, Santa Fe 87505, tel. 505/988–7575).

New Mexico State Fair, Albuquerque. One of the nation's liveliest state fairs takes place at the New Mexico State Fairgrounds, with arts, crafts, livestock shows, entertainment, a midway, a rodeo, and living early Spanish and Native American villages. Tel. 505/265–1791.

October **Fall Festival of the Arts,** Santa Fe. This 10-day fall arts festival highlights New Mexico's finest painters, sculptors, ceramicists, weavers, and woodworkers. Contact Santa Fe Festival Foundation (1524 Paseo de Peralta, Santa Fe 87501, tel. 505/988–3924).

International Balloon Fiesta, Albuquerque. More than 650 hot-air and gas balloons will participate in a mass ascension at sunrise during the first two weekends in October. This major event in the world of ballooning—you'll never see anything like it—takes place at Balloon Fiesta Park. Tel. 505/821–1000.

November   **Arts and Crafts Fair,** Santa Fe. Over 50 local and statewide artists offer folk dolls, Spanish colonial woodwork, *santos* (saint) carvings, *retablos* (religious paintings on tin or wood), wooden toys, fabric crafts, jewelry, and other hand-made goods for sale in an annual charity event that takes place at the famous La Fonda Hotel. Tel. 505/471–7873.

Indian National Finals Rodeo, Albuquerque. The biggest Indian rodeo takes place at the New Mexico State Fairgrounds in mid-November, along with a powwow, ceremonial dances, and Native American arts and crafts. Tel. 505/265–1791.

December   **Christmas Native American Dances,** various pueblos. The Spanish dance-drama *Los Matachines* is performed at Picuris and San Juan pueblos. There are also pine-torch processions at San Juan and Taos pueblos, the Kachina Dance at Taos, and Basket, Buffalo, Deer, Harvest, Rainbow, and Turtle dances at Acoma, Cochiti, San Ildefonso, San Juan, Santa Clara, and Taos pueblos. Tel. 505/843–7270.

Procession of the Virgin, Taos Pueblo. After vespers on Christmas Eve, the procession of the Virgin Mary takes place, with dancers and bonfires. Tel. 505/758–8626.

Christmas Season, Santa Fe. During the Christmas holidays the New Mexico capital is at its most festive, with incense and piñon smoke sweetening the air and the darkness of winter illuminated by thousands of *farolitos*, lunch sack-size paper bags weighted with sand and bearing a candle. A custom believed to have derived from the Chinese lanterns the conquistadores brought with them, the glowing farolitos are everywhere, lining walkways, doorways, rooftops, walls, windowsills, and sometimes even gravesites with soft puddles of light. The songs of Christmas are sung around corner bonfires (*luminarias*, as the holiday bonfires are called in Santa Fe), and mugs of hot cider and melt-in-your-mouth Christmas cookies, *biscochitos*, are offered to all who pass by. With glowing lights reflected on the snow, Santa Fe is never lovelier. Numerous religious pageants and processions take place. Early in the month are 10 days of **Las Posadas** at San Miguel Mission (401 Old Santa Fe Trail, tel. 505/983–3974), during which the story of Mary and Joseph's journey to Bethlehem is reenacted. The **Feast Day of Our Lady of Guadalupe,** December 12, is grandly celebrated at Santuario de Guadalupe, and **Christmas at the Palace** resounds with hours of festive music emanating from the Palace of the Governors.

What to Pack

Clothing Typical of the Southwest, even when the days are warm, evenings and nights are chilly to cold. You should pack accordingly.

The areas of higher elevation are, of course, considerably cooler than are Carlsbad and other low-lying southern portions of the state. That means winter visitors should pack warm clothes—coats, parkas, and whatever else your body's thermostat and your ultimate destination dictate. Sweaters and jackets will also be needed for summer visitors because while days are warm, nights at the higher altitudes can be extremely chilly. And bring comfortable shoes; you're likely to be doing a lot of walking.

New Mexico is one of the most informal and laid-back areas of the country, which for many is much a part of its appeal. Probably no more than three or four restaurants in the entire state enforce a dress code, even for dinner meals, though men are likely to feel more comfortable wearing a jacket in the major hotel dining rooms, and women in tennis shoes may receive a look of stern disapproval from the maître d'.

The Western look, popular throughout the country a few years back has, of course, never lost its hold on the West. But Western dress has become less corny and more subtle and refined. Western-style clothes are no longer a costume; they're being mixed with tweed jackets, for example, for a more conservative, sophisticated image. Which is to say, you can dress Western with your boots and big belt buckles in even the best places in Santa Fe, Taos, Albuquerque, or Carlsbad, but if you come strolling through the lobby of the Eldorado Hotel looking like Hopalong Cassidy, you'll get some funny looks.

Miscellaneous Depending on where you're headed in New Mexico, you may find the sun strong, the air dry, and the wind hot and relentless. Bring skin moisturizers if dry skin's a problem, and sunglasses to protect your eyes from the glare of lakes or ski slopes. High altitude can be a problem (it may cause headaches and dizziness), so check with your doctor about special medication.

Bring an extra pair of eyeglasses or contact lenses. If you have a health problem that may require you to purchase a prescription drug, pack enough to last the duration of the trip, or have your doctor write a prescription. And don't forget to pack a list of the addresses of offices that supply refunds for lost or stolen traveler's checks.

Luggage Free baggage allowances on an airline depend on the air-
Regulations line, the route, and the class of your ticket. In general, on
domestic flights you are entitled to check two bags—nei-
ther exceeding 62 inches, or 158 centimeters (length +
width + height), or weighing more than 70 pounds (32 kilograms). A third piece may be brought aboard as a carryon;
its total dimensions are generally limited to less than 45
inches (114 centimeters), so it will fit easily under the seat
in front of you or in the overhead compartment. There are
variations, so ask in advance. The single rule, a Federal
Aviation Administration safety regulation that pertains to
carry-on baggage on U.S. airlines, requires only that
carryons be properly stowed and allows the airline to limit
allowances and tailor them to different aircraft and opera-
tional conditions. Charges for excess, oversize, or over-
weight pieces vary, so inquire before you pack.

Safeguarding Your Before leaving home, itemize your bags' contents and their
Luggage worth; this list will help you estimate the extent of your loss
if your bags go astray. To minimize that risk, tag them inside and out with your name, address, and phone number.
(If you use your home address, cover it so that potential
thieves can't see it.) At check-in, make sure that the tag attached by baggage handlers bears the correct three-letter
code for your destination. If your bags do not arrive with
you, or if you detect damage, do not leave the airport until
you've filed a written report with the airline.

Insurance In the event of loss, damage, or theft on domestic flights,
airlines limit their liability to $1,250 per passenger. Ex-
cess-valuation insurance can be bought directly from the
airline at check-in but leaves your bags vulnerable on the
ground. Your own homeowner's policy may fill the gap; or
you may want special luggage insurance. Sources include
The Travelers Companies (1 Tower Sq., Hartford, CT 06183,
tel. 203/277–0111 or 800/243–3174) and **Wallach and Company, Inc.** (107 W. Federal St., Box 480, Middleburg, VA
22117, tel. 703/687–3166 or 800/237–6615), underwritten
by Lloyds, London.

Traveler's Checks Although you will want cash when visiting small cities or
rural areas, traveler's checks are usually preferable. The
most widely recognized are **American Express, Barclay's,
Thomas Cook,** and those issued by major commercial banks
such as **Citibank** and **Bank of America.** American Express
also issues *Traveler's Cheques for Two*, which can be signed
and used by you or your traveling companion. Some checks
are free; usually the issuing company or the bank at which
you make your purchase charges 1% of the checks' face value as a fee. Always record the numbers of checks as you
spend them, and keep this list separate from the checks.

Getting Money from Home

Cash Machines Automated-teller machines (ATMs) are proliferating; many are tied to international networks such as **Cirrus** and **Plus.** You can use your bank card at ATMs away from home to withdraw money from an account and get cash advances on a credit-card account (providing your card has been programmed with a personal identification number, or PIN). Check in advance on limits on withdrawals and cash advances within specified periods. Remember that on cash advances you are charged interest from the day you get the money from ATMs as well as from tellers. And note that transaction fees for ATM withdrawals outside your home turf will probably be higher than for withdrawals at home.

For specific Cirrus locations in the United States and Canada, call 800/424-7787 (for U.S. Plus locations, 800/843-7587), and press the area code and first three digits of the number you're calling from (or the calling area where you want an ATM).

American Express Cardholder Services The company's **Express Cash** system lets you withdraw cash and/or traveler's checks from a worldwide network of 57,000 American Express dispensers and participating bank ATMs. You must *enroll first* (call 800/CASH-NOW for a form and allow two weeks for processing). Withdrawals are charged not to your card but to a designated bank account. You can withdraw up to $1,000 per seven-day period on the basic card, more if your card is gold or platinum. There is a 2% fee (minimum $2.50, maximum $10) for each cash transaction, and a 1% fee for traveler's checks (except for the platinum card), which are available only from American Express dispensers.

At AmEx offices, cardholders can also cash personal checks for up to $1,000 in any seven-day period; of this $200 can be in cash, more if available, with the balance paid in traveler's checks, for which all but platinum cardholders pay a 1% fee. Higher limits apply to the gold and platinum cards.

Wiring Money You don't have to be a cardholder to send or receive an **American Express MoneyGram** for up to $10,000. To send one, go to an American Express MoneyGram agent, pay up to $1,000 with a credit card and anything over that in cash, and phone a transaction reference number to your intended recipient, who needs only present identification and the reference number to the nearest MoneyGram agent to pick up the cash. There are MoneyGram agents in more than 60 countries (call 800/543-4080 for locations). Fees range from 5% to 10%, depending on the amount and how you pay. You can't use American Express, which is really a convenience card—only Discover, MasterCard, and Visa credit cards.

You can also use **Western Union.** To wire money, take either cash or a check to the nearest office. (Or you can call and use a credit card.) Fees are roughly 5%-10%. Money sent from the United States or Canada will be available for pick up at agent locations in New Mexico within minutes. (Note that once the money is in the system it can be picked up at *any* location. You don't have to miss your train waiting for it to arrive in City A, because if there's an agent in City B, where you're headed, you can pick it up there, too.) There are approximately 20,000 agents worldwide (call 800/325–6000 for locations).

Traveling with Cameras, Camcorders, and Laptops

Film and Cameras
If your camera is new or if you haven't used it for a while, shoot and develop a few rolls of film before leaving home. Pack some lens tissue and an extra battery for your built-in light meter, and invest in an inexpensive skylight filter, to both protect your lens and provide some definition in hazy shots. Store film in a cool, dry place—never in the car's glove compartment or on the shelf under the rear window.

Films above ISO 400 are more sensitive to damage from airport security X-rays than others; very high speed films, ISO 1,000 and above, are exceedingly vulnerable. To protect your film, don't put it in checked luggage; carry it with you in a plastic bag and ask for a hand inspection. Such requests are honored at American airports. Don't depend on a lead-lined bag to protect film in checked luggage—the airline may very well turn up the dosage of radiation to see what you've got in there. Airport metal detectors do not harm film, although you'll set off the alarm if you walk through one with a roll in your pocket. Call the Kodak Information Center (tel. 800/242–2424) for details.

Camcorders
Before your trip, put new or long-unused camcorders through their paces, and practice panning and zooming. Invest in a skylight filter to protect the lens, and check the lithium battery that lights up the LCD (liquid crystal display) modes. As for the rechargeable nickel-cadmium batteries that are the camera's power source, take along an extra pair, so while you're using your camcorder you'll have one battery ready and another recharging.

Videotape
Unlike still-camera film, videotape is not damaged by X-rays. However, it may well be harmed by the magnetic field of a walk-through metal detector. Airport security personnel may want you to turn the camcorder on to prove that that's what it is, so make sure the battery is charged when you get to the airport.

Laptops
Security X-rays do not harm hard-disk or floppy-disk storage. Most airlines allow you to use your laptop aloft but request that you turn it off during takeoff and landing so as not to interfere with navigation equipment. Make sure the battery is charged when you arrive at the airport, because you may be asked to turn on the computer at security checkpoints to prove that it is what it appears to be. If

you're a heavy computer user, consider traveling with a backup battery.

Car Rentals

All major car-rental companies are represented in New Mexico, including **Avis** (tel. 800/331–1212, 800/879–2847 in Canada), **Budget** (tel. 800/527–0700), **Dollar** (tel. 800/800–4000), **Hertz** (tel. 800/654–3131, 800/263-0600 in Canada), and **National** (tel. 800/227–7368). Other rental agencies in New Mexico include **Alamo** (tel. 800/327–9633), **General** (tel. 800/327–7607), **PayLess** (tel. 800/541–1566), **Rent Rite** (tel. 800/554–7483), **Rich Ford** (tel. 800/331–3271), and **Thrifty** (tel. 800/367–2277). In cities, unlimited-mileage rates range from $35 per day for an economy car to $45 for a large car; weekly unlimited-mileage rates range from $135 to $180.

Requirements Your U.S., Canadian, or U.K. driver's license is acceptable.

Extra Charges Picking up the car in one city or state and leaving it in another may entail drop-off charges or one-way service fees, which can be substantial. The cost of a collision or loss-damage waiver (*see below*) can be high, also.

Cutting Costs If you know you will want a car for more than a day or two, you can save by planning ahead. Major international companies have programs that discount their standard rates by 15%–30% if you make the reservation before departure (anywhere from two to 14 days), rent for a minimum number of days (typically three or four), and prepay the rental. Ask about these advance-purchase schemes when you call for information. More economical rentals are those that come as part of fly/drive or other packages, even those as bare-bones as the rental plus an airline ticket (*see* Tours and Packages, *above*).

Other sources of savings are companies that operate as wholesalers—companies that do not own their own fleets but rent in bulk from those that do and offer advantageous rates to their customers. Rentals through such companies must be arranged and paid for in advance. Among them is **Auto Europe** (Box 1097, Camden, ME 04843, tel. 207/236–8235 or 800/223–5555, 800/458–9503 in Canada). You won't see these wholesalers' deals advertised; they're even better in summer, when business travel is down. Always ask whether unlimited mileage is available. Find out about any required deposits, cancellation penalties, and drop-off charges, and confirm the cost of the collision damage waiver (CDW).

One last tip: Remember to fill the tank when you turn in the vehicle to avoid being charged for refueling at what you'll swear is the most expensive pump in town.

Insurance and The standard rental contract includes liability coverage (for
Collision Damage damage to public property, injury to pedestrians, etc.) and
Waiver coverage for the car against fire, theft (not included in certain countries), and collision damage with a deductible—
most commonly $2,000–$3,000, occasionally more. In the
case of an accident, you are responsible for the deductible
amount unless you've purchased the CDW, which costs an
average $12 a day, although this varies depending on what
you've rented, where, and from whom.

Because this adds up quickly, you may be inclined to say "no
thanks"—and that's certainly your option, although the
rental agent may not tell you so. Planning ahead will help
you make the right decision. By all means, find out if your
own insurance covers damage to a rental car while traveling
(not simply a car to drive when yours is in for repairs). And
check whether charging car rentals to any of your credit
cards will get you a CDW at no charge. Note before you de-
cline that deductibles are occasionally high enough that to-
taling a car would make you responsible for its full value. In
many states, laws mandate that renters be told what the
CDW costs, that it's optional, and that their own auto insurance may provide the same protection.

Traveling with Children

Publications *Family Travel Times,* published 10 times a year by **Travel**
Newsletter **With Your Children** (TWYCH, 45 W. 18th St., 7th Floor
Tower, New York, NY 10011, tel. 212/206–0688; annual
subscription $55), covers destinations, types of vacations,
and modes of travel.

Books *Great Vacations with Your Kids,* by Dorothy Jordan and
Marjorie Cohen ($13; Penguin USA, 120 Woodbine St.,
Bergenfield, NJ 07621, tel. 800/253–6476) and *Traveling
with Children—And Enjoying It,* by Arlene K. Butler
($11.95 plus $3 shipping per book; Globe Pequot Press, Box
833, Old Saybrook, CT 06475, tel. 800/243–0495, or 800/
962–0973 in CT), both help plan your trip with children,
from toddlers to teens.

Tour Operators **GrandTravel** (6900 Wisconsin Ave., Suite 706, Chevy
Chase, MD 20815, tel. 301/986–0790 or 800/247–7651) of-
fers international and domestic tours for grandparents
traveling with their grandchildren. The catalogue, as
charmingly written and illustrated as a children's book,
positively invites armchair traveling with lap-sitters
aboard. **Rascals in Paradise** (650 5th St., Suite 505, San
Francisco, CA 94107, tel. 415/978–9800, or 800/872–7225)
specializes in programs for families.

Getting There On domestic flights, children under 2 not occupying a seat
Air Fares travel free, and older children currently travel on the "lowest applicable" adult fare.

Baggage The adult baggage allowance applies for children paying half or more of the adult fare. Check with the airline for particulars.

Safety Seats The FAA recommends the use of safety seats aloft and details approved models in the free leaflet "**Child/Infant Safety Seats Recommended for Use in Aircraft**" (available from the Federal Aviation Administration, APA–200, 800 Independence Ave. SW, Washington, DC 20591, tel. 202/267–3479). Airline policy varies. U.S. carriers must allow FAA-approved models, but because these seats are strapped into a regular passenger seat, they may require that parents buy a ticket even for an infant under 2 who would otherwise ride free.

Facilities Aloft Airlines do provide other facilities and services for children, such as children's meals and freestanding bassinets (to those sitting in seats on the bulkhead, where there's enough legroom to accommodate them). Make your request when reserving. The annual February/March issue of *Family Travel Times* gives details of the children's services on dozens of airlines ($10; *see above*). "Kids and Teens in Flight" (free from the U.S. Department of Transportation, tel. 202/366–2220) offers tips for children flying alone.

Lodging At the **Best Western Hotels** (tel. 800/528–1234) in Albuquer-
Hotels que and Santa Fe, children under 12 stay free. All **Holiday Inns** (tel. 800/465–4329) allow children under 12 to stay free when sharing a room with their parents, and some offer "Family Plans" that provide the same privileges for children 18 and younger. During holiday periods and on weekends, the new **Hyatt Hotel** in Albuquerque (tel. 505/842–1234, ext. 51) offers special games and activities—including classes in Southwestern cooking—for young guests. **Bishop's Lodge** in Santa Fe (tel. 505/983–6377) has a summer riding and horsemanship program for children.

Condominiums **Campanilla Compound** (334 Otero St., Santa Fe 87501, tel.
and Resorts 505/988–7585) and **Pueblo Hermosa** (501 Rio Grande, Santa Fe 87501, tel. 505/984–2590) offer excellent facilities for families with children. In many cases, especially for larger families, resort accommodations work out to be much cheaper than hotels.

Adventure In the Southwest region, children's- and family-adventure
Holidays holidays abound. **Santa Fe Adventures, Inc.** (Box 15086, Santa Fe 87506–5086, tel. 505/983–0111 or 800/766–5443) provides half-day educational trips and activities for children over 4, leaving parents free to relax and explore. A separate Family Adventure Group offers hot-air ballooning, animal tracking, and overnight family backpacking trips. **Santa Fe Detours** (La Fonda Hotel, 100 E. San Francisco St., Santa Fe 87501, tel. 800/DETOURS) organizes wagon rides and safaris for children.

Baby-Sitting Baby-sitters are available at many hotels and resorts. In
Services Santa Fe, both **Enchanting Land Babysitting Service** (tel.

505/988–2718) and **The Kid Connection** (tel. 505/471–3100) offer reputable services. **Trudy's Discovery House** in Taos (tel. 505/758–1659) provides drop-in day care for visiting families.

Hints for Travelers with Disabilities

Most of the region's national parks and recreational areas have accessible visitor centers, rest rooms, campsites, and trails, and more are being added every year. For information on accessible facilities at specific parks and sites in New Mexico, contact the **National Park Service, Southwest Region** (Box 728, Santa Fe 87504, tel. 505/988–6375).

Organizations Several organizations provide travel information for people with disabilities, usually for a membership fee, and some publish newsletters and bulletins. Among them are the **Information Center for Individuals with Disabilities** (Fort Point Pl., 27–43 Wormwood St., Boston, MA 02210, tel. 617/727–5540 or 800/462–5015 in MA between 11 and 4, or leave message; TDD/TTY tel. 617/345–9743); **Mobility International USA** (Box 3551, Eugene, OR 97403, voice and TDD tel. 503/343–1284), the U.S. branch of an international organization based in Britain and present in 30 countries; **MossRehab Hospital Travel Information Service** (1200 W. Tabor Rd., Philadelphia, PA 19141, tel. 215/456–9603, TDD tel. 215/456–9602); the **Society for the Advancement of Travel for the Handicapped** (SATH, 347 5th Ave., Suite 610, New York, NY 10016, tel. 212/447–7284, fax 212/725–8253); the **Travel Industry and Disabled Exchange** (TIDE, 5435 Donna Ave., Tarzana, CA 91356, tel. 818/368–5648); and **Travelin' Talk** (Box 3534, Clarksville, TN 37043, tel. 615/552–6670).

Travel Agencies and Tour Operators **Directions Unlimited** (720 N. Bedford Rd., Bedford Hills, NY 10507, tel. 914/241–1700), a travel agency, has expertise in tours and cruises for the disabled. **Evergreen Travel Service** (4114 198th St. SW, Suite 13, Lynnwood, WA 98036, tel. 206/776–1184 or 800/435–2288) operates Wings on Wheels Tours for those in wheelchairs, White Cane Tours for the blind, and tours for the deaf and makes group and independent arrangements for travelers with any disability. **Flying Wheels Travel** (143 W. Bridge St., Box 382, Owatonna, MN 55060, tel. 800/535–6790 or 800/722–9351 in MN), a tour operator and travel agency, arranges international tours, cruises, and independent travel itineraries for people with mobility disabilities. **Nautilus,** at the same address as TIDE (*see above*), packages tours for the disabled internationally.

Publications In addition to the fact sheets, newsletters, and books mentioned above are several free publications available from the Consumer Information Center (Pueblo, CO 81009): "New Horizons for the Air Traveler with a Disability," a U.S. Department of Transportation booklet describing changes resulting from the 1986 Air Carrier Access Act and those still to come from the 1990 Americans with Disabilities Act (include Department 608Y in the address), and the Airport Operators Council's *Access Travel: Airports* (Dept. 5804), which describes facilities and services for the disabled at more than 500 airports worldwide.

Twin Peaks Press (Box 129, Vancouver, WA 98666, tel. 206/694–2462 or 800/637–2256) publishes the *Directory of Travel Agencies for the Disabled* ($19.95), listing more than 370 agencies worldwide; *Travel for the Disabled* ($19.95), listing some 500 access guides and accessible places worldwide; the *Directory of Accessible Van Rentals* ($9.95) for campers and RV travelers worldwide; and *Wheelchair Vagabond* ($14.95), a collection of personal travel tips. Add $2 per book for shipping. The Sierra Club publishes *Easy Access to National Parks* ($16 plus $3 shipping; 730 Polk St., San Francisco, CA 94109, tel. 415/776–2211).

Hints for Older Travelers

Organizations The **American Association of Retired Persons** (AARP, 601 E St. NW, Washington, DC 20049, tel. 202/434–2277) provides independent travelers the Purchase Privilege Program, which offers discounts on hotels, car rentals, and sightseeing, and the AARP Motoring Plan, provided by Amoco, which furnishes domestic trip-routing information and emergency road-service aid for an annual fee of $39.95 per person or couple ($59.95 for a premium version). AARP also arranges group tours, cruises, and apartment living through AARP Travel Experience from American Express (400 Pinnacle Way, Suite 450, Norcross, GA 30071, tel. 800/927–0111); these can be booked through travel agents, except for the cruises, which must be booked directly (tel. 800/745–4567). AARP membership is open to those 50 and over; annual dues are $8 per person or couple.

Two other membership organizations offer discounts on lodgings, car rentals, and other travel products, along with such nontravel perks as magazines and newsletters. The **National Council of Senior Citizens** (1331 F St. NW, Washington, DC 20004, tel. 202/347–8800) is a nonprofit advocacy group with some 5,000 local clubs across the United States; membership costs $12 per person or couple annually. **Mature Outlook** (6001 N. Clark St., Chicago, IL 60660, tel. 800/336–6330), a Sears Roebuck & Co. subsidiary with 800,000 members, charges $9.95 for an annual membership.

Note: When using any senior-citizen identification card for reduced hotel rates, mention it when booking, not when checking out. At restaurants, show your card before you're seated; discounts may be limited to certain menus, days, or hours. If you are renting a car, ask about promotional rates that might improve on your senior-citizen discount.

Educational Travel **Elderhostel** (75 Federal St., 3rd floor, Boston, MA 02110, tel. 617/426–7788) is a nonprofit organization that has offered inexpensive study programs for people 60 and older since 1975. Programs take place at more than 1,800 educational institutions in the United States, Canada, and 45 countries overseas, and courses cover everything from marine science to Greek myths and cowboy poetry. Participants generally attend lectures in the morning and spend the afternoon sightseeing or on field trips; they live in dorms on the host campuses. Fees for programs in the United States and Canada, which usually last one week, run about $300, not including transportation.

Interhostel (University of New Hampshire, 6 Garrison Ave., Durham, NH 03824, tel. 800/733–9753), a slightly younger enterprise than Elderhostel, caters to a slightly younger clientele—that is, 50 and over—and runs programs overseas in some 25 countries. But the idea is similar: Lectures and field trips mix with sightseeing, and participants stay in dormitories at cooperating educational institutions or in modest hotels. Programs are usually two weeks in length and cost $1,500–$2,100, not including airfare from the United States.

Tour Operators **Saga International Holidays** (222 Berkeley St., Boston, MA 02116, tel. 800/343–0273), which specializes in group travel for people over 60, offers a selection of variously priced tours and cruises covering five continents. If you want to take your grandchildren, look into **GrandTravel** (*see* Traveling with Children, *above*).

Further Reading

General Interest A list of classic books on New Mexico would include *Death Comes for the Archbishop*, by Willa Cather, a novel based on the life of Archbishop Jean Baptiste Lamy, who built, among other churches, the Cathedral of St. Francis in Santa Fe. *Big River*, by Paul Horgan; *Wind Leaves No Shadow*, by Ruth Laughlin; *Miracle Hill*, by Barney Mitchell; *Navajos Have Five Fingers*, by T. D. Allen; *Sante Fe*, by Oliver La Farge; *New Mexico*, by Jack Schaefer; and *Moon Over Adobe*, by Dorothy Pillsbury, are all good choices as well. *Lautree*, by Norman Zollinger, is an entertaining mystery set in Albuquerque. Zollinger, who owns the Professor Book Center on Lomas Boulevard NE, in Albuquerque, also wrote *Riders to Cibola*, which chronicles the conquistadores' search for the legendary Seven Cities of Gold. Albuquerque author Tony Hillerman received an Edgar Allan Poe Award from the Mystery Writers of America in 1974 for his book *Dance Hall of the Dead*. *The Wood Carvers of Cordova, New Mexico*, by Charles L. Briggs, is a prize-winning study of the making and selling of religious images in a northern New Mexico village. *Eliot Porter's Southwest* is the famed photographer's poetic view of the Southwest, much of it focused around his Tesuque, New Mexico, home.

Indian Lore and Pueblo Life
The Man Who Killed the Deer, by Frank Waters, is a classic of Pueblo life. *Masked Gods,* by the same author, has a following that reaches cult proportions. J. J. Brody's profusely illustrated book *Anasazi and Pueblo Painting* is an indispensable volume for art historians and students of Southwestern culture. *Mornings in Mexico,* by D. H. Lawrence, contains a number of essays pertaining to Taos and the Pueblo ritual dances. *Pueblo Style and Regional Architecture,* edited by Nicholas C. Markovich, Wolfgang F. E. Preiser, and Fred G. Strum, covers the evolution of architecture in the Southwest, with particular emphasis on New Mexico. *Pueblos: Prehistoric Indian Cultures of the Southwest,* by Sylvio Acatos, with photos by Maximilien Bruggman, is a portrait of the peace-loving people who carved out a civilization in the region. *Nacimientos: Nativity Scenes by Southwest Indian Artists,* by Guy and Doris Monthan, offers photographs and descriptions of ceramic Nativity scenes produced by Pueblo Native Americans.

New Mexican Personalities
Billy the Kid: A Short and Violent Life, by Robert M. Utley, a noted historian, is considered the definitive work on the notorious outlaw. *The Life of D. H. Lawrence,* by Keith Sagar, published in 1980, is a good biography of the world-renowned author so strongly associated with (and buried in) New Mexico. Taos is also Georgia O'Keeffe country, and there is a wealth of books about the artist. Among the best is *Georgia O'Keeffe: Arts and Letters,* published by the New York Graphic Society in conjunction with a retrospective of her work at the National Gallery of Art, Washington, D.C. Also worthy of note is the reissue of the coffee-table book, *Georgia O'Keeffe,* with text by the artist herself. *Portrait of an Artist: A Biography of Georgia O'Keeffe,* by Laurie Lisle, spans the artist's life and career. *Georgia O'Keeffe: Some Memories of Drawings,* edited by Doris Bry, is a collection of the artist's major 1915–1963 drawings, with comments on each.

On Albuquerque, Santa Fe, and Taos
Albuquerque—A Narrative History, by Marc Simmons, is a fascinating look at the city's birth and development. *The Wingspread Collectors Guide to Santa Fe and Taos* and *The Wingspread Collectors Guide to Albuquerque and Corrales* (Wingspread, Box 13566-T, Albuquerque 87192) provide high-quality reproductions and useful information about art galleries, art, and crafts of the region; they also include listings of museums, hotels, restaurants, and historic sites. *Taos: A Pictorial History,* by John Sherman, contains numerous black-and-white historical photographs of the major characters, events, and structures that formed the backbone of Taos, as well as of Native Americans, Hispanics, and Anglo immigrants, with accompanying text.

Arriving and Departing

By Plane

Flights are either nonstop, direct, or connecting. A **nonstop** flight requires no change of plane and makes no stops. A **direct** flight stops at least once and can involve a change of plane, although the flight number remains the same; if the first leg is late, the second waits. This is not the case with a **connecting** flight, which involves a different plane and a different flight number.

Airports and Airlines **Albuquerque International Airport,** 65 miles southwest of Santa Fe and 130 miles south of Taos, is the gateway to New Mexico. Airlines serving Albuquerque International Airport are **America West** (tel. 800/247–5692), **American** (tel. 800/433–7300), **Continental** (tel. 800/525–0280), **Delta** (tel. 800/221–1212), **Mesa Air** (tel. 800/637–2247), **Southwest** (tel. 800/531–5601), **TWA** (tel. 800/221–2000), **United** (tel. 800/241–6522), and **USAir** (tel. 800/428–4322).

Air-shuttle service via Mesa Air operates four times a day between Albuquerque and Santa Fe; the flying time aboard the nine-passenger Cessna Caravan is 25 minutes, and the fare ranges from $59 to $110 for round-trip flights, depending on the time of day and the time of year, and half that for one-way flights. Interline buses at the airport link Mesa Airlines with all Albuquerque connections.

Cutting Flight Costs The Sunday travel section of most newspapers is a good source of deals. When booking, particularly through an unfamiliar company, call the Better Business Bureau to find out whether any complaints have been registered against the company, pay with a credit card if you can, and consider trip-cancellation and default insurance (*see* Insurance, *above*).

Promotional Airfares All the less expensive fares, called promotional or discount fares, are round-trip and involve restrictions. The exact nature of the restrictions depends on the airline, the route, and the season and on whether travel is domestic or international, but you must usually buy the ticket—commonly called an APEX (advance purchase excursion) when it's for international travel—in advance (seven, 14, or 21 days are usual). You must also respect certain minimum- and maximum-stay requirements (for instance, over a Saturday night or at least seven and no more than 30, 45, or 90 days), and you must be willing to pay penalties for changes. Airlines generally allow some changes for a fee. But the cheaper the fare, the more likely the ticket is nonrefundable; it would take a death in the family for the airline to give you any of your money back if you had to cancel. The cheapest fares are also subject to availability; because only a certain percentage of the plane's total seats will be sold at that price, they may go quickly.

Consolidators Consolidators or bulk-fare operators—also known as bucket shops—buy blocks of seats on scheduled flights that airlines anticipate they won't be able to sell. They pay wholesale prices, add a markup, and resell the seats to travel agents or directly to the public at prices that still undercut the airline's promotional or discount fares. You pay more than on a charter but ordinarily less than for an APEX ticket, and, even when there is not much of a price difference, the ticket usually comes without the advance-purchase restriction. Moreover, although tickets are marked nonrefundable so you can't turn them in to the airline for a full-fare refund, some consolidators sometimes give you your money back. Carefully read the fine print detailing penalties for changes and cancellations. If you doubt the reliability of a company, call the airline once you've made your booking and confirm that you do, indeed, have a reservation on the flight.

The biggest U.S. consolidator, C.L. Thomson Express, sells only to travel agents. Well-established consolidators selling to the public include **UniTravel** (Box 12485, St. Louis, MO 63132, tel. 314/569–0900 or 800/325–2222); **Council Charter** (205 E. 42nd St., New York, NY 10017, tel. 212/661–0311 or 800/800–8222), a division of the Council on International Educational Exchange and a longtime charter operator now functioning more as a consolidator; and **Travac** (989 6th Ave., New York, NY 10018, tel. 212/563–3303 or 800/872–8800), also a former charterer.

Charter Flights Charters usually have the lowest fares and the most restrictions. Departures are limited and seldom on time, and you can lose all or most of your money if you cancel. (Generally, the closer to departure you cancel, the more you lose, although sometimes you will be charged only a small fee if you supply a substitute passenger.) The charterer, on the other hand, may legally cancel the flight for any reason up to 10 days before departure; within 10 days of departure, the flight may be canceled only if it becomes physically impossible to operate it. The charterer may also revise the itinerary or increase the price after you have bought the ticket, but if the new arrangement constitutes a "major change," you have the right to a refund. Before buying a charter ticket, read the fine print for the company's refund policy and details on major changes. Money for charter flights is usually paid into a bank escrow account, the name of which should be on the contract. If you don't pay by credit card, make your check payable to the escrow account (unless you're dealing with a travel agent, in which case, his or her check should be payable to the escrow account). The Department of Transportation's Consumer Affairs Office (I–25, Washington, DC 20590, tel. 202/366–2220) can answer questions on charters and send you its "Plane Talk: Public Charter Flights" information sheet.

Charter operators may offer flights alone or with ground arrangements that constitute a charter package. Well-established charter operators include **Council Charter** (*see* above), now largely a consolidator, despite its name, and **Travel Charter** (1120 E. Long Lake Rd., Troy, MI 48098, tel. 313/528–3570 or 800/521–5267), with Midwestern departures. **DER Tours** (Box 1606, Des Plains, IL 60017, tel. 800/782–2424), a charterer and consolidator, sells through travel agents.

Discount Travel Clubs Travel clubs offer their members unsold space on airplanes, cruise ships, and package tours at nearly the last minute and at well below the original cost. Suppliers thus receive some revenue for their "leftovers," and members get a bargain. Membership generally includes a regular bulletin or access to a toll-free telephone hot line giving details of available trips departing anywhere from three or four days to several months in the future. Packages tend to be more common than flights alone, so if airfares are your only interest, read the literature before joining. Reductions on hotels are also available. Clubs include **Discount Travel International** (114 Forrest Ave., Suite 203, Narberth, PA 19072, tel. 215/668–7184; $45 annually, single or family), **Moment's Notice** (425 Madison Ave., New York, NY 10017, tel. 212/486–0503; $45 annually, single or family), **Travelers Advantage** (CUC Travel Service, 49 Music Sq. W, Nashville, TN 37203, tel. 800/548–1116; $49 annually, single or family), and **Worldwide Discount Travel Club** (1674 Meridian Ave., Miami Beach, FL 33139, tel. 305/534–2082; $50 annually for family, $40 single).

Smoking Since February 1990, smoking has been banned on all domestic flights of less than six hours duration. On U.S. carriers flying to New Mexico, a seat in a no-smoking section must be provided for every passenger who requests one, and the section must be enlarged to accommodate such passengers if necessary as long as they have complied with the airline's deadline for check-in and seat assignment. If smoking bothers you, request a seat far from the smoking section.

By Car

I–40 runs east–west across the middle of the state; I–10 cuts across the southern part of the state from the Texas border at El Paso to the Arizona line, through Las Cruces, Deming, and Lordsburg; I–25 runs north from the state line at El Paso through Albuquerque and Santa Fe, then angles northeast to the Colorado line near Raton.

U.S. highways connect all major cities and towns with a good network of paved roads. State roads go to the smaller towns; most of them are paved, two-lane thoroughfares. Roads on Native American lands are designated by wooden, arrow-shape signs; these, like roads in national forests, are usually not paved.

Technically, there may not be a lot of true desert in New Mexico, but there is a lot of high, dry, lonesome country. Keep your gas tank full and abide by the signs, and you shouldn't have any trouble.

Arroyos, dry washes or gullies, are bridged on major roads, but lesser roads often dip down through them. These can be a hazard during the rainy season of July, August, and September. If water is running through an arroyo, don't try to cross it, even if it looks shallow—it may have an axle-breaking hole in the middle. Just wait a little while, and it will drain off almost as quickly as it filled. If you stall in a running arroyo, get out of the car and onto high ground if possible. If you are in backcountry, never drive (or walk) in a dry arroyo bed if the sky is dark anywhere upstream. A sudden thunderstorm 15 miles away could send a raging flash flood down a wash that was perfectly dry a few minutes earlier.

Avoid unpaved roads in New Mexico, unless they are well graded and graveled, when they are wet. The soil has a lot of *caliche*, or clay, in it that gets very slick when mixed with water.

By Bus

Frequent ground-shuttle service between Albuquerque and Santa Fe is available via **Greyhound/Trailways** (tel. 505/471–0008 or 800/231–2222); the cost is $11.13. Continuing on to Taos costs $10.50 more. **Shuttlejack** (tel. 800/452–2665) also offers bus service between Albuquerque and Santa Fe, $20 one-way, but doesn't go to Taos.

Staying in New Mexico

Shopping

Antiques Though the American West is still relatively young, antiques shops and roadside museums dot the desert landscape. You'll find everything in New Mexico's antiques shops, from early Mexican typewriters to period saddles, ceramic pots, farm tools, pioneer aviation equipment, and yellowed newspaper clippings about Kit Carson and D. H. Lawrence.

Art Santa Fe is the fine-arts capital of the Southwest, with over 150 galleries. Albuquerque and Taos are not far behind. Native American art, Western art, fine art, junk art—you'll find everything for sale in New Mexico, and in all media: sculptures, prints, posters, ceramics, etchings, drawings, photographs, and exquisite miniatures, by artists of both international and local renown.

Crafts Hispanic handcrafted furniture, religious carvings and paintings, *santos* (representations of saints) and *retablos* (holy images painted on wood or tin) command high prices from collectors. Colorful handwoven Hispanic textiles are much in demand. Native American blankets, rugs, kachina dolls, baskets, silver jewelry, turquoise, pottery, beadwork, ornamental shields, drums, and ceramics can be found almost everywhere in New Mexico, from Santa Fe Plaza to the Indian pueblos that range across the entire state. Prices range from thousands of dollars for a rare 1930s kachina doll to just a few cents for hand-wrapped bundles of sage, juniper, sweet grass, and lavender that are used by Native Americans in healing ceremonies, gatherings, and daily cleansing of the home. Ignited like incense, this herbal combination gives off a sacred smoke; passing it once around the room is enough to change and charge the air.

Spices You'll find stands beside the road selling *chile ristras*, strings of crimson chiles to hang in your kitchen or beside the front door, and you'll find shops everywhere selling chile powder and other spices. You can smell them from the road; walk in, and your eyes begin to water and your mouth to salivate. For many, especially natives of the Southwest, *picante* is the purest, finest word in the Spanish language. It means hot—spicy hot. All around you, in boxes, bags, packets, jars, and cans, there's everything *picante*— salsas, chile pastes, powders, herbs, spices, peppers, barbecue sauce, and fiery potions in bottles.

Sports and the Outdoors

Bicycling Albuquerque is a biker's paradise, with miles and miles of bike lanes and trails crisscrossing and skirting the city. Not only is Albuquerque's Parks and Recreation Department aware of bikers' needs, but bike riding is heavily promoted as a means of cutting down on traffic congestion and pollution. Santa Fe and Taos, because of hilly terrain and narrow, frequently congested downtown streets, are less hospitable to cyclists. However, mountain biking is popular in both areas. With low gears and knobby tires, mountain bikes open back roads and trails to bike excursions of all kinds.

Cycling events in New Mexico include the Santa Fe Century (50- or 100-mile recreational rides), the Sabusco Hill Climb (an annual race to the Santa Fe Ski Area), and the Tour de Los Alamos (road race and criterium).

Bird-Watching Bird-watchers have wonderful opportunities to spot birds migrating from the jungles of South America to the tundra of the Arctic Circle. The **Bosque del Apache National Wildlife Refuge** (Box 1246, Socorro 87801, tel. 505/835–1828), 90 miles south of Albuquerque, is the winter home of thousands of migrating birds, including one of only two wild flocks of the rare whooping crane.

Camping New Mexico has over a million acres of wilderness areas, with hundreds of campgrounds, picnic areas, and recreational sites. For information on New Mexico's five national forests and the Kiowa National Grasslands (part of the Cibola National Forest), contact the **USDA Forest Service** (*see* Visitor Information, *above*), **Carson National Forest** (Forest Service Bldg., 208 Cruz Alta Rd., Box 558, Taos 87571, tel. 505/758–6200), **Cibola National Forest** (2113 Osuna Rd. NE, Suite A, Albuquerque 87113, tel. 505/761–4650), **Gila National Forest** (2610 N. Silver St., Silver City 88061, tel. 505/388–8201), **Lincoln National Forest** (Federal Bldg., 11th and New York Sts., Alamogordo 88310, tel. 505/437–6030), and **Santa Fe National Forest** (1220 St. Francis Dr., Box 1689, Santa Fe 87504, tel. 505/988–6940).

Canoeing, Kayaking, and River Rafting New Mexico's rivers offer a choice: A lazy glide along a serpentine waterway, past colorful mesas and soaring cliffs, or a heart-thumping ride through white-water rapids. **The Taos Box,** a 17-mile run through the churning rapids of the upper **Rio Grande,** is one of New Mexico's most exciting rafting experiences. Most of the hard-core river rafting is done in the Taos area; the **Taos County Chamber of Commerce** (Drawer 1, Taos 87571, tel. 505/732–3873 or 800/732–TAOS) can supply a list of local outfitters. More leisurely trips can be had aboard the sightseeing crafts that ply the **Pecos, Rio Charma,** and other meandering rivers. For statewide information concerning river recreational activities, contact the **New Mexico Department of Tourism** (*see* Visitor Information, *above*).

Fishing Fishing spots include the **Rio Grande,** which traverses New Mexico north to south; **Abiquiu Lake,** 40 miles northwest of Santa Fe; **Heron Lake,** 20 miles southwest of Chama via U.S. 64 and NM 96; and **Blue Water Lake** in the northwest closer to Albuquerque, 28 miles west of Grants via NM 371. The **San Juan**'s high-quality-water regulations make for some of the best trout fishing in the country. Six-thousand-acre **Heron Lake** offers rainbow trout, lake trout, and kokanee salmon. Trout fishermen will also find nirvana in the sparkling streams of the Sangre de Cristo range, bordering Santa Fe. The **Pecos River** and its tributaries offer excellent backcountry fishing.

Anyone over 12 must have a New Mexico fishing license. Including a trout-validation stamp, the license costs out-of-state visitors $25 per year. Temporary licenses are also available. Nearly 300 stores, in addition to game-and-fish offices, sell fishing and hunting licenses.

Fishing on Native American reservations is not subject to regulations but may require special permits; the **Indian Pueblo Cultural Center** (*see* Visitor Information, *above*) can provide further information.

For additional information, or to obtain copies of state fishing regulations and maps, contact the **New Mexico Game and Fish Department** (Villagra Bldg., 408 Galisteo St., Santa Fe 87503, tel. 505/827–7911). Another source of information is the **New Mexico Council of Outfitters and Guides** (160 Washington St. SE, No. 175, Albuquerque 87108, tel. 505/248–4461), representing independent guides and outfitters throughout the state.

Golfing The state has a respectable share of turf, with over 60 courses offering recreation throughout the year. The dry climate here makes playing more comfortable than in many other states. There are excellent public courses in Albuquerque, Angel Fire, Las Vegas, Los Alamos, and Santa Fe; Taos joined the ranks in August 1992 with the opening of a new course at the Taos Country Club. **The Golf Association** (10035 Golf Course La. NW, Albuquerque 87114, tel. 505/897–0864) can provide a list of courses, along with details on the greens fees and hours for each club.

Hiking Bring your walking shoes: Few states in the nation are as blessed with such a diverse network of trails. New Mexico's air is clean and crisp, and its ever-changing terrain is aesthetically rewarding as well. The **State Parks and Recreation Division** (Energy, Minerals, and Natural Resources Department, 408 Galisteo St., Santa Fe 87503, tel. 505/827–0291) can provide further information and maps.

Hunting The New Mexico Game and Fish Department has instituted many innovative game-management and wildlife-restoration programs. As a result, hunters have a diverse selection of wildlife to pursue, including sizable herds of mule deer and elk. Waterfowl and upland game-bird hunting is also excellent. There are antelope in the wide, windswept eastern New Mexican plains, and bear in the mountainous backcountry. In addition, there are limited special hunts for Barbary and bighorn sheep, oryx, javelina, and Siberian and Persian ibex.

Four Native American reservations conduct hunts separate from the regular state hunts: the Jicarilla and Mescalero Apaches, the Navajos, and the Zunis all have extensive landholdings in the state and offer the opportunity to hunt certain species when the regular state season is closed.

Out-of-state hunters must check with the New Mexico Game and Fish Department for hunting dates in the area they plan to visit. General big-game hunting licenses are not available to nonresidents, but separate licenses may be bought for turkey and all big game. A general license for small game (squirrels and birds other than turkey) is available to nonresidents for $51. Indian tribes have their own fee schedules. For more information, contact the New Mexico Game and Fish Department (*see* Fishing, *above*).

Skiing New Mexico offers many world-class ski areas. Snowmaking equipment is used in most areas to ensure a long season, usually from Thanksgiving through Easter. Check with the **Bureau of Land Management** (224 Cruz Aulta Rd., Taos 87571, tel. 505/758–8851) and state park officials for local snow and trail conditions and weather updates.

Downhill   The major downhill ski areas in New Mexico include **Angel Fire Resort** (Drawer B, Angel Fire 87710, tel. 505/377–6401 or 800/633–7463), **Pajarito Mountain Ski Area** (Box 155, Los Alamos 87544, tel. 505/662–SNOW or 505/662–5725), **Red River Ski Area** (Box 900, Red River 87558, tel. 505/754–2382), **Sandia Peak Ski Area** (10 Tramway Loop NE, Albuquerque 87122, tel. 505/296–9585 or 505/242–9052), **Santa Fe Ski Area** (1210 Louisa St., Suite 10, Santa Fe 87501, tel. 505/982–4429), **Sipapu Lodge and Ski Area** (Rte. Box 29, Vadito 87579, tel. 505/587–2240), **Ski Apache** (Box 220, Ruidoso 88345, tel. 505/336–4356 or 505/336–4357), **Snow Canyon** (Box 53, Cloudcroft 88317, tel. 505/682–2333 or 505/682–2733), and **Taos Ski Valley** (Box 90, Taos Ski Valley 87525, tel. 505/776–2291). For information about the state's ski areas or to order a 40-page *Skier's Guide*, call **Ski New Mexico,** tel. 800/446–3898.

Cross-Country   **Enchanted Forest** near Red River has groomed trails in the state's best-known Nordic ski area. Head to the Sangre de Cristo Mountains for high-altitude terrain. There are also exciting cross-country trails north of Chama along the New Mexico–Colorado border, in the **Tularosa Mountains** in the Gila Wilderness, and to the south in the **Sacramento Mountains** adjacent to White Springs National Monument. The **Sandia** and **Manzano Mountains** near Albuquerque are easily accessible for skiers.

Spectator Sports

Horse Racing   Horse racing with pari-mutuel betting is very popular in New Mexico. The state's tracks include: **Downs at Santa Fe** (5 mi south of Santa Fe, tel. 505/471–3311, open early June–Labor Day, Wed., Fri.–Sun., holidays), **Downs at Albuquerque** (New Mexico State Fairgrounds, East Central Ave., tel. 505/262–1188, open Jan.–June 15, Wed., Fri.–Sun., holiday Mon.), **Ruidoso Downs Racetrack** (tel. 505/378–4431, open early May–Labor Day, Thurs.–Mon., holidays), **San Juan Downs** (7 mi east of Farmington, tel. 505/326–4551, open last weekend in Apr.–Labor Day, Sat., Sun., and holidays), and **Sunland Park Racetrack** (5 mi north of El Paso, Texas, tel. 505/589–1131, open mid-Oct.–mid-May, Wed., Fri.–Sun., holidays).

Quarterhorse racing's Triple Crown events—Kansas Futurity, Rainbow Futurity, and All-American Futurity—take place in mid-June, mid-July, and Labor Day, respectively, at Ruidoso Downs (*see* Chapter 6, Excursion to Lincoln County and White Sands National Monument).

Hot-Air Balloons Kodak's International Balloon Fiesta, held in Albuquerque in early October, draws the largest number of spectators (an estimated 1.5 million people) of any sporting event in the state (*see* Festivals and Seasonal Events, *above*).

Rodeos Rodeos are a big draw from early spring through autumn. Besides big events in Santa Fe, Albuquerque, and Gallup, every county in the state has a rodeo competition during its county fairs. Major Native American rodeos take place at Stone Lake on the Jicarilla Reservation, on the Mescalero Apache Reservation, at the Inter-Tribal Ceremonial in Gallup, and at the National Indian Rodeo Finals in Albuquerque.

National and State Parks and Monuments

National Parks **Carlsbad Caverns National Park** (3225 National Parks Hwy., Carlsbad 88220, tel. 505/785–2232 or 505/785–2107 for 24-hr recorded information), in the southeastern part of the state (27 mi southwest of Carlsbad on U.S. 62/180), contains one of the largest and most spectacular cave systems in the world. Of the more than 70 caves in the park, only two, Carlsbad Cavern and Slaughter Canyon Cave, are open to the public. No camping is permitted in the park, but nearby Brantley Lake State Park and Lincoln National Forest have camping facilities. Commercial sites in Carlsbad and at White's City, 7 miles northeast of the caverns, are also available. (*See* Chapter 6.)

National Monuments There are 12 national monuments in New Mexico: **Aztec Ruins National Monument** (Box 640, Aztec 87410, tel. 505/334–6174); **Bandelier National Monument** (Box 1, Suite 15, Los Alamos 87544, tel. 505/672–3861); **Capulin Volcano National Monument** (Box 94, Capulin 88414, tel. 505/278–2201); **Chaco Culture National Historic Park** (Star Rte. 4, Box 6500, Bloomfield 87413, tel. 505/988–6716); **El Malpais National Monument and Conservation Area** (Box 939, Grants 87020, tel. 505/285–4641); **El Morro National Monument** (Rte. 2, Box 43, Ramah 87321–9603, tel. 505/783–4226); **Fort Union National Monument** (Watrous 87753, tel. 505/425–8025); **Gila Cliff Dwellings National Monument** (Rte. 11, Box 100, Silver City 88061, tel. 505/536–9461); **Pecos National Historical Park** (Drawer 418, Pecos 87552, tel. 505/757–6032); **Petroglyph National Monument** (contact National Park Service, Southwest Region, Box 728, Santa Fe 87504, tel. 505/988–6430); **Salinas Pueblo Missions National Monument** (Box 496, Mountainair 87036, tel. 505/847–2585); and **White Sands National Monument** (Box 458, Alamogordo 88310, tel. 505/479–6124).

State Monuments New Mexico's state monuments include: **Coronado State Monument** (NM 44, off I–25, tel. 505/867–5351), 18 miles north of Albuquerque, preserves ruins of a prehistoric Native American pueblo; it has self-guided trails, a visitor center and a museum. **Jemez State Monument** (NM 4, 1 mi north of Jemez Springs, tel. 505/829–3530) has ruins of a 17th-century mission church and pueblo. **Lincoln State Monument** (U.S. 380, 12 mi east of Capitan, tel. 505/653–4500), **Fort Selden** (Radium Springs exit off I–25, 13 mi north of Las Crucas, tel. 505/526–8911), and **Fort Sumner** (2 mi east of the town Fort Sumner, on Billy the Kid Rd., tel. 505/355–2573) all give insight into the 19th-century territorial period of New Mexico. For more information, contact the **Monument Division, Museum of New Mexico** (Box 2087, Santa Fe 87504, tel. 505/827–6334).

State Parks Established in the 1930s, New Mexico's state park system is composed of 45 parks throughout the state, ranging from high mountain lakes and pine forests in the north to the Chihuahuan Desert lowlands of the south. Pristine and unspoiled, they offer all outdoor recreational facilities. For maps and brochures, contact the **State Parks and Recreational Division** (*see* Hiking in Sports and Outdoor Activities, *above*).

Reservations

Two general classifications of Native Americans live in New Mexico: Pueblos, who established an agricultural civilization here many centuries ago, and the descendants of the nomadic tribes who came into the area much later—the Navajos, Mescalero Apaches, and Jicarilla Apaches. The **Jicarilla Apaches** live on a reservation of ¾ million acres in north-central New Mexico, the capital of which is Dulce. The terrain varies from mountains, mesas, and lakes to high grazing land, suited to cattle and horse ranching. The tribe has a well-defined tourist program promoting big-game hunting, fishing, and camping on a 20,000-acre game preserve. Nearly all the tribe members gather at Stone Lake on September 14 and 15 for the fall festival—two days of dancing, races, and a rodeo. For more information, contact the **Tourism Department, Jicarilla Apache Tribe** (Box 507, Dulce 87528, tel. 505/759–3242).

A reservation of ½ million acres of timbered mountains and green valleys is home to the **Mescalero Apaches** in southeastern New Mexico. The tribe owns and operates the famous resort, Inn of the Mountain Gods, as well as Ski Apache, 16 miles from Ruidoso. For detailed information, *see* Chapter 6, Excursion to Lincoln County and White Sands National Monument.

The **Navajo** Reservation, home to the largest Native American group in the United States, covers 16 million acres in New Mexico, Arizona, and Utah. More than any other tribe, the Navajos are still nomadic, following flocks from place to place and living in hogans (mud and pole houses). There are a few towns on the reservation, but for the most part it is a vast area of stark pinnacles, colorful rock formations, high desert, and mountains; the land encompasses several national and tribal parks, some of which include campgrounds. Navajos are master silversmiths and rug weavers, and their work is available at trading posts scattered throughout the reservation. The tribe encourages tourism; for more information, contact the **Navajo Tribal Tourism Office** (Box 663, Window Rock, AZ 86515, tel. 602/871–4941).

For detailed information about New Mexico's Pueblo peoples and their villages, *see* Chapter 7, Pueblos of the Rio Grande.

Dining

A delicious and extraordinary mixture of Pueblo, Spanish Colonial, and Mexican and American frontier cooking, the regional cuisine is not only good, it's good for you. Mexican restaurants are especially popular and are almost universally inexpensive. Nutrition experts say that the basic staple diet of the Mexican peasant is among the healthiest in the world. Beans provide carbohydrates and protein; corn offers protein and calcium; and chiles, one of the most versatile seasonings known, contain an entire storehouse of vitamins and minerals—they're particularly rich with vitamin C.

New Mexico also has numerous Chinese restaurants, where freshness is the key to everything served. Many of the dishes are steamed, all brimming with natural vitamins and goodness. Many New Mexico restaurants offer buffalo meat (stews, steaks, and burgers). Of course, there is a fair share of trendy and contemporary restaurants, particularly in the Santa Fe and Taos areas, as well as a respectable offering of gourmet grill rooms, French, Italian, Japanese, Greek, and other ethnic establishments.

The following list of names and terms may prove helpful for the newcomer to New Mexico who doesn't know what a great taste treat lies in store:

Aguacate. Spanish for avocado, the key ingredient of guacamole. Also may be served halved at breakfast time, with a squeeze of lemon, or quartered or sliced as a garnish.

Albondigas. Meatballs, usually served with vegetables in a broth.

Burrito. A warm flour tortilla wrapped around meat, beans, or vegetables. Burritos are occasionally crisp-fried; filled with meat, fish, or chicken; and topped with refried beans, shredded lettuce, and chopped tomatoes.

Chayote. A light green, pear-shape vegetable (it looks like a squash) with edible seeds.

Chile relleno. A large, mild green chile pepper, peeled, stuffed with cheese or a special mixture of spicy ingredients, dipped in batter, and fried.

Chiles. Mexico's infamous hot peppers, which come in an endless variety of sizes and in various degrees of hotness, from the thumb-size jalapeño to the smaller and often hotter serrano. They can be canned or fresh, dried or cut up into salsa.

Chimichanga. The same as a burrito above, only deep-fried and topped with a dash of sour cream or salsa.

Chorizo. Well-spiced Spanish sausage, made with red chile.

Enchilada. A rolled corn tortilla, filled with meat, chicken, seafood, chiles, or cheese; covered with salsa; and baked. The ultimate enchilada is made with blue Indian corn tortillas. New Mexicans order them flat, sometimes topped with a fried egg.

Flauta. A tortilla filled with cheese or meat and rolled into a flutelike shape (*flauta* means flute) and lightly fried. When eaten, they're usually dipped into a spicy sauce.

Frijoles refritos. Refried beans, often seasoned with lard, cheese, or a little river of pumpkin-seed oil.

Guacamole. Mashed avocado, mixed with tomatoes, garlic, onions, lemon juice, and hot sauce, used as a dip, a sauce, or a side dish.

Huevos rancheros. New Mexico's answer to eggs Benedict—eggs doused with chile and sometimes melted cheese, served on top of a tortilla. They're good accompanied by chorizos.

Jicama. A large, brown-skinned root, shaped like a turnip. Sweet and crisp, it's either cooked or peeled and eaten raw.

Nopales. Leaves of the prickly-pear cactus, available canned (*nopalitos*) or fresh.

Posole. Resembling popcorn soup, this is a sublime marriage of lime hominy, pork, chile, garlic, and spices.

Quesadilla. A folded tortilla, filled with cheese and warmed or lightly fried so the cheese melts.

Sopapilla. Puffy deep-fried bread, served with honey.

Taco. A corn or flour tortilla, fried and made into a shell that's then stuffed with spicy meat or chicken, and garnished with shredded lettuce, radishes, chopped tomatoes, onions, olives, and grated cheese.

Tamale. Crushed Indian corn and finely chopped meat, seasoned with red pepper, rolled in a corn shuck, then steamed or baked.

Tortilla. Thin pancake made of corn or wheat flour, used as bread, as an edible "spoon," and as a container for other foods. Locals place butter in the center of a hot tortilla, roll it up, and eat it as a scroll. It is also useful for scooping up the last bit in a bowl of chili.

Verde. Spanish for "green." Salsa chile verde is a green chile sauce.

Lodging

In the early days of the American West, it wasn't uncommon for a cowboy, with one too many tequilas under his belt, to ride his horse right through the front door of a hotel and into the lobby. Hotels were more informal in those days, and scarce—so scarce, in fact, that guests frequently not only had to share rooms with total strangers but had to share beds with them as well. Traces of that informality remain in New Mexico to this day, albeit not to such extremes; you'll never be intimidated by management or staff, by dress codes, or by menus you can't read. Bellboys usually wear clean white shirts and jeans, and the switchboard operator or the desk clerk may call you by your first name.

However, New Mexico is a hot tourist destination that attracts lots of upscale travelers. As a result, prices have been escalating steadily and are likely to continue to climb as long as a steady stream of tourists continues to pay them. Low-season rates, which fluctuate, tend to be 20% lower than during the peak tourist months of July and August. Reservations are also easier to obtain during low season. In addition to hotels, New Mexico offers a broad range of alternative accommodations, from charming bed-and-breakfasts in quaint residential areas to small alpine lodges near the primary ski resorts.

Home Exchange This is obviously an inexpensive solution to the lodging problem, because house-swapping means living rent-free. You find a house, apartment, or other vacation property to exchange for your own by becoming a member of a home-exchange organization, which then sends you its annual directories listing available exchanges and includes your own listing in at least one of them. Arrangements for the actual exchange are made by the two parties to it, not by the organization. Principal clearinghouses include **Intervac U.S./International Home Exchange** (Box 590504, San Francisco, CA 94159, tel. 415/435–3497), the oldest, with thousands of foreign and domestic homes for exchange in its three annual directories; membership is $62, or $72 if you want to receive the directories but remain unlisted. The **Vacation Exchange Club** (Box 650, Key West, FL 33041, tel. 800/638–3841), also with thousands of foreign and domestic listings, publishes four annual directories plus updates; the $50 membership includes your listing in one book. **Loan-a-Home** (2 Park La., Apt. 6E, Mount Vernon, NY 10552, tel. 914/664–7640) specializes in long-term exchanges; there is no charge to list your home, but the directories cost $35 or $45 depending on the number you receive.

If you want a home base that's roomy enough for a family and comes with cooking facilities, a furnished rental may be the solution. It's generally cost-wise, too, although not always—some rentals are luxury properties (economical only when your party is large). Home-exchange directories do list rentals—often second homes owned by prospective house swappers— and there are services that not only look for a house or apartment for you (even a castle if that's your fancy) but also handle the paperwork. Some send an illustrated catalogue and others send photographs of specific properties, sometimes at a charge; up-front registration fees may apply.

Among the companies is **Rent a Home International** (7200 34th Ave. NW, Seattle, WA 98117, tel. 206/789–9377 or 800/ 488–7368), which handles properties in Santa Fe. **Hideaways International** (767 Islington St., Box 4433, Portsmouth, NH 03802, tel. 603/430–4433 or 800/843–4433) functions as a travel club. Membership ($79 yearly per person or family at the same address) includes two annual guides plus quarterly newsletters; rentals are arranged directly between members, not by the club staff.

Credit Cards

The following credit card abbreviations are used: AE, American Express; D, Discover; DC, Diners Club; MC, MasterCard; and V, Visa. It's a good idea to call ahead to check on an establishment's credit-card policies.

2 Portrait of New Mexico

New Mexico

By D. H.
Lawrence

Superficially, the world has become small and known. Poor little globe of earth, the tourists trot round you as easily as they trot round the Bois or round Central Park. There is no mystery left, we've been there, we've seen it, we know all about it. We've done the globe, and the globe is done.

This is quite true, superficially. On the superficies, horizontally, we've been everywhere and done everything, we know all about it. Yet the more we know, superficially, the less we penetrate, vertically. It's all very well skimming across the surface of the ocean, and saying you know all about the sea. There still remain the terrifying under-deeps, of which we have utterly no experience.

The same is true of land travel. We skim along, we get there, we see it all, we've done it all. And as a rule, we never once go through the curious film which railroads, ships, motor-cars, and hotels stretch over the surface of the whole earth. Peking is just the same as New York, with a few different things to look at; rather more Chinese about, etc. Poor creatures that we are, we crave for experience, yet we are like flies that crawl on the pure and transparent mucous-paper in which the world like a bon-bon is wrapped so carefully that we can never get at it, though we see it there all the time as we move about it, apparently in contact, yet actually as far removed as if it were the moon.

As a matter of fact, our great-grandfathers, who never went anywhere, in actuality had more experience of the world than we have, who have seen everything. When they listened to a lecture with lantern-slides, they really held their breath before the unknown, as they sat in the village school-room. We, bowling along in a rickshaw in Ceylon, say to ourselves: "It's very much what you'd expect." We really know it all.

We are mistaken. The know-it-all state of mind is just the result of being outside the mucous-paper wrapping of civilization. Underneath is everything we don't know and are afraid of knowing.

I realized this with shattering force when I went to New Mexico.

This essay is taken from Phoenix: The Posthumous Papers of D. H. Lawrence. *Lawrence visited New Mexico with his wife, Frieda, in the early 1920s as part of an extended tour of Europe, Mexico, and the American Southwest. The couple lived on a ranch north of Taos, where Lawrence continued to write.*

New Mexico, one of the United States, part of the U.S.A. New Mexico, the picturesque reservation and playground of the eastern states, very romantic, old Spanish, Red Indian, desert mesas, pueblos, cowboys, penitentes, all that film-stuff. Very nice, the great South-West, put on a sombrero and knot a red kerchief round your neck, to go out in the great free spaces!

That is New Mexico wrapped in the absolutely hygienic and shiny mucous-paper of our trite civilization. That is the New Mexico known to most of the Americans who know it at all. But break through the shiny sterilized wrapping, and actually *touch* the country, and you will never be the same again.

I think New Mexico was the greatest experience from the outside world that I have ever had. It certainly changed me for ever. Curious as it may sound, it was New Mexico that liberated me from the present era of civilization, the great era of material and mechanical development. Months spent in holy Kandy, in Ceylon, the holy of holies of Southern Buddhism, had not touched the great psyche of materialism and idealism which dominated me. And years, even in the exquisite beauty of Sicily, right among the old Greek paganism that still lives there, had not shattered the essential Christianity on which my character was established. Australia was a sort of dream or trance, like being under a spell, the self remaining unchanged, so long as the trance did not last too long. Tahiti, in a mere glimpse, repelled me; and so did California, after a stay of a few weeks. There seemed a strange brutality in the spirit of the western coast, and I felt: O, let me get away!

But the moment I saw the brilliant, proud morning shine high up over the deserts of Santa Fe, something stood still in my soul, and I started to attend. There was a certain magnificence in the high-up day, a certain eagle-like royalty, so different from the equally pure, equally pristine and lovely morning of Australia, which is so soft, so utterly pure in its softness, and betrayed by green parrot flying. But in the lovely morning of Australia one went into a dream. In the magnificent fierce morning of New Mexico one sprang awake, a new part of the soul woke up suddenly, and the old world gave way to a new.

There are all kinds of beauty in the world, thank God, though ugliness is homogeneous. How lovely is Sicily, with Calabria across the sea like an opal, and Etna with her snow in a world above and beyond! How lovely is Tuscany, with little red tulips wild among the corn: or bluebells at dusk in England, or mimosa in clouds of pure yellow among the grey-green dun foliage of Australia, under a soft, blue, unbreathed sky! But for a *greatness* of beauty I have never experienced anything like New Mexico. All those mornings when I went with a hoe along the ditch to the Cañon, at the ranch, and stood, in the fierce, proud silence of the Rockies,

on their foothills, to look far over the desert to the blue
mountains away in Arizona, blue as chalcedony, with the
sage-brush desert sweeping grey-blue in between, dotted
with tiny cube-crystals of houses, the vast amphitheatre of
lofty, indomitable desert, sweeping round to the ponderous
Sangre de Cristo mountains on the east, and coming up
flush at the pine-dotted foot-hills of the Rockies! What
splendor! Only the tawny eagle could really sail out into the
splendor of it all. Leo Stein once wrote to me: It is the most
aesthetically-satisfying landscape I know. To me it was
much more than that. It had a splendid silent terror, and a
vast far-and-wide magnificence which made it way beyond
mere aesthetic appreciation. Never is the light more pure
and overweening than there, arching with a royalty almost
cruel over the hollow, uptilted world. For it is curious that
the land which has produced modern political democracy at
its highest pitch should give one the greatest sense of overweening, terrible proudness and mercilessness: but so
beautiful, God! so beautiful! Those that have spent morning
after morning alone there pitched among the pines above
the great proud world of desert will know, almost unbeara-
bly how beautiful it is, how clear and unquestioned is the
might of the day. Just day itself is tremendous there. It is so
easy to understand that the Aztecs gave hearts of men to
the sun. For the sun is not merely hot or scorching, not at
all. It is of a brilliant and unchallengeable purity and
haughty serenity which would make one sacrifice the heart
to it. Ah, yes, in New Mexico the heart is sacrificed to the
sun and the human being is left stark, heartless, but un-
dauntedly religious.

And that was the second revelation out there. I had
looked over all the world for something that would
strike *me* as religious. The simple piety of some English people, the semi-pagan mystery of some Catholics in
southern Italy, the intensity of some Bavarian peasants,
the semi-ecstasy of Buddhists or Brahmins: all this had
seemed religious all right, as far as the parties concerned
were involved, but it didn't involve me. I looked on at the
religiousness from the outside. For it is still harder to feel
religion at will than to love at will.

I had seen what I felt was a hint of wild religion in the so-
called devil dances of a group of naked villagers from the
far-remote jungle in Ceylon, dancing at midnight under the
torches, glittering wet with sweat on their dark bodies as if
they had been gilded, at the celebration of the Pera-hera, in
Kandy, given to the Prince of Wales. And the utter dark absorption of these naked men, as they danced with their
knees wide apart suddenly affected me with a *sense* of religion. I *felt* religion for a moment. For religion is an experience, an uncontrollable sensual experience, even more so
than love: I use sensual to mean an experience deep down in
the senses, inexplicable and inscrutable.

But this experience was fleeting, gone in the curious turmoil of the Pera-hera, and I had no permanent feeling of religion till I came to New Mexico and penetrated into the old human race-experience there. It is curious that it should be in America, of all places, that a European should really experience religion, after touching the old Mediterranean and the East. . . . A vast old religion which once swayed the earth lingers in unbroken practice there in New Mexico, older, perhaps, than anything in the world save Australian aboriginal taboo and totem, and that is not yet religion.

You can feel it, the atmosphere of it, around the pueblos. Not, of course, when the place is crowded with sight-seers and motor-cars. But go to Taos pueblo on some brilliant snowy morning and see the white figure on the roof: or come riding through at dusk on some windy evening, when the black skirts of the silent women blow around the white wide boots, and you will feel the old, old root of human consciousness still reaching down to depths we know nothing of: and of which, only too often, we are jealous. It seems it will not be long before the pueblos are uprooted.

But never shall I forget watching the dancers, the men with the fox-skin swaying down from their buttocks, file out at San Geronimo, and the women with seed rattles following. The long, streaming, glistening black hair of the men. Even in ancient Crete long hair was sacred in a man, as it is still in the Indians. Never shall I forget the utter absorption of the dance, so quiet, so steadily, timelessly rhythmic, and silent, with the ceaseless downtread, always to the earth's centre, the very reverse of the upflow of Dionysiac or Christian ecstasy. Never shall I forget the deep singing of the men at the drum, swelling and sinking, the deepest sound I have heard in all my life, deeper than thunder, deeper than the sound of the Pacific Ocean, deeper than the roar of a deep waterfall: the wonderful deep sound of men calling to the unspeakable depths.

Never shall I forget coming into the little pueblo of San Filipi one sunny morning in spring, unexpectedly, when bloom was on the trees in the perfect little pueblo more old, more utterly peaceful and idyllic than anything in Theocritus, and seeing a little casual dance. Not impressive as a spectacle, only, to me, profoundly moving because of the truly terrifying religious absorption of it.

Never shall I forget the Christmas dances at Taos, twilight, snow, the darkness coming over the great wintry mountains and the lonely pueblo, then suddenly, again, like dark calling to dark, the deep Indian cluster-singing around the drum, wild and awful, suddenly arousing on the last dusk as the procession starts. And then the bon-fires leaping suddenly in pure spurts of high flame, columns of sudden flame forming an alley for the procession. . . . Never shall I forget the Indian races, when the young men, even the boys, run naked, smeared with white earth and stuck with bits of eagle fluff for the swiftness of the heavens, and the old men brush them with eagle feathers, to give them power. And they run in the strange hurling fashion of the primitive world, hurled forward, not making speed deliberately. And the race is not for victory. It is not a contest. There is no competition. It is a great cumulative effort. The tribe this day is adding up its male energy and exerting it to the utmost—for what? To get power, to get strength: to come, by sheer cumulative, hurling effort of the bodies of men, into contact with the great cosmic source of vitality which gives strength, power, energy to the men who can grasp it, energy for the zeal of attainment.

It was a vast old religion, greater than anything we know: more starkly and nakedly religious. There is no God, no conception of a god. All is god. But it is not the pantheism we are accustomed to, which expresses itself as "God is everywhere, God is in everything." In the oldest religion, everything was alive, not supernaturally but naturally alive. There were only deeper and deeper streams of life, vibrations of life more and more vast. So rocks were alive, but a mountain had a deeper, vaster life than a rock, and it was much harder for a man to bring his spirit, or his energy, into contact with the life of the mountain, and so draw strength from the mountain, as from a great standing well of life, than it was to come into contact with the rock. And he had to put forth a great religious effort. For the whole life-effort of man was to get his life into direct contact with the elemental life of the cosmos, mountain-life, cloud-life, thunder-life, air-life, earth-life, sun-life. To come into immediate *felt* contact, and so derive energy, power, and a dark sort of joy. This effort into sheer naked contact, *without an intermediary or mediator*, is the root meaning of religion, and at the sacred races the runners hurled themselves in a terrible cumulative effort, through the air, to come at last into naked contact with the very life of air, which is the life of the clouds, and so of the rain.

It was a vast and pure religion, without idols or images, even mental ones. It is the oldest religion, a cosmic religion the same for all peoples, not broken up into specific gods or saviours or systems. It is the religion which precedes the god-concept, and is therefore greater and deeper than any god-religion.

And it lingers still, for a little while in New Mexico: but long enough to have been a revelation to me. And the Indian, however objectionable he may be on occasion, has still some of the strange beauty and pathos of the religion that brought him forth and is now shedding him away into oblivion. When Trinidad, the Indian boy, and I planted corn at the ranch, my soul paused to see his brown hands softly moving the earth over the maize in pure ritual. He was back in his old religious self, and the ages stood still. Ten minutes later he was making a fool of himself with the horses.

Horses were never part of the Indian's religious life, never would be. He hasn't a tithe of feeling for them that he has for a bear, for example. So horses don't like Indians.

But there it is: the newest democracy ousting the oldest religion! And once the oldest religion is ousted, one feels the democracy and all its paraphernalia will collapse, and the oldest religion, which comes down to us from man's pre-war days, will start again. The skyscraper will scatter on the winds like thistledown, and the genuine America, the America of New Mexico, will start on its course again. This is an interregnum.

3 Santa Fe and Vicinity

With its crisp, clear air and bright, sunny weather, Santa Fe couldn't be more welcoming. Perched on a 7,000-foot-high plateau at the base of the Sangre de Cristo Mountains, the city is surrounded by the remnants of a 2,000-year-old Pueblo civilization, and filled with evidence of Spanish rule. Add rows of chic art galleries, smart restaurants, and shops selling Southwestern furnishings and cowboy gear, and you have a uniquely appealing destination that is growing increasingly popular every year.

La Villa Real de la Santa Fe de San Francisco de Asis (the Royal City of the Holy Faith of St. Francis of Assisi) was founded in 1609 by Don Pedro de Peralta, who planted his banner in the name of Spain; St. Augustine, Florida, is the only city in the United States that's older. Santa Fe's Paseo de Peralta—a paved loop that approximates the former boundaries of the original Spanish Colonial outpost—still protects the vital core of the city, if only symbolically. The town plaza, laid out in 1609 and now filled with Native American vendors, has been the site of bullfights, public floggings, gunfights, tribal wars, political rallies, and promenades, as well as public markets.

In 1680, the Native Americans of San Juan drove the Spanish out, burning their churches and missions and turning the Palace of the Governors into a tribal dwelling. But the tide turned again 12 years later, when General Don Diego de Vargas returned with a new army from El Paso and recaptured Santa Fe without firing a shot. To commemorate Don Diego's triumph, Las Fiestas de Santa Fe has been held every year since 1712. The country's oldest community celebration traditionally takes place the weekend after Labor Day, with parades, mariachis, pageants, melodramas, arts-and-crafts shows, and nonstop private parties. Though the best-known, Las Fiestas de Santa Fe is but one of numerous opportunities for revelry throughout the year—everything from a celebration to start the rodeo season in mid-July to traditional Pueblo dances at Christmas.

The road from the south, one of the two main arteries into town, is the once-grand Camino Real (Royal Highway). As spectacular for its time as the transcontinental Pan American Highway is today, El Camino Real originally stretched from Mexico City to Santa Fe, bringing an army of conquistadores to the northernmost reaches of their New World conquest. Now, however, visitors who drive along the last 5-mile stretch into town from the south will find it lined with motels, gas stations, fast-food restaurants, launderettes, and convenience stores.

The Old Santa Fe Trail from the northeast also brought newcomers—first traders to sell goods to the Spanish, then settlers from Missouri and beyond. The covered-wagon days of this famous route ended with the arrival of the railroad—the Atchison, Topeka and Santa Fe, a line made far more famous, perhaps, by the Andrews Sisters' hit recording than by its initial arrival in town in 1880. The Old Santa Fe Trail has survived the ravages of time and progress with far more grace than has El Camino Real, giving first-time visitors a more accurate impression of the town that lies ahead: The route is lined with splendid Southwest-style homes made of adobe and stucco. As one approaches town, the buildings become larger and closer together, but Santa Fe remains mercifully free of skyscrapers; a town ordinance keeps all buildings within a five-story limit.

Melded into the landscape with their earthen colors and rounded, flowing lines—and thus difficult to see from afar—the adobe pueblos of the area's original inhabitants were so styled as a means of protection from enemy tribes and, later, from Spanish explorers. Today the distinct Pueblo-style architecture that has come to characterize Santa Fe and its environs attracts rather than repels visitors—although the predominance of adobe, pure or ersatz, flat-roofed Colonial style or climbing pueblo fashion, can be a bit overwhelming. As a result of the tendency to build in this style, the State Capitol, the Santa Fe Hilton, the Camera Shop of Santa Fe, and One Hour Martinizing all look pretty much alike.

Santa Fe is among the smallest state capitals in the country and is without a major airport. The city's population, an estimated 55,000, swells to nearly double that figure during the peak summer season and again in the winter, when skiers arrive, lured by the challenging slopes of the Santa Fe Ski Area and those of nearby Taos Ski Valley. Geared for tourists, Santa Fe can put a serious dent in your travel budget. Prices are highest in June, July, and August. September–October and the shoulder months, November and April, are lower. Rates are lowest (except for the major holidays) December–March. In general, hotel rates are on a par with top hotels and resorts in popular spots all over the globe, and prices charged for contemporary artwork in Santa Fe—the third major art center in the country after New York and Los Angeles—can be astonishingly high.

Essential Information

Important Addresses and Numbers

Tourist Information
The **Santa Fe Convention and Visitors Bureau** (201 W. Marcy St., Box 909, 87504, tel. 505/984–6760 or 800/777–2489) has Santa Fe visitor guides, brochures, maps, and calendar listings. The **Santa Fe Chamber of Commerce** (510 N. Guadalupe St., De Vargas Center N., 87501, tel. 505/983–7317) is geared more toward the traveling businessperson and individuals relocating to Santa Fe, providing assistance and general information. The **New Mexico Department of Tourism** (Lamy Bldg., 491 Old Santa Fe Trail, 87503, tel. 505/827–7400) offers a wealth of booklets and printed mate-

rial on all areas of New Mexico. The **BBS Bulletin Board** (tel. 505/988–5867), a computerized library, carries ski and tourist information for Santa Fe. Except for long-distance calls, the 24-hour service is free to anyone with a modem-equipped computer.

Another good source of information is the **Santa Fe Public Library,** whose main branch (145 Washington Ave., tel. 505/984–6780) is just off the Plaza in a historic building that has served at various times as city hall and police and fire stations (the large windows in front are where the fire engines used to rush out). Here you'll find bus route maps, discount taxi coupons, and a wealth of local literature.

Emergencies **Fire, ambulance, police** (tel. 911).

Medical Emergency Room. St. Vincent Hospital (455 St. Michaels Dr., tel. 505/983–3361; 24-hour hospital hot line, tel. 505/989–5242).

Medical Clinics. Ambulatory Surgical Center of Santa Fe (102 Faithway St., tel. 505/982–6317), **Lovelace Urgent Care** (901 W. Alameda, tel. 505/986–3656; 440 St. Michaels Dr., tel. 505/986–3566).

Dental Clinics. Medical Dental Center (465 St. Michaels Dr., tel. 505/982–2578) will see walk-in patients on an emergency basis.

Late-Night **Lee Pharmacies (Medical Center Pharmacy,** 465 St. Mi-
Pharmacies chaels Dr., tel. 505/983–4359, and **Fraser Pharmacy,** 505 Old Santa Fe Trail, tel. 505/982–5524) and **Medicap Pharmacy** (2801 Rodeo Rd., tel. 505/471–6177) all offer 24-hour emergency service. Pharmacies at Lovelace (*see above*) are open until 8 PM.

Other Numbers Weather information (tel. 505/988–3437).

Time and temperature (tel. 505/473–2211).

Arriving and Departing

By Plane *See* Arriving and Departing in Chapter 1.

By Rail **Amtrak's** (tel. 800/872–7245) *Southwest Chief* serves Santa Fe via the village of Lamy, 17 miles from town, daily on routes from Chicago and Los Angeles. A connecting Amtrak shuttle-bus service (tel. 505/982–8829 in Santa Fe, tel. 505/988–4511 in Lamy) is available to and from town. The one-way fare is $14.

By Bus **Greyhound/Trailways** (858 St. Michaels Dr., tel. 505/471–0008) offers comprehensive daily service to and from Santa Fe.

By Car Although located in a secluded mountain setting, Santa Fe is easily accessible; it's a day's drive from several metropolitan areas from points north and south via I–25 or U.S. 84/285.

Getting around Santa Fe

Downtown Santa Fe is easily maneuvered on foot, with the majority of its museums, galleries, shops, and restaurants located within a comfortable radius of the famous Santa Fe Plaza. But you'll need transportation for the city's outer reaches, including such attractions as the International Folk Art Museum and the Museum of Indian Arts and Culture. Even a tour of the art galleries along Canyon Road can be a hilly 2-mile stretch. Fortunately, the city has inaugurated its first major bus system, **Santa Fe Trails.** So far, the line's smart tan buses cover four major routes: West Alameda, Southside, Eastside, and Galisteo. For information, tel. 505/984–6730. Tell the operator where you are and where you want to go, and advice will be forthcoming. Fares are 50¢ adults, 25¢ students under 18 (with school ID) and seniors. Buses run approximately every 30 minutes weekdays, every hour weekends, and there's no service after 7:30 PM.

By Car Following is a list of car-rental services in Santa Fe: **Adopt-A-Car** (3570 Cerrillos Rd., tel. 505/473–3189), **Agency** (3157 Cerrillos Rd., tel. 505/473–2983), **Avis** (Garrett's Desert Inn, 311 Old Santa Fe Trail, tel. 505/982–4361), **Budget** (1946 Cerrillos Rd., tel. 505/984–8028), **Hertz** (100 Sandoval St., in the Hilton of Santa Fe lobby, tel. 505/982–1844), **Snappy** (3012 Cielo Ct., tel. 505/473–2277), and **Thrifty** (1718 Cerrillos Rd., tel. 505/984–1961).

By Taxi Public transportation in town is monopolized by **Capital City Cab Company** (tel. 505/438–0000), the only taxi service in Santa Fe. The taxis aren't metered; you pay a flat fee determined by the distance you're going. There are no official cab stands in town; you must phone to arrange a ride—and if you're lucky, a cab will show up. Rates for various points within the city range from $4 to $7. You can pick up a 40% taxi discount coupon at the Santa Fe Public Library (*see* Tourist Information, *above*).

By Limo If you're feeling flush or the occasion warrants it, you can call the **Dream Limousine Service** (tel. 505/884–6464), **Elegante Luxury Transportation Service** (tel. 505/473–1115), or **Limotion VIP Limousine Service** (tel. 505/982–5466). Fares average about $35 per hour, generally with a two-hour minimum.

Opening and Closing Times

Store and commercial hours may vary from place to place and season to season (remaining open longer in summer than in winter), but the following is a general guide: banks, weekdays 9–3; museums, daily 10–5; stores, Monday–Saturday 10–6; post office, weekdays 8–5.

Guided Tours

General-Interest **Aboot About/Santa Fe Walks** (Box 452, 87504, tel. 505/988–
Tours 2774) is a 2½-hour walking tour through the "City Differ-
ent" led by a long-time resident historian. It leaves the
Eldorado Hotel daily at 9:30 and 1:30.

Afoot in Santa Fe Walking Tours (211 Old Santa Fe Trail,
87501, tel. 505/983–3701) offers a 2½-hour get-acquainted,
close-up look at the city with the help of resident guides. It
leaves from the Inn at Loreto.

Gray Line of Santa Fe (1330 Hickock St., 87501, tel. 505/
983–9491) features a variety of daily tours leaving from and
returning to the Santa Fe Bus Depot (hotel and motel pickups by advance arrangement). Taos, Bandelier Cliff Dwellings, Los Alamos, and the Santa Clara Pueblo are among
the company's destinations. In winter, the availability of
tours is subject to road and weather conditions.

Recursos (826 Camino de Monte Rey, Suite A-3, 87501, tel.
505/982–9301) runs historical, cultural, and nature tours.

Santa Fe Detours (La Fonda Hotel lobby, 100 E. San Francisco St., 87501, tel. 505/983–6565) includes tours by bus,
river, and rail; city walks; trail rides; and ski packages.

Special-Interest **Art Tours of Santa Fe** (310 E. Marcy St., 87501, tel. 505/
Tours 988–3527) specializes in visits to historic sites, museums,
galleries, artists' studios, private homes, and collections;
tours are accompanied by authorities on art, archaeology,
and New Mexican history.

Ghost Tours of Santa Fe (142 Lincoln Ave., Suite 103, 87502,
tel. 505/984–2080) takes its often-apprehensive group of evening travelers on an eerie, 90-minute journey through the
alleyways, hidden graveyards, and haunted buildings of
downtown Santa Fe, where, it is believed, witches once
roamed and the ghosts of broken-hearted women and gam-
blers still linger.

House and garden tours have always been popular in Santa
Fe and are scheduled periodically, depending on the mood
and disposition of property owners and guides. The **Santa
Fe Architect Society** (tel. 505/983–7421) opens a different
home each year to visitors, usually in August, a week after
the Sunday of Indian Market Weekend. **Behind Adobe Walls
and Garden Tours** (tel. 505/983–6565 or 800/338–6877) generally schedules tours during the last two Tuesdays of July
and the first two Tuesdays of August. Contact the Santa Fe
Convention and Visitors Bureau (*see* Important Addresses
and Numbers, *above*) for late-breaking house-tour an-
nouncements.

Native American Tours (142 Lincoln Ave., Suite 103, Box
22658, 87502, tel. 505/986–0804 or 800/5–PUEBLO, fax
505/986–0812) is a newly formed group, completely operated by Native Americans, covering such sights and attrac-

tions as the ruins of Bandelier, pueblos, petroglyphs, Indian arts and crafts, storytelling sessions, Chaco Canyon, and Canyon de Chelley. Founder Elaina Ortiz of the San Juan Pueblo is the daughter of an archaeologist. Both standard and customized tours are available.

Rojo Tours (228 Old Santa Fe Trail, 87501, tel. 505/983–8333) offers a variety of specialized trips—to view wildflowers, pueblo ruins and cliff dwellings, galleries and studios, Native American arts and crafts, and private homes—as well as adventure tours, such as ballooning, white-water rafting, hiking, and horseback riding, all with hotel and motel pickups.

Southwest Adventure Group (142 Lincoln Ave., Suite 103, 85702, tel. 505/984–2080 or 800/766–5443), along with adventure tours, also has a number of special-interest offerings, such as guided photo walks, studio tours of artists' galleries and workshops, craft tours, and cooking-tasting tours.

Studio Entrada (Box 4934, Santa Fe 87502, tel. 505/983–8786) gives informal tours of the studios and ateliers of some of Santa Fe's best-known artists and craftspeople, enabling visitors to buy directly from the artists, often at considerable savings over gallery prices.

Learning Experiences

Santa Fe School of Cooking (116 W. San Francisco St., tel. 505/983–4511) offers both night and day classes that allow visitors to capture the flavor of regional New Mexican fare. Classes range from a two-hour basic demonstration exploring the rich flavors and history of northern New Mexican and Southwestern cuisine to more elaborate undertakings, with particular emphasis on exploring the wonders of special chile sauces. The results, good or bad, may be eaten. The beginners' class is $30; other rates vary depending on the class. The school is headed by Susan Curtis and Jennifer Livesay, who suggest that reservations be made in advance, and is located on the upper level of Plaza Mercado, only a block from the main Plaza.

Travel Photography Workshop is a week-long photography blitz headed by Lisl Dennis, a noted photographer whose work appears regularly in *Outdoor Photographer* and other major publications and who has authored a number of books on photographic techniques. A tuition of $1,125 includes workshop sessions; photo field trips to Chimayo, Rancho de Taos, and Taos; critiques; lodging and some meals. Lisl Dennis and her husband, author Landt Dennis, also offer a number of international photography workshop tours. For inquiries, contact Travel Photography Workshop in Santa Fe (Box 2847, Santa Fe 87504, tel. 505/982–4979, fax 505/983–9489).

Exploring Santa Fe

Humorist Will Rogers said on his first visit to Santa Fe, "Whoever designed this town did so while riding on a jackass, backwards and drunk." While the maze of narrow streets and alleyways may confound motorists, it's a delight for shoppers and pedestrians, who will find attractive shops and restaurants, a flowered courtyard, or yet another eye-catching gallery to explore at just about every turn.

Highlights for First-time Visitors

Beneath the portales of the Palace of the Governors (*see* Tour 1)
Canyon Road art galleries (*see* Tour 2)
Cathedral of St. Francis (*see* Tour 2)
Loretto Chapel (*see* Tour 3)
Museum of International Folk Art (*see* Tour 3)
Santa Fe Plaza (*see* Tour 1)

Tour 1: Santa Fe Plaza

Numbers in the margin correspond to points of interest on the Santa Fe map.

❶ A get-acquainted stroll of the city begins logically enough with the historic **Plaza** that forms its heart. Originally laid out in 1609–10 as the city's center for religious and military activities by New Mexico governor Don Pedro de Peralta, it witnessed the revolt of the Pueblos in 1680 and the peaceful recapture of Santa Fe in 1692. It once held a bullring, was the site of fiestas and fandangos, and was the actual end of the Santa Fe Trail, where freight wagons would unload after completing their arduous journeys. The American flag was raised over it in 1846, as was the standard of the Confederate army, some 20 years later, before Santa Fe was recaptured by Union forces. For a time it was a tree-shaded park, complete with a white picket fence, and later, in the Gay '90s, an expanse of lawn, where uniformed bands played from within the ornate gazebo at its center. Today, lined with shops, art galleries, and restaurants, it is as much the heart of the city as ever.

❷ The Pueblo-style **Palace of the Governors,** bordering the northern side of the Plaza on Palace Avenue, is the oldest public building in the United States. Built at the same time that the Plaza was laid out, it has been the key seat of government for four separate flags—Spain, Mexico, the Confederacy, and the U.S. territory that preceded New Mexico's statehood in 1912—serving as the residence for 100 Spanish, Native American, Mexican, and American governors.

Since 1913, the palace has been the central headquarters of the **Museum of New Mexico,** a state museum system that in-

Santa Fe

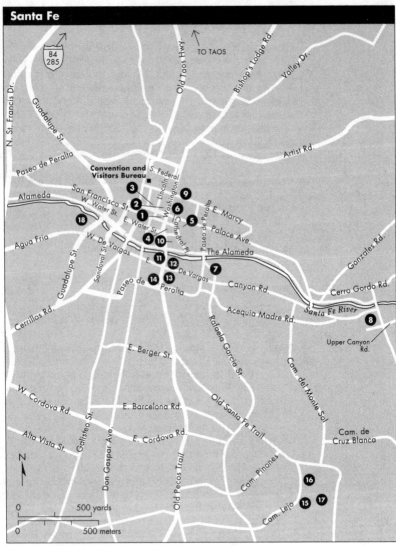

cludes four museums in Santa Fe—the on-site **History Museum,** the adjacent **Museum of Fine Arts,** the **Museum of Indian Arts and Culture,** and the **Museum of International Folk Art**—and five state monuments scattered about New Mexico: the prehistoric ruins at **Jemez** and **Coronado,** the historic frontier forts **Sumner** and **Selden,** and the historic community of **Lincoln.** There's no separate admission; a three-day pass for $5 allows admission to all state museums and monuments. For information, call 505/827–6474.

Permanent exhibits at the **History Museum** in the Palace of the Governors chronicle 450 years of New Mexico history. In addition to displays of furniture, clothing, and housewares, a collection of rare mural-size works, painted on elk and bison hides, depicts key historical events. Themes of changing exhibits may include frontier firearms and the Civil War in New Mexico. In the same building, the Museum of New Mexico Press prints books, cards, and booklets on antique presses and offers bookbinding demonstrations, lectures, and slide shows. With advance permission, students and researchers have access to an extensive historical-research library and collections of rare maps and manuscripts, as well as photographs (more than 120,000 prints and negatives). *Box 2087, 87504–2087, north side of the Plaza (Palace Ave.), tel. 505/827–6474. Admission: 3-day pass $5, children under 17 free. Open daily 10–5. Closed Mon. during Jan. and Feb.; Thanksgiving, Christmas, and New Year's Day.*

Under the shaded portals of the Palace of the Governors, **local Native American vendors** display and sell their wares as they've been doing for centuries. With few exceptions, the more than 500 vendors who are registered to sell under the portals are all members of New Mexico Pueblos or tribes. All merchandise on sale is required to meet Museum of New Mexico standards: Items are all handmade or hand-strung in Native American households; silver jewelry is either sterling (92.5% pure) or coin silver (90% pure); all metal jewelry bears the maker's mark, which is registered with the museum. Prices tend to reflect the high quality of the merchandise and the mastery of art forms that require years of apprenticeship and learning. Books, regional magazines, owners and salesclerks at reputable shops, and the vendors themselves are all good sources of information about Native American arts and crafts. No bargaining is allowed (except perhaps discreetly when purchasing two or more items), and no photographs should be taken unless permission is requested and granted.

Across from the Palace of the Governors (turn right upon exiting and cross Lincoln Ave.), the **Museum of Fine Arts,** dating from 1917, was Santa Fe's first Pueblo Revival–style structure. More than any other building, it inspired the architectural trend in the region that continues to this day. Inside, the ceilings are made of split cedar *latillas* (branches set in a cross-hatched pattern) and hand-hewn *vigas* (beams); many excellent examples of Spanish Coloni-al–style furniture are on display. The 8,000-piece perma-nent collection emphasizes the work of regional artists, including Georgia O'Keeffe and the Taos Masters (Ernest Blumenschein, Bert Geer Philips, Joseph Henry Sharp, and Eanger Irving Couse, among them), as well as that of Mexican (such as Diego Rivera), Southwestern, and Native American artists. Sculpture is displayed in three adjoining courtyards. *107 W. Palace Ave., tel. 505/827–4455. Admis-sion: 3-day pass $5, children under 17 free. Open daily 10–5. Closed Mon. during Jan. and Feb.; Thanksgiving, Christmas, and New Year's Day.*

If you cross to the far corner of the Plaza, where Shelby and East San Francisco streets meet, you'll find yourself virtu-ally in the lobby of Santa Fe's landmark hotel, **La Fonda** (*see* Lodging, *below*). Built in 1864 and refurbished several times in recent years, the hotel is still known fondly as "The Inn at the End of the Trail" because of its history as a gath-ering place for cowboys, trappers, pioneers, soldiers, drummers, and frontier politicians. It's still a major social setting for many of the town's activities.

Time Out Stop in at the lunch counter of **Woolworth's** on the Plaza (58 E. San Francisco St., tel. 505/982–1062)—the only Wool-worth's in New Mexico, opened in 1931—for some of its fa-mous Frito pie. A small portion of this tasty concoction of Fritos, chile, and cheese costs $2.35 and a large portion is $3.79.

Tour 2: Cathedral of St. Francis, Canyon Road

If the day's not too hot and you're in good physical condi-tion, this tour can be done on foot. Be aware, however, that Canyon Road is a long stretch, all uphill. In most cases, it's a good idea to drive.

A block east of the Plaza is the magnificent **Cathedral of St. Francis,** one of the rare departures from the city's steadfast pueblo design: Founded by Jean Baptiste Lamy, Santa Fe's first archbishop, it was built by French architects in 1869 in a French Romanesque style, with Italian stonemasons add-ing the finishing touches. The inspiration for Willa Cather's novel *Death Comes for the Archbishop*, the circuit-riding young Lamy, credited with resuscitating the Catholic faith in New Mexico, is buried in the crypt beneath the church's high altar. A small adobe chapel on the northeast side, the remnant of an earlier church built on the site, reveals the Spanish architectural influence so noticeably missing from the cathedral itself. Inside the chapel, *Nuestra Señora de la Paz* (Our Lady of Peace), is the oldest representation of the Madonna in the United States. This statue accompanied Don Diego de Vargas on his peaceful reconquest of Santa Fe

in 1692, a feat attributed to the statue's spiritual interven-
tion. Every Friday the faithful adorn *Nuestra Señora de la
Paz*, now the patron saint of New Mexico, with a new dress.
*131 Cathedral Pl., tel. 505/982–5619. Open daily. Mass cel-
ebrated daily at 6, 7, and 7:45 AM, 5:15 PM; Sun. at 6, 8, and
10 AM, noon and 7 PM.*

Across the street, in an expanded state-of-the-art facility in
❻ the renovated former Federal Post Office, is the **Museum of
the Institute of American Indian Arts,** which has the largest
collection of contemporary Native American art in the
United States. Its paintings, photography, and traditional
crafts showcase the work of the students and teachers, past
and present, of the prestigious Institute of American Indian Arts, located across town on Cerrillos Road, where it
was founded as a one-room studio classroom in the early
1930s. Established by Dorothy Dunn, a well-known teacher
and promoter of the Native American cause, the school was
taken over by the Bureau of Indian Affairs in 1962 and has
since blossomed into the major learning center for Native
American arts in the country. Famed artist Fritz Scholder
taught here for years. (Straining against the bonds of rigid
academia, he also taught informally at a compound on lower
W. Alameda.) Among his best-known disciples was T. C.
Cannon, who was killed in Santa Fe in 1978 at the age of 38
when his pickup truck crashed into a shallow ravine. Today,
Earl Biss, another Scholder protégé, paints dreamlike impressions of Native Americans on horseback moving relent-
lessly toward distant horizons, and he hasn't sold a dry
painting in years. Long hair flying in the wind, he's frequently seen whipping around town in a white Cadillac convertible. Kevin Red Star, born on the Crow Reservation in
Montana, as was Earl Biss, paints stylized warriors and
chiefs in full regalia, using strong earth colors and bold in-
terpretations. His work hangs in the Smithsonian and is
sold in major galleries throughout the country. Allan
Houser, a Chiricahua Apache (he Anglicized his original
name, Alan Haozous, thinking it would broaden his appeal),
has become one of America's legendary sculptors. He is
now in his mid-seventies and lives just outside of Santa Fe.
Painter Harrison Begay, a classmate of Houser's, is yet another illustrious alumnus of the institute. These artists are
all represented in the permanent collection. *Cathedral
Place, tel. 505/988–6281, or 505/988–6211 for events and
parking information. Admission: $3.50 adults, $2 children
under 16, students, and senior citizens. Open summer,
Mon.–Sat. 9–6 (Wed. 9–8), Sun. noon–5; winter, weekdays
10–5, weekends noon–5.*

If you walk south to the end of Cathedral Place and turn left
on Alameda for another block, crossing Paseo de Peralta,
❼ you'll come to **Canyon Road,** which once served as an Indian
trail. During the early part of the century, woodcutters
with their loaded burros used El Camino de Cañón as a
route into town, where they sold bundles of chopped wood

door to door. The road's 2-mile stretch from the center of town is now Santa Fe's most fashionable street, lined with many of the city's finest art galleries, shops, and restaurants—described affectionately by locals as "the art and soul of Santa Fe." If you're driving, remember that parking is at a premium on Canyon Road. A shopping complex at the lower end (225 Canyon Rd.) provides parking and rest rooms for customers only. The municipal parking lot at the juncture of Canyon Road and Camino del Monte Sol costs $1 per hour.

Upper Canyon Road is the city's high-rent district, containing some of its most elegant homes. At its terminus is the historic **Randall Davy House** (Upper Canyon Rd., tel. 505/983–4609), once the home and studio of one of the most prolific early Santa Fe artists and, since 1975, the regional headquarters of the National Audubon Society. It's open to the public daily 9–5 for self-guided tours.

❽ The **Cristo Rey Church,** at the corner of Upper Canyon Road and Cristo Rey, 1.5 miles from the Plaza, was built in 1939 to commemorate the 400th anniversary of Coronado's exploration of the Southwest. Built the old-fashioned way, with parishioners mixing the more than 200,000 mud-and-straw adobe bricks themselves and hauling them into place, it's the largest adobe structure in the United States and is considered by many to be the finest example of Pueblo-style architecture anywhere. No less impressive is the church's magnificent 225-ton stone *reredos* (altar screen). *1107 Cristo Rey, tel. 505/983–8528. Open daily 8–6.*

Time Out When you need a respite from shopping, drop into the **Bookroom Coffeebar** (616 Canyon Rd., tel. 505/988–5323) for a light snack and something to read.

If you don't want to spend the day along Canyon Road, another option when you're at St. Francis Cathedral is to head north. Within 600 yards of the Plaza, on a hill northeast of **❾** the city, lie the ruins of **Fort Marcy,** the first American military post in the Southwest (the entrance is near the corner of Paseo de Peralta and Otero St.). Something of a white elephant that never justified its massive size (the walls are 9 feet high and 5 feet thick), the adobe fort—named after William L. Marcy, the secretary of war under President Polk—was eventually abandoned. Only a few mounds of earth mark its former existence, but the overview from the hilltop of the city and of nearby mountain ranges (and, on a clear day, of the Sandia Mountains bordering Albuquerque) is spectacular. Also on the Fort Marcy hilltop, the huge white **Cross of the Martyrs,** raised and dedicated during the fiesta, September 1920, commemorates the lives of the 23 Franciscan monks who were killed by Native Americans in the Pueblo Revolt of 1680.

Tour 3: Along the Old Santa Fe Trail

The first part of this tour can be done on foot, but you'll need a car to go beyond the State Capitol building. Most of the sights noted are along the route of the Old Santa Fe Trail, but the final two, the Wheelright Museum of the American Indian and Santuario de Guadalupe, are at opposite ends of town, both south of the Plaza, but not particularly accessible from the Old Santa Fe Trail.

10 Behind the La Fonda Hotel and just to the left on the Old Santa Fe Trail is the **Loretto Chapel.** Started in 1873, the French-Romanesque chapel, modeled after the famous Parisian church Sainte-Chapelle, was built concurrently with the Cathedral of St. Francis; the same French architects and Italian stonemasons worked on both projects. The chapel is known for the "Miraculous Staircase" that leads to the choir loft. Legend has it that the chapel was almost finished when it became obvious that there wasn't room enough to complete a staircase to the choir loft. In answer to the prayers of the cathedral's sisters, an old, bearded man arrived on a donkey, built a 20-foot staircase—using only a square, a saw, and a tub of water to season the wood—and then disappeared as quickly as he came. Many of the faithful believe it was St. Joseph himself. Considered an engineering marvel, the staircase contains two complete 360-degree turns, a double helix with no central or visible support; no nails were used in its construction and the wood is like none found in the region. The chapel is maintained by the Inn at Loretto (*see* Lodging, *below*), which adjoins it. The corridor from the chapel vestibule to the hotel lobby and shops adds a bit of a tacky taste, even if all the money raised goes to a retirement home for nuns. *212 Old Santa Fe Trail, tel. 505/984–7971. Admission: $1 adults, children 12 and under free. Open daily 9–5.*

11 Continuing south along the Old Santa Fe Trail, crossing the bridge over the Santa Fe River, one block farther, you'll come to **Barrio de Analco** (now called E. De Vargas St.), believed to be one of the oldest continuously inhabited streets in the United States. Settled in the early 1600s by Mexican Indian mercenaries and Spanish colonists, it's also the oldest Spanish settlement in Santa Fe, with the exception of the Plaza area. Interpretive plaques highlight some of the more historic houses, including the Crespin, Alarid, Bandelier, and Boyle homes.

12 Here too, on the right, you'll find **The Oldest House,** little more than a tacky curiosity. Claimed to be the most ancient dwelling in America, built by Native Americans more than 800 years ago, it is constructed of "puddled" adobe, which predates the brick type. The building is now leased to a gift shop and museum, where T-shirts and souvenirs are sold. In the rear, a lifelike Native American dummy sits at a table with its head atilt beside a half-open coffin that supposedly contains the remains of a Spanish soldier. A few antique pots and pans, a lamp, and some tools complete the "museum" display. *215 E. De Vargas St., tel. 505/983–3883. Admission free, donation suggested. Open daily 9–5.*

Across the street, heading back toward the Old Sante Fe Trail, you'll see the **San Miguel Mission.** The oldest church still in use in the United States, the earth-hued adobe structure was built in 1636 by the Tlaxcalas (they originally came to New Mexico as servants of the Spanish troops and clergymen). Badly damaged in the 1680 Pueblo Revolt, the church was rebuilt in 1710. On display in the chapel is the San José Bell, weighing nearly 800 pounds, believed to have been cast in Spain in 1356 and brought to Santa Fe via Mexico several centuries later. This simple church, filled with priceless statues and paintings, is a must for any visitor to Santa Fe. *401 Old Santa Fe Trail, tel. 505/983–3974. Admission free. Open Mon.–Sat. 11:30–4, Sun. 1–4:30.*

Time Out   Next door to the San Miguel Mission, **Upper Crust Pizza** (329 Old Santa Fe Trail, tel. 505/983–4140) is a good place to sit and enjoy a slice out on the patio, watching the passing parade on Old Santa Fe Trail.

A block south of the San Miguel Mission, across the Old Santa Fe Trail, is the **State Capitol building,** built in 1966. Known as "the Roundhouse" (and sometimes "the Bullring"), it is modeled after a Southwestern Native American *zia,* representing the Circle of Life; four short walls symbolizing the four winds, four directions, four seasons, and the four sacred obligations of Native American mythology radiate from the central circular structure. Visitors may view the Governor's Gallery, as well as numerous historical and cultural displays, and enjoy 6 acres of landscaped gardens containing roses, sequoia, plum, and almond trees. *715 Alta Vista, tel. 505/984–9600. Admission free. Guided tours offered. Open weekdays 8–5.*

About a mile farther south along the Old Santa Fe Trail, take the Camino Lejo turnoff. On the right, perched on a hillside overlooking the city, is the **Museum of International Folk Art,** the premier museum of its kind in the world. You'll need a car or taxi to get there; it's 2 miles from the Plaza and almost all uphill. Charming, handmade creations are everywhere you look—a Madonna painted on tin; papier-mâché pears and apples; a devil made from bread dough; rag dolls; clay pots; and much, much more. Founded by Florence Dibell Barttless, a collector who built the museum and donated it and her collection of over 4,000 pieces of folk art to the state, the museum opened in 1953. In 1978, designer and architect Alexander Girard turned over to the museum his lifelong collection of folk art—over 106,000 items. The Museum of International Folk Art was again enriched in 1989 with the opening of a new $1.1 million Hispanic Heritage Wing, designed to display Hispanic folk art from the

Spanish Colonial period (in New Mexico, 1598–1821) to the present. The 5,000-piece exhibit includes religious folk art—particularly *bultos* (carved wooden statues of saints) and *retablos* (holy images painted on wood or tin). Along with the permanent collection, the museum frequently presents visiting exhibits, such as the recent "Folk Art of Brazil's Northeast" and "Mud, Mirror, and Thread: Adornment in Rural India." A gift shop carries textiles, dolls, jewelry, ornaments, and other folk-art objects, as well as the excellent color-illustrated book *The Spirit of Folk Art*, to help explain it all. *706 Camino Lejo, tel. 505/ 827–6350. Admission: 3-day pass $5, children under 17 free. Open daily 10–5. Closed Christmas, New Year's Day, Thanksgiving, and Mon. during Jan. and Feb.*

⑯ Next door, the **Museum of Indian Arts and Culture,** the newest (1987) addition to the museums of Santa Fe, focuses on the history and contemporary culture of New Mexico's Pueblo, Navajo, and Apache Native Americans. Along with its extensive collection of Southwestern Native American arts and crafts, the museum offers art demonstrations; Native American food concessions; and a Learning and Research Center, where visitors can weave on a Navajo loom or beat a Pueblo drum. Workshops and classes for children and adults are offered regularly. *710 Camino Lejo, tel. 505/ 827–6344. For hours and prices,* see *Museum of International Folk Art, above.*

⑰ The privately owned **Wheelwright Museum of the American Indian,** housed in a building shaped like a traditional Navajo hogan behind the Museum of International Folk Art, first opened in 1937. Founded by Boston scholar Mary Cabot Wheelwright and Navajo medicine man Hastiin Klah, it houses the works of all Native American cultures, exhibited on a single-subject rotating basis—silverwork, jewelry, pottery, basketry, paintings. On the lower level, the Case Trading Post, the museum shop, is modeled after those that dotted the Southwestern frontier over a hundred years ago. *704 Camino Lejo, tel. 505/982–4636. Admission free, donation suggested. Open Mon.–Sat. 10–5, Sun. 1–5.*

Another of Santa Fe's historic gems lies at the other side of
⑱ town. **Santuario de Guadalupe,** at the terminus of El Camino Real, 3½ blocks southwest of the Plaza, is the oldest shrine to Our Lady of Guadalupe, patron saint of Mexico, in the United States. It was built by Franciscan missionaries between 1776 and 1795 and has adobe walls nearly 3 feet thick. A museum administered by the nonprofit Guadalupe Historic Foundation, the Santuario contains several noteworthy paintings, including a priceless 16th-century work by Venetian painter Leonardo de Ponte Bassano, depicting Jesus driving the money changers from the temple, and a portrait of Our Lady of Guadalupe, one of the largest and finest oil paintings of the Spanish Southwest, by Mexico's renowned Colonial painter José de Alzibar. Other high-

lights are an authentic 19th-century sacristy; a pictorial-history archives; a library devoted to Archbishop Lamy, furnished with many of his personal possessions; and gardens containing a number of plants from the Holy Land. Many local religious ceremonies, dramatic performances, art and educational events, and concerts are held at the Santuario. Adjacent is Agua Fria Street, filled with colorful shops and restaurants, all part of the Guadalupe Historic District. *100 Guadalupe St., tel. 505/988–2027. Admission free, donation suggested. Open daily (weekdays only during the winter) 9–4.*

Santa Fe for Free

Although Santa Fe can be a very expensive town indeed, much of the joy and exuberance expressed during the city's many fiestas and festivals spills over onto the visiting public, without charge. *See* Festivals and Seasonal Events in Chapter 1 to find out what's in town when you're planning to visit. In addition to the festivals noted there, the Spanish Colonial Arts Society (Box 1611, 87501, tel. 505/983–4038) sponsors the **Traditional Spanish Market** each year on the Plaza during the last full weekend in July. **Las Fiestas de Santa Fe,** beginning the Friday morning after Labor Day and lasting three days (tel. 505/988–7575), and the spectacular **Indian Market,** held for two days each August (tel. 505/983–5220) with more than 800 Native American artists participating in juried competition, are both free. So is the 10-day **Santa Fe Festival of the Arts** (tel. 505/988–3924 for information), which twice each year—in the middle of May and October—showcases the finest paintings, lithography, and sculpture of area artists. *See also* The Arts and Nightlife, *below,* for a listing of free concerts.

There's no charge for admission to the **Governor's Gallery** in the State Capitol (*see* Tour 3, *above*). And it's free to enter the **pueblos** outside Santa Fe, with their colorful ceremonial dances and tempting handicraft shops, excluding fees charged for parking and camera permits. A festive culmination of the Christmas season takes place with many matachines and other holiday dances at the surrounding pueblos. *See* Chapter 7, Pueblos of the Rio Grande, for full details.

What to See and Do with Children

The **Museum of International Folk Art** (*see* Tour 3, *above*), with its colorful and fantasy-filled exhibits, is a great place to take children any day, but its **Saturdays Are for Kids** program is especially fun for them. Activities range from adobe making to wood carving to creating Valentines, clay fishes, or Polish snowflakes. Minimasterpieces are displayed in the museum's special **Children's Gallery.** Advance registration is required; prices range from $3 to $4, depending on the age and grade of the child, with discounts for combined sessions, each of which lasts two to four hours. For registration or inquiries, call Judy Lokenvitz, Coordinator of Children's Programs, Museum of International Folk Art, tel. 505/827-6350.

Santa Fe Adventures for Kids (142 Lincoln Ave., Suite 103, 85702, tel. 505/984-2080) runs a variety of exciting—and well-supervised—programs for children. Youngsters can float down the Rio Grande with a Native American storyteller, journey back to the days of the Old West on a horse-drawn wagon driven by a stuntman, or learn Native American sand painting and pottery making. During the ski season, supervised full-day downhill-skiing packages are available to the Chipmunk ski area for children aged 7–12. Groups are generally limited to 20; the minimum age for participation in some programs is 4, for others, 7. Fees range from $20 for a two-hour visit to the Children's Museum, with snacks, to $60 for the Raft Ride on the Rio Grande and Pueblo Visit, to $72 for the ski packages. Parents are welcome to participate as well, and many do.

Santa Fe Children's Museum, next to the New Mexico Repertory Theater, less than a mile from the Plaza, offers stimulating hands-on exhibits in the arts and sciences. A solar greenhouse, waterworks, giant bubbles, oversize geometric forms, and a climbing area with a simulated 18-foot mountain-climbing wall all contribute to the museum's great popularity. Special performances—puppets, storytellers, and the like—and programs—including talks by scientists and artists—are offered on different days. A gift shop is open during museum hours. *1050 Old Pecos Trail, tel. 505/989-8359. Admission: $2.50 adults, $1.50 children old enough to walk. Open Tues.–Sat. 10–5.*

Wild Oats Market (1090 S. St. Francis Dr., 85701, tel. 505/983-5333) offers free events for children 12 and under from 9 to 3 on the last Saturday of each month. Programs vary from arts and crafts and face painting to clowns, puppet shows, and the like.

Off the Beaten Track

The **Cumbres & Toltec Scenic Railroad** (in Chama, a 2-hr drive from Santa Fe via I–84) runs the 64 miles each way between Chama and Antonio, Colorado, on the only surviving portion of track alongside the old 1,200-mile mountain route that the Denver and Rio Grande Railroad was forced to build when the Santa Fe beat it to Ratan Pass. A veritable rolling museum of antique narrow-gauge engines, equipment, and stock—including snow-fighting attachments that date from 1889 and are still working—the train provided the setting for key scenes in the film *Butch and Sundance: The Early Years*. It snakes back and forth over the Colorado border, whistle blowing and coal smoke belching; the climb up Cumbres Pass is so steep that a second engine is required to pull it up the grade. During the ride, the brakeman and conductor deliver a lively nonstop commentary about the history of the line and interesting sidelights about passing scenes. Dress warmly; the train is drafty. And take along sunglasses to protect your eyes from soot and cinders. *500 Terrace Ave., Chama, tel. 505/756–2151. Fares: one-way, returning by bus, $50 adults, $26 children 2–11. The train leaves at 10:30 daily, Memorial Day weekend–mid-Oct.*

A kind of Williamsburg of the Southwest, **El Rancho de las Golondrinas** (the Ranch of the Swallows), some 15 miles south of Santa Fe, is a reconstruction of a small New Mexican agricultural village. Originally a *paraje*, or stopping place, on El Camino Real, the village has restored buildings from the 17th and 18th centuries. Guided tours highlight Spanish Colonial lifestyles in New Mexico from 1660 to 1890; visitors view a molasses mill, threshing grounds, and wheelwright and blacksmith shops, as well as a mountain village and a *morada*, meeting place of the order of Penitentes. Sheep, goats, and other farm animals wander about the sprawling 200-acre complex. During the Spring and Harvest Festivals, on the first weekends of June and October, respectively, the village comes alive with traditional music, Spanish folk dancing, and food and crafts demonstrations. There's a museum gift shop on the premises, but the nearest restaurant is 4 miles away. *Cienega, 15 mi south of Santa Fe on I–25, tel. 505/471–2261. Admission: $3.50 adults, $2 senior citizens, $1 children 5–12; during festivals, the rates are $5 for adults, $3 for senior citizens, and $2 for children 5–12. Open Apr. 1–Oct. 31, daily 8–4.*

Founded as a Spanish Colonial outpost in 1614, when it was built largely from the rocks of Pueblo Native American ruins, **Galisteo** is now a charming little village popular with artists and with equestrians who keep their animals boarded here (trail rides and rentals are available). There's a small church, open only on Sunday for services, a graveyard, and an old working brewery that welcomes visitors for tours and an occasional sampling. Twenty-three miles south of Santa Fe (take I–25 east to U.S. 285 south, then NM 41 south), Galisteo is mercifully free of fast-food and souvenir shops.

Ojo Caliente Mineral Springs (take I–25 to Espanola, then U.S. 285 to Ojo Caliente, tel. 505/583–2233) was considered a sacred spot by the Native Americans who inhabited this area centuries ago. Today this famous turn-of-the-century resort, with its five bubbling hot springs, one hour north of Santa Fe, offers mineral baths, massages, facials, herbal wraps, a hotel-motel, gift shop, and a restaurant. This isn't Canyon Ranch; don't expect an up-to-date luxury spa. Come if you want to take a trip back in time when it was fashionable to come and "take the waters" (they contain healthful doses of some minerals not usually associated with beneficial effects, such as arsenic).

Ten Thousand Waves (3½ miles outside town on Hyde Park Rd., tel. 505/982–9304) is the perfect place to unwind after a day's cavorting on the slopes or in the dusty desert. Tucked into a pine-and-juniper-covered mountainside, this Japanese-style spa offers private and communal indoor and outdoor hot tubs, therapeutic massages, facials, herbal wraps, Japanese body scrubs, salt glows, hiking, and stretch classes. Full-day programs are also available. Towels, kimonos, soaps, shampoos, sandals, and lockers are provided. Hot teas, juices, and pastries are available, too. Depending on the treatment, you'll part with anywhere from $12 to $50.

National Parks and Monuments

Chaco Culture National Historic Park, set in a canyon 17 miles long and 1 mile wide, with cliff faces rising 330 feet, protects the remains of 13 fully developed pueblos and about 400 smaller settlements. Pueblo Bonito, the largest prehistoric Southwest Indian dwelling ever excavated, contains 800 rooms covering more than 3 acres. This dwelling, the magnificent kivas, and other ancient structures, including a 1,200-mile network of paved roads and a solstice marker, all testify that the area was the highest point in the Anasazi culture, which peaked about AD 1150. Located at the park site is a visitor center, museum, and petroglyph displays. Overnight camping is permitted April through October.

To get here from Santa Fe, heading south–southwest via NM 44, in the direction of Bloomfield, drive to Cuba, NM, and continue on to Anasazi. At Anasazi, head west (right) and drive on the dirt road all the way to Chaco Culture National Historic Park. The trip takes about 3½ to 4 hours. *Star Rte. 4, Box 6500, Bloomfield 87413, tel. 505/988–6716. Admission: $4 per car, $2 per bus passenger. (The Golden Age Passport, issued to U.S. citizens 62 and older, allows free admission to all occupants of the same car, regardless of their age.)*

Shopping

Santa Fe has been a trading post for a long, long time. The great pueblos of the Hohokam and Anasazi civilizations 2,000 years ago were strategically located between the buffalo-hunting tribes of the Great Plains and the Native Americans of Mexico, who exchanged shells, metals, and parrots for sky-colored turquoise, which was thought to have magical properties. After the arrival of the Spanish in 1610 and the subsequent development of the West, Santa Fe became the place in which to exchange silver, hides, and fur from Mexico for manufactured goods, whiskey, and green-backs from the East. And following the building of the rail-road in 1880, all manner of products came and went.

The legacy remains, but today Santa Fe's major commodity is something known as Santa Fe style, as distinctive as the city's architecture. The clean lines, strong colors, and Na-tive American patterns that characterize the style have a great deal of charm. True, because of its popularity, it's be-come a bit of a cliché; a locally produced poster shows a San-ta Fean lying faceup on a Native American rug, surrounded by howling-coyote carvings, a kiva fireplace, a beamed ceil-ing, a sun-bleached cattle skull, a string of red chile pep-pers, and other trendy ornaments. But the style remains highly infectious just the same—visitors can't seem to get enough of it and can't wait to take it home.

Santa Fe may strike newcomers as one massive shopping mall, with stores and shopping nooks sprouting up in the least likely places. Nevertheless, a few shopping areas stand out. Canyon Road is the most famous and most expen-sive. The downtown district offers a mix of shops, galleries, restaurants, and crafts nooks within a five-block radius of the Plaza. At the southwest perimeter of town, the Guada-lupe neighborhood is great for strolling and for relaxing at a sidewalk café as a break from shopping.

Specialty Stores

Home Furnishings

Artesanos (222 Galisteo St., tel. 505/983–5563 or 505/983–1743), a Mexican marketplace only a block from the Santa Fe Plaza, has a warehouse-size showroom and an open courtyard filled with arts and crafts from south of the bor-der—everything from leather chairs to papier-mâché *cala-veras* (skeletons used in Day of the Dead celebrations), tinware, Colonial furniture, Talavera tiles, lighting fix-tures, and more. The prices are reasonable, too.

Foreign Traders (202 Galisteo St., tel. 505/983–6441), a San-ta Fe landmark—founded as the Old Mexico Shop in 1927 and still run by the same family—offers high-quality handi-crafts, antiques, and accessories from Mexico and other parts of the world. A section of outstanding collectible pieces includes mesquite *escritorio* (writing tables), an-tique wooden tortilla presses, and burro pack saddles.

Montez Gallery (Sena Plaza Courtyard, 125 E. Palace Ave., tel. 505/982–1828) offers "masterpieces" of New Mexican art, including retablos, bultos, tinwork, furniture, paint-ing, pottery, weaving, and jewelry, all by Hispanic artists.

Spanish Pueblo Doors (1091 Siler Rd., tel. 505/473–0464), established in 1952, is the buyer's gateway to a wide selec-tion of handcrafted wood doors and gates in Spanish Coloni-al and custom designs.

Santa Fe Shopping

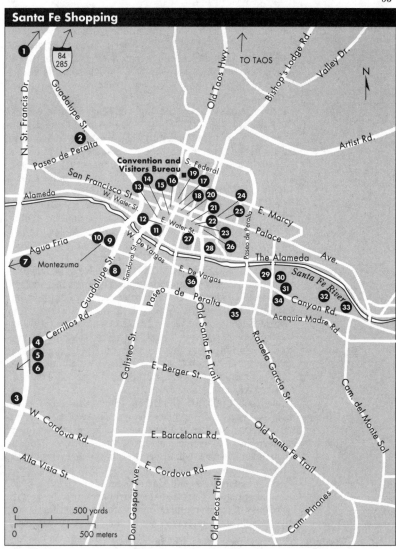

Altermann & Morris Gallery, **31**

Arrowsmith's, **36**

Artesanos, **11**

Bellas Artes, **33**

Canyon Road Fine Arts, **32**

Caxton Books, **14**

Cerillos Road Mercantile and Trading Company, **4**

Cline Fine Art, **34**

Coopers Western Warehouse, **2, 6**

Deborah Hudgins Gallery, **23**

Dewey Galleries, **22**

Elaine Horwitch Galleries, **19**

Fenn Galleries, **35**

Footsteps Across New Mexico, **28**

Foreign Traders, **12**

Frank Patania, **17**

Glenn Green Galleries, **21**

Joshua Baer & Co., **24**

Kachina House and Gallery, **29**

Montecristi Custom Hat Works, **15**

Montez Gallery, **25**

Morning Star Gallery, **30**

Prairie Edge, **27**

Sambusco Outfitters, **10**

Santa Fe Boot Company, **3**

Santa Fe Western Mercantile, **5**

Scheinbaum & Russek, **9**

Spanish Pueblo Doors, **7**

Tom Taylor Boots, **26**

Trade Roots Collection, **16**

Trader Jack's Flea Market, **1**

21st Century Fox Fine Art, **13**

Wadle Galleries, **18**

William R. Talbot Fine Art, **20**

Worldly Possessions, **8**

Native American Arts and Crafts

Arrowsmith's (402 Old Santa Fe Trail, tel. 505/989–7663), neighboring the popular Pink Adobe restaurant, offers an eclectic collection of artifacts and early crafts from cowboy-and-Indian days. Prices range from a few dollars for arrowheads and Indian fetishes to $24,000 for a saddle embellished with 200 pounds of silver. The buffalo head on the wall isn't for sale.

Cerrillos Road Mercantile and Trading Company (3741 Cerrillos Rd., tel. 505/471–6329) is one of the leading suppliers of movie props for Hollywood Westerns filmed on location in the area. Peace pipes, tomahawks, Hopi masks, Navajo blankets, muskets, and oil lamps—they're all here at some of the best prices in town. This museumlike shop is 4 miles from the Plaza, but well worth the drive.

Frank Patania (119 E. Palace Ave., tel. 505/983–2155), just off the Plaza, carries on the name of the Tucson-based family long known for excellence in sterling silver and top-of-the-line Indian jewelry and crafts. This shop offers New Guinea art and Oceanic art and artifacts as well.

Kachina House and Gallery (236 Delgado Rd., tel. 505/982–8415) features an incomparable collection of authentic Hopi kachina dolls, along with a vast selection of Navajo pottery, sculpture, and jewelry.

Prairie Edge (102 E. Water St., El Centro, tel. 505/984–1336) offers classic Lakota art, artifacts, and jewelry, created by contemporary Sioux artists and craftspeople in the style and tradition of the past. Hides, beaded and quilled clothing, shields, weapons, buffalo skulls, and sterling and bead jewelry are all sold here.

Trade Roots Collection (38 Burro Alley, tel. 505/982–8168) is the place to go if you're heavily into Native American ritual objects—outstanding fetishes, fetish jewelry, and Hopi rattles. This handsome showroom, one block west of the Plaza, also has an extensive collection of handwoven rugs, pillows, fabrics, and accessories.

Worldly Possessions (330 Garfield St., tel. 505/983–6090) takes shoppers on a round-the-world treasure hunt, with its bounty of outstanding tribal and folk art, artifacts, textiles, wood carvings, fine art, gifts, and decorative items.

Clothing Function dictates form in cowboy fashions. A wide-brimmed hat is essential in sun country; not only does it protect the wearer from heat, but it's effective in warding off gnats, flies, and other insects. Cowboy hats made by Resistol, Stetson, Bailey, and other leading firms range in price from $50 to $500, but hats made of exotic materials, such as fur, can go for thousands. Small wonder that when it rains in Santa Fe or Albuquerque, a man is more apt to be concerned with protecting his hat than with letting it protect him.

While tenderfeet may guess that cowboy boots are worn to protect against rattlesnakes, they serve other practical purposes as well. Pointed toes slide easily in and out of the stirrups, and high heels—worn for the same reason by

Mongolian tribesmen—help keep feet in the stirrups. Tall tops protect ankles and legs on rides through brush and cactus country and can save the wearer a nasty shin bruise from a skittish horse.

Some Western accessories, now mostly worn to be stylish, were once also functional. A colorful bandanna protected an Old West cowboy from sunburn and windburn and served as a mask in windstorms; when riding drag behind a herd; or, on occasions far rarer than Hollywood would have us believe, when robbing trains. A cowboy's sleeveless vest offered maneuverability during roping and riding chores and provided pocket space that his skintight pants—snug to prevent wrinkles in the saddle area—didn't. Of all the accessories today, however, belt buckles are probably the most important to Western dressers, and it's not unusual for them to spend thousands of dollars for gold ones. Hey, Mama, for all those children who grow up to be cowboys, here's a few places to send them.

Coopers Western Warehouse (De Vargas Center, tel. 505/982–3388, and Villa Linda Mall, tel. 505/471–8775) features all the top names and top lines—hats, boots, belts, buckles, and complete outfits for the well-dressed cowboy and cowgirl.

Montecristi Custom Hat Works (118 Galisteo St., tel. 505/983–9598) is where the smart set goes for custom-made straw hats that fit so perfectly they're all but guaranteed to stay on, even when driving in an open convertible. Felt toppers with bejeweled and unusual hatbands are also available. The smooth-talking sales force will make you feel like a movie star—like those whose autographed photos hang on the wall.

Sambusco Outfitters (550 Montezuma Ave., tel. 505/988–1664), located in the Sambusco Market Center, is where all those tall-in-the-saddle fellas head for jeans, boots, belts, Western shirts, jewelry, and accessories.

Santa Fe Boot Company (950 W. Cordova Rd., tel. 505/983–8415) features boots by all major manufacturers, as well as more exotic styles designed by owner Marian Trujillo. The store also sells hats and Western outerwear.

Santa Fe Western Mercantile (6820 Cerrillos Rd., tel. 505/471–3655) offers a seemingly inexhaustible supply of hats, boots, jeans, English and Western saddles, buckles, belts, and feed and health-care products for horses and livestock.

Tom Taylor Boots (La Fonda Hotel, tel. 505/924–2231) specializes in fine handmade cowboy boots, belts (ostrich, alligator, and other exotic leathers), and sculptured sterling-silver buckles designed by Jean Taylor.

Books **Caxton Books** (216 W. San Francisco St., tel. 505/982–8911), with a new address and expanded space, is perhaps the hottest book nook in New Mexico. It's a meeting place for local writers and the scene of frequent book signings and receptions, with a trio of Spanish folk musicians often playing over the intellectual buzz.

At **Footsteps Across New Mexico** (211 Old Santa Fe Trail, tel. 505/982–9297), the emphasis is on the Land of Enchantment. The shop easily contains the most comprehensive selection of books and guidebooks on Santa Fe and New Mexico, from regional cookbooks to area histories.

Flea Markets

Trader Jack's Flea Market (7 mi north of Santa Fe on U.S. 84/285; tel. 505/455–7874), also known as the Santa Fe Flea Market, has been dubbed the best flea market in America by its habitual legion of bargain hunters. It's open dawn to dusk every Friday, Saturday, and Sunday except during December, January, and February—and sometimes even then if the weather's right. You can buy everything here from a half-wolf puppy or African carvings to vintage cowboy boots, fossils, or a wall clock made out of an old hubcap. Sprawled over 12 acres on land belonging to the Tesuque Pueblo, the flea market is located right next to the Santa Fe Opera. ("There goes the neighborhood," says Trader Jack, when the opera season starts.)

Art Galleries

Santa Fe's brilliant light, limpid skies, and timeless landscape of mountains and mesas have long hypnotized artists. "The world is wide here," said Georgia O'Keeffe, in her usual get-right-to-the-point manner. "It's very hard to feel that it's wide in the East."

Well before the arrival of such artists as Ernest Blumenschein and John Sloan to the state in the early 20th century, an earlier form of art was popular in northern New Mexico. Bultos and retablos, both commonly known as *santos*, or saints, remain a unique, little-heralded art form as indigenous to the Southwest as is an oil painting by Ted DeGrazia. Except for black spirituals, santos are the only non-Native American religious art to originate in America. These devotional images were part of everyday life in Mexico and the American Southwest in the years following the conquistadores and the founding of Christianity in the New World. Today they have captured the attention of serious art collectors and leading museums. Although the santos now being made seem destined more for the tourist trade than for regional churches, no attempt has been made to mass-produce them, and no two are exactly alike. As a result, they still retain their unique charm.

Santa Fe is also the epicenter of contemporary Native American art, the breakaway and sometimes satirical styles of Fritz Scholder, R. C. Gorman, Earl Biss, Kevin Red Star, Robert Redbird, Amado Maurilio Pena, and others who are strongly identified with the Santa Fe movement. Before the introduction of blurred images and shocking colors, Native American art was traditionally flat and static, with Bambi-like deer with big, sad eyes, and Corn dancers in lifeless pueblo rituals. Today, top Native American painters, such as Gorman and Cherokee artist Bert Seabourn, are as celebrated in the galleries of Berlin and Tokyo as they are on Canyon Road.

Santa Fe has 125 art galleries (and no one knows how many painters). The following selection represents a good cross section; the Santa Fe Convention and Visitors Bureau (*see* Essential Information, *above*) has a fuller listing, and *The Wingspread Collectors Guide to Santa Fe and Taos* (*see* Further Reading in Chapter 1) is a good bet for those who are seriously interested in buying art in Santa Fe.

Altermann & Morris Gallery (225 Canyon Rd., tel. 505/983–1590) is among the city's newest, featuring works of the Cowboy Artists of America, original Remingtons and Bierstadts, the Wyeths, and the Hurds. It occupies the former Janus Gallery, which closed.

Bellas Artes (653 Canyon Rd., tel. 505/983–2745), a landmark crafts gallery and sculpture garden, located next to the popular Compound Restaurant, carries a wide selection of contemporary arts and crafts, pre-Columbian works, ceramics, and textiles.

Canyon Road Fine Arts (621 Canyon Rd., tel. 505/988–9511, fax 505/988–2108) is one of the city's newest art galleries. Owner Lisa Otis specializes in works by early Santa Fe and Taos artists, as well as by selected contemporary impressionist painters.

Cline Fine Art (526 Canyon Rd., tel. 505/982–5328), located in a 200-year-old landmark adobe, specializes in early to mid-20th-century American art, with an emphasis on pre–World War II New Mexico. Selected contemporary artists are also represented.

Deborah Hudgins Gallery (80 E. San Francisco St., tel. 505/988–9298) was formed with the merger of two previous galleries, El Taller Santa Fe and the Plaza Gallery. A full range of original paintings, drawings, and graphics is available here. Among the artists represented is Amado Peña, a master painter of Mexican and Yaqui ancestry, noted for his bold color schemes and strong graphic use of lines.

Dewey Galleries (74 E. San Francisco St., tel. 505/982–8632 or 800/327–7721) is housed in the historic Spiegelberg Building on the south side of the Plaza. In a spacious showroom under the original 20-foot-high pressed tin ceilings, a huge collection of historic Navajo textiles and jewelry, plus paintings and sculpture by contemporary and past artists, are offered.

Elaine Horwitch Galleries (129 W. Palace Ave., tel. 505/988–8997) sells paintings, sculptures, and graphics by internationally known artists as well as by up-and-coming painters from the Southwest. Ms. Horwitch's death in 1991 hasn't slowed the gallery's activities down a bit; a recent expansion, including the opening of an upstairs showroom, has doubled its exhibit space. The Horwitch firm also has a gallery in Scottsdale.

Fenn Galleries (1075 Paseo de Peralta, tel. 505/982–4631) specializes in works of the celebrated Taos Society of Artists and their successors, in addition to those of early Santa Fe painters, including such luminaries as Maxfield Parrish, Maynard Dixon, and Georgia O'Keeffe. One of the best-known galleries in the Southwest, its list of clients includes former president Gerald Ford, Jacqueline Onassis, Cher, and Cybill Shepherd.

Glenn Green Galleries (50 E. San Francisco St., tel. 505/ 988–4168) features paintings and photographs by internationally known artists. Founded in 1975, the spectacular two-story gallery exclusively represents the work of Native American sculptor Allan Houser, as well as other noted Native American and Anglo artists.

Joshua Baer & Co. (116½ E. Palace Ave., tel. 505/988–8944), a half block from the Plaza, focuses on 19th-century Navajo wall hangings, serapes, and blankets, as well as prehistoric Mimbres pottery.

Morning Star Gallery (513 Canyon Rd., tel. 505/982–8187) is the largest gallery in the world specializing in antique Native American art and artifacts. Located in a landmark Spanish hacienda and shaded by a huge cottonwood tree, it's a virtual museum of antique basketry, pre-1940 Navajo silver jewelry, Eskimo ivories, Northwest Coast Native American carvings, classic Navajo weavings, and art of the Plains Buffalo culture. (Gallery director Joe Rivera operated trading posts on the Rosebud Sioux Reservation for 12 years.)

Scheinbaum & Russek (328 S. Guadalupe St., Suite M, tel. 505/988–5116) handles contemporary and rare fine-art photographs and limited-edition portfolios. Among photographers represented are Eliot Porter and Mexican master Manuel Alvarez-Bravo.

21st Century Fox Fine Art (217 W. Water St., tel. 505/983–2002), founded by Stephen Fox in 1980, is a huge street-level showroom filled with contemporary Native American paintings and antique pawn jewelry, signed posters and prints, and an excellent collection of photographs of Southwestern and Native American subjects by Yousuf Karsh, Myron Wood, Tracey Pierre, and Edward Curtis. One of Santa Fe's best-known dealers, Fox has also turned to jewelry crafting of late and offers his own fine line of Native American pawn–style jewelry.

Wadle Galleries (128 W. Palace Ave., tel. 505/983–9219) features works of national and regional painters, bronze and stone sculpture, Pueblo pottery, jewelry, and American folk art. This spacious gallery, with plenty of chairs and seating space, is a good place for unwinding and soaking up the arty Southwestern ambience.

William R. Talbot Fine Art (129 W. San Francisco St., tel.

505/982–1559) features antique maps of the Americas and natural-history paintings.

Sports and the Outdoors

Participant Sports

Bicycling   The streets of Santa Fe are narrow and winding, but the roads and byways are generally level, and the scenery is spectacular. While the city is an ideal size for biking, unfortunately no special bike lanes are available. A suggested route map for bikers can be picked up at the information desk of the Convention and Visitors Bureau (201 W. Marcy St., tel. 505/984–6760). Because of the high density of out-of-state tourist traffic and erratic drivers, bikers are cautioned to stay alert.

Rentals are available at the **Tennis and Sports Shop** (107 Washington Ave., tel. 505/983–5637) and **Rob and Charlie's** (1632 St. Michael's St., tel. 505/471–9119).

Golf   **Cochiti Lake Golf Course** (5200 Cochiti Hwy., Cochiti Lake, tel. 505/465–2239) was designed by Robert Trent Jones, Jr., and is set against a stunning backdrop of steep canyons and red-rock mesas. A 45-minute drive southwest of the city, it's rated among the top 25 public golf courses in the country.
Quail Run (3101 Old Pecos Trail, tel. 505/986–2255), opened in 1987, is a beautiful, well-balanced course set amid piñon pine and juniper. It has the only kiva-shaped bunkers in the country, designed in the style of local fireplaces. The club is private, so you'll have to find a member to take you.
Santa Fe Country Club (Airport Rd., tel. 505/471–0601), a close-to-town, tree-shaded, semiprivate course, was designed over 50 years ago. There's a pro shop, club and electric-cart rentals, and private lessons by appointment.
Valle Grande (288 Prairie Star Rd. [I–25/NM 44 West], tel. 505/867–9464), about 45 minutes south of Santa Fe, offers 18 holes of golf, a driving range, a putting area, a fully stocked pro shop, the Prairie Star restaurant, and a bar and grill.

Horseback Riding   New Mexico's rugged mountain country has been the scene of many Hollywood Westerns, including, in recent years, *Silverado*. Whether you want to ride the range that Kevin Kline and Gregory Peck rode or just go out and feel tall in the saddle, try the following. Rentals average about $20 an hour.

Pool Wells Station (40 mi north of Santa Fe on NM 68, tel. 505/852–2013) is a former stagecoach stop where you can make reservations for trail rides, hayrides, barbecues, mock hangings, gunfights, and barn dancing.
Runaway Lodge and Riding (Madrid Hwy., south of Santa

Fe, tel. 505/438–7333) offers Western trail rides for all levels, from beginner to expert, plus bed-and-breakfast.

Vientos Encantados (Round Barn Stables, Ojo Caliente, one hour north of Santa Fe on U.S. 84/285, no phone) features trail rides and pack trips near the hot mineral springs of northern New Mexico (*see* Off the Beaten Track, *above*). After a long ride, a hot soak?

River Rafting The mention of no other sport conjures up as much excitement as does white-water rafting, and justly so. White-water rafting provides the kind of walloping action-packed thrill that belongs to the rocky, bone-thumping country that gave birth to it. Of course, if you prefer something less invigorating than heart-stopping, hair-raising Class V rapids, there are always more leisurely sightseeing possibilities on a river trip along the Rio Chama or one of the more gentle riverways of northern New Mexico, gliding past colorful mesas, ancient ruins, and fields ripening in the sun. Unless you're a polar bear, the river trips are an option only in the summertime.

Los Rios River Runners (desk in La Fonda Hotel, tel. 505/983–6565 or 800/338–6877) offers a variety of white-water adventures, including the famous Taos Box, a 17-mile run on the rolling rapids of the upper Rio Grande.

Native American Tours (142 Lincoln Ave., Suite 103, Box 22658, tel. 505/986–0804 or 800/5–PUEBLO, fax 505/986–0812) offers rafting trips on the Rio Grande and the Rio Chama. Half-day, full-day, and overnight trips are available, all with Native American guides, gourmet meals, and storytelling.

New Wave Rafting Company (107 Washington Ave., tel. 505/984–1444) features full, half-day, and overnight river trips, with daily departures from Santa Fe.

Rio Bravo River Tours (Hwy. 87, between Taos and Espanda, tel. 505/758–0762 or outside New Mexico, 800/525–4966) has professionally guided tours that leave daily from Santa Fe and Taos.

Santa Fe Rafting Company and Outfitters (Box 28525-3525, tel. 505/988–4914 or 800/584–6011) features personalized rafting tours. Tell them what you want, they'll do it.

Southwest Wilderness Center (information and reservations through Galisteo News and Ticket Center, tel. 505/983–7262) handles local and international river tours, from the Rio Chama to China.

For a complete list of outfitters who guide trips on the Rio Grande and the Rio Chama, write the **Bureau of Land Management, Taos Resource Area Office** (224 Cruz Alta Dr., Taos 97571, tel. 505/758–8851).

Running With the city's 7,000-foot altitude, newcomers to Santa Fe may feel as if they're running in the Chilean Andes. Once they adjust, however, they'll find it a great place to slip into their Nikes or Reeboks. The city obliges its runners with a jogging track that runs along the Santa Fe River, parallel to

Alameda, and one on Washington Avenue near Fort Marcy.
There's lots of local organized activity as well, in which visitors may participate. **The Santa Fe Runaround,** a 10-kilometer race held in early June, begins and ends at the Plaza.
The **Women's Five-Kilometer Run** is held in early August,
and joggers turn out in droves on Labor Day for the most
popular run of all, the annual **Old Santa Fe Trail Run.** More
a weekly social event than a minimarathon is the **Fun Run**
that starts out every Wednesday evening from the Plaza;
starting time is 6 PM in summer, 5:30 in winter months. Almost all Santa Fe's running events are organized by the **Santa Fe Striders Running Club** (tel. 505/989–7423).

Skiing The ski season in Santa Fe runs from Thanksgiving through
Easter and averages 250 inches of dry-powder snow a year.
The **Santa Fe Ski Area,** with blue skies above, blue-silver
snow below, and green pines dotting the horizon like exclamation marks, has a 1,650-foot vertical rise and more than
40 trails (20% beginner, 40% intermediate, 40% advanced).
The resort's six ski lifts include an Easy Street beginner's
chair lift and a swift, breath-halting 5,000-foot triple chair
to the summit. New Mexico's first quad chair lift, The Santa
Fe Super Chief, makes the ride up almost as much fun as the
downhill run. Chipmunk is a free run for small fry who measure less than 46 inches in their ski boots, provided they're
in the company of a paying adult. Open bowls at the peak
and more sheltered runs through the trees make for pleasant skiing even when the high winds blow. A ski-area restaurant, **Evergreen** (High Park Rd., tel. 505/984–8190),
offers warming soups and chowders, as well as other hearty
dishes.

For ski-area information, call the Santa Fe Ski Area (tel.
505/982–4429 or 505/983–9155) or Santa Fe Central Reservations (tel. 505/983–8200 or 800/776–SNOW outside New
Mexico). Snow-condition information is available by calling
505/984–0606. For cross-country skiing conditions, contact
the **Santa Fe National Forest** office, tel. 505/988–6940.

Tennis Santa Fe has 27 public tennis courts, including four asphalt
courts at **Alto Park** (1035½ Alto St.), four concrete courts at
Herb Martinez/La Resolana Park (Camino Carlos Rey),
three asphalt courts at **Ortiz Park** (Camino de las Crusitas),
and two asphalt courts at **Old Fort Marcy Commemorative
Park** (Prince and Kearney Aves.). They are all available on
a first-come, first-served basis. For the location of additional public facilities, call the City Recreation Department
(tel. 505/984–6864). Among the major private tennis facilities, including indoor, outdoor, and lighted courts, are **Club
at El Gancho** (Las Vegas Hwy., tel. 505/988–5000), **Sangre
De Cristo Racquet Club** (1755 Camino Corrales, tel. 505/
983–7978), **Santa Fe Country Club** (Airport Rd., tel. 505/
471–3378), and **Shellaberger Tennis Center** (St. Michaels
Dr., tel. 505/473–6411). Check for limited membership
privileges.

Windsurfing Strong summer breezes and a proximity to numerous lakes have made northern New Mexico a popular destination for windsurfers. **Abiquiu Lake** (40 mi northwest of Santa Fe, via U.S. 84/285; Drawer D, Abiquiu, 87510, tel. 505/685–4371), **Cochiti Lake** (off U.S. 85 between Los Alamos and Santa Fe; Cochiti Lake, PenaBlanca, 87041, tel. 505/242–8302), **Conchas Lake** (3 hours east of Santa Fe, via I–25 to Las Vegas and NM 104 to Conchas Lake; Box 976, Conchas Dam, 88416, tel. 505/868–2270), and **Storrie Lake** (an hour east, via I–25 to Las Vegas; Box 3157, Las Vegas, 87701, tel. 505/425–9231), all with warm water and good winds, have developed a legion of devoted regulars. Most of the windsurfing lakes have no on-site rental facilities, so you'll have to bring your own equipment, which can be rented or purchased from sporting-goods and water-sports stores in Santa Fe. **Santa Fe Windsurfing** (905 St. Francis Dr., tel. 505/986–1611) and **Water Sports** (1301 Escalante St., tel. 505/982–8085) both have good selections.

Northern New Mexico is in a constant thunderstorm pattern during the summer, so early morning sessions are recommended for beginning windsurfers or anyone who can't get off the lakes in a hurry. For more information, contact Jeff Backi of **Santa Fe Sailboard Fleet** by calling 505/471–2176 or by writing to him at Box 15931, Santa Fe, 87506.

Spectator Sports

Horse Racing Horse racing at the Santa Fe Downs, a beautiful 1-mile track in the foothills of the towering Sangre de Cristo Mountains (on I–25, just 6 minutes west of town), attracts nearly a quarter-million spectators each year. The racing season begins in the middle of June and runs through Labor Day. Races are held each Wednesday, Friday, Saturday, and Sunday and on holidays, with the first race starting at 1:30 or, on Wednesday and Friday, at 3. The $100,000 Santa Fe Futurity for two-year-olds is New Mexico's richest Thoroughbred purse. There's pari-mutuel betting, of course, a Jockey Club, a Turf Club, ultramodern grandstands, and plenty of parking, something rare in Santa Fe. For more information, contact **Santa Fe Racing, Inc.** (tel. 505/471–3311).

Dining

A delicious mixture of Pueblo, Spanish Colonial, Mexican, and American-frontier cooking, Santa Fe cuisine is like none other. Recipes that came from Spain via Mexico were adapted generations ago for local ingredients—chiles, corn, pork, beans, honey, apples, piñon nuts, jicama, and leaves of the prickly pear cactus—and have remained much the same ever since. Mexican dishes, such as *carne adovada* (marinated meat), burritos, chiles rellenos, *flautas* (rolled corn tortillas filled with shredded beef or chicken), and *chalupas* (literally a "boat" made from a shaped corn tortilla and filled with shrimp, beef, or chicken), are distinct because the flavor is baked in, not poured over. Pinto beans and blue corn or flour tortillas are usually served as side orders.

In northern New Mexico, even Anglo babies cut their teeth on fresh, warm tortillas. And how quickly they develop a taste for *sopapillas*, deep-fried, puff-pastry pillows, drizzled with butter and honey. But it is the chile, whether red or green, that is the heart and soul of northern New Mexican cuisine. Visitors from other parts of the country are always a bit surprised to learn that *ristras*, those strings of bright red chile peppers that seem to hang everywhere, are sold more for eating here than for decoration. More varieties of chiles—upwards of 90—are grown in New Mexico than anywhere else in the world.

But if you can't stand the heat, you don't have to get out of the Santa Fe kitchen. The city has nearly 200 restaurants to suit all tastes and budgets, from a riot of fast-food outlets on the outskirts of town, particularly along Cerrillos Road, to elegant downtown restaurants near the Plaza, where you can hobnob with film stars and publishers. There are also health-food and vegetarian restaurants and a wide selection of ethnic eating places.

Highly recommended restaurants in each price category are indicated by a star ★.

Category	Cost*
Expensive	over $25
Moderate	$10–$25
Inexpensive	under $10

per person, excluding drinks, service, and sales tax (5.8%)

Expensive

★ **The Compound.** With its crisp white linen tablecloths, heavy crystal, gleaming silver, elaborate floral arrangements, white-glove service—and perhaps the only rigidly enforced dress code in Santa Fe—this restaurant shimmers with Old World elegance. The main dining room, draped with colorful fabrics, overlooks an Italian garden where a playful fountain splashes; the other, with Navajo-rug hangings, overlooks a Spanish patio. Described as American Continental, the menu includes breast of chicken in champagne, fresh foie gras, roast loin of lamb, baked salmon, Russian caviar, and raspberries from New Zealand. *653 Canyon Rd., tel. 505/982-4353. Reservations required. Jacket and tie required. AE. Open Tues.–Sat., dinner only.*

★ **Coyote Cafe.** Formerly a Greyhound bus depot, this is now one of the trendiest spots in town, thanks to its great food and cheerful ambience: bright, flashy colors; modern art;

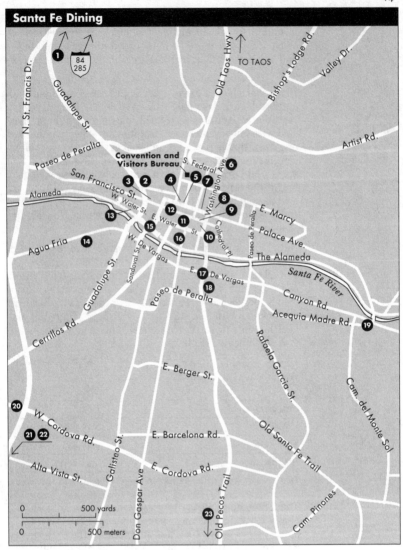

Santa Fe Dining

The Bull Ring, **18**
Burrito Company, **8**
Cafe Pasqual's, **16**
The Compound, **19**
Coyote Cafe, **11**
El Nido, **1**
Encore Provence, **14**
La Tertulia, **15**

Legal Tender, **23**
Maria Ysabel
Restaurante, **13**
Maria's New Mexico
Kitchen, **20**
The Old House, **12**
Ore House on the
Plaza, **9**
The Palace, **4**

Pink Adobe, **17**
Plaza Cafe, **10**
Santacafe, **6**
The Shed, **5**
Shohko-Cafe, **2**
Staab House, **7**
Tecolote Cafe, **21**
Tortilla Flats, **22**
Vanessie, **3**

oversize folk art figures; and howling-coyote silhouettes everywhere you look. The imaginative menu, which changes every other week, offers dishes based on the history and tradition of northern New Mexican cuisine. The signature steak is a 26-ounce ribeye called The Cowboy, served with barbecued black beans and onion rings. Other crowd-pleasers include lobster enchiladas; lobster, scallops, and vanilla in corn husks; and ravioli filled with wild-boar-and-goat-cheese sausage. The wine list offers over 500 selections. Weather permitting, a rooftop cantina is open during the summer months. A shop adjoining the café offers a wide variety of Southwestern spices, salsas, cookbooks, and kitchenware. *132 W. Water St., tel. 505/983–1615. Reservations recommended. Dress: casual at lunch, informal to formal in the evening. AE, MC, V. Closed Tues. during the winter.*

Encore Provence. *The* new French restaurant is in an unpretentious little pale yellow wooden house with a stone front porch. (You park and enter in the rear.) But inside, its 15 tables are immaculately set with linens, flowers, and crystal. Every night chef-owner Patrick Benrezkellah offers a selection of some seven fish dishes and three meat dishes, from steamy, tantalizing bouillabaisse to a seven-hour leg of lamb. The wine list is half-French, half-Californian. *548 Agua Fria, tel. 505/983–7470. Open Mon.–Sat. 6–10. Reservations strongly advised. Dress: smart casual. AE, MC, V. Dinner only.*

The Old House. Pride of the Eldorado Hotel, the Old House specializes in such dishes as cut-to-order New York sirloin, oysters Rockefeller, and a special mixed grill. The masculine setting matches the menu: Dining rooms are Southwestern style, with hardwood floors, beamed ceilings, mohair-covered chairs, and a dominating mural-size painting, *The Rio Grande*, as well as a piano bar and fireplaces. Adjoining the main room is a smaller dining room, decorated with a colorful collection of carved animals from Mexico and New Mexico. *309 W. San Francisco St., tel. 505/988–4455. Reservations required. Jacket and tie advised. AE, DC, MC, V.*

★ **Pink Adobe.** Rosalea Murphey has been the owner of this Santa Fe gold mine—easily the best-known restaurant in town—for nearly 50 years. (She's the one in the photos on the reception-area wall with George Bush and Larry Hagman.) She still takes a hand in the kitchen; her grandson is one of the managers. Located in a historic three-centuries-old adobe, it's creatively decorated with antique copper pots, wooden shipping chests, painted pine chairs, and early Spanish pottery. Continental, New Orleans Creole, and local New Mexican favorites are served in several cozy dining rooms with fireplaces. Steak with green chiles and mushrooms is a perennial special; so is Key lime pie. A less formal dining area (with a bar), the Dragon Room, adjoins the restaurant. No smoking is allowed. *406 Old Santa*

Fe Trail, tel. 505/983–7712. Reservations required. Dress: informal. AE, DC, MC, V.

Santacafe. This romantic, low-keyed restaurant, in a thick-walled 200-year-old adobe (the Pedro Gallegos House, two blocks north of the Plaza), is simply decorated with floral bouquets. The menu is inspired by an eclectic array of international cuisines and changes with the season. Chef Laszlo Gyermek offers up such specialties as Chinese dumplings, venison with juniper-berry sauce, fresh grilled fish, and a wide variety of breads and desserts. *231 Washington Ave., tel. 505/984–1788. Reservations required. Jacket and tie advised. MC, V. Lunch weekdays, dinner daily.*

Staab House. Beautiful, handcrafted Southwestern furniture, a Victorian bar complete with a brass foot rail, and a large fireplace help set the elegant tone at this well-known restaurant, adjacent to La Posada de Santa Fe. In a delightful conservatory setting, you can dine on seafood and such northern New Mexican favorites as *fajitas del norte* (tortillas filled with chunks of pork, beef, or chicken); in summer you can sit out on the patio beside a bubbling fountain. *330 E. Palace Ave., tel. 505/986–0000. Reservations suggested for dinner. Jacket and tie advised. AE, DC, MC, V.*

Moderate **The Bull Ring.** This relaxed, dimly lighted establishment, set in a rambling old Spanish adobe (ca. 1886) next door to the State Capitol, includes steak, pasta, and Spanish red shrimp among its wide selection of New Mexican specialties. In addition to the six crowded dining rooms, there's a popular adjoining lounge, with dancing and entertainment, and a patio, open to diners in the summer. If you're fussy about whom you eat with, avoid this place in January, when the New Mexico Legislature is in session, or you'll be elbow-to-elbow with politicians, lobbyists, and lawyers. *414 Old Santa Fe Trail, tel. 505/983–3328. Reservations suggested. Dress: casual. MC, V.*

El Nido. This Santa Fe institution has been serving seafood—including excellent broiled salmon and swordfish steak—choice aged beef, prime rib, and New Mexican specialties in cozy, firelit rooms for more than 50 years. (The place was a dance hall and trading post before that.) Located in Tesuque, only five minutes from the Santa Fe Opera, El Nido has long been a favorite of opera fans—and often of the stars themselves. *NM 592 (22) at Bishop's Lodge Rd., 1 mi from Tesuque, tel. 505/988–4340. Reservations advised. Dress: casual but neat. MC, V. Closed Mon.*

★ **La Tertulia.** At this lovely restaurant in a converted 19th-century convent, the six small dining rooms are always crowded, but you won't hear your neighbors talking: The walls are 3 feet thick in places, and there's wall-to-wall carpeting throughout. The restaurant is almost as well known for its splendid Spanish Colonial art collection, including some rare early *santos* (carvings representing saints), as for its fine New Mexican cuisine, tangy margaritas, and extraordinary house sangria. *416 Agua Fria St., tel. 505/988–2769. Reservations a must. Dress: dressy to informal. AE, MC, V. Closed Mon.*

Legal Tender. It's worth taking a drive 18 miles southeast of town to this saloon and restaurant, opposite the Santa Fe Railroad junction in Lamy. Built as a general store in 1881, it's a Victorian period piece, with its stained-glass lamps, bawdy oil paintings, and turn-of-the-century memorabilia. The menu offers lots of variations on steaks, chops, and chicken, plus a generous selection of spicy regional dishes. This large place (it seats 250) is popular with locals for Sunday brunch. *In Lamy, just off U.S. 285, tel. 505/982–8425. Reservations not necessary. Dress: informal. MC, V. Closed Mon.*

Maria Ysabel Restaurante. This little jewel of a restaurant in an old adobe is a favorite of locals. It's not on one of Santa Fe's most fashionable streets (you can get there by taking a shortcut through the parking lot of the Hilton of Santa Fe), but a string of twinkling lights outside sets a festive mood. Inside is a series of small dining rooms, pleasantly furnished and decorated with colorful Mexican touches. Chef/owner Bell Mondragon appears frequently on local and national television shows talking up the marvels of New Mexican cuisine, and she knows of what she speaks. From her kitchen come green-chile chicken enchiladas, burritos, carnitas, and *taquitos compuestos* (one with refritos topped with guacamole, sour cream, and melted cheese, and two with beef and chile verde). Dinner courses come with two free appetizers. *409 W. Water St., tel. 505/986–1662. Reservations advised. Dress: informal. MC, V.*

Ore House on the Plaza. This restaurant is notable for its perfect location, with a dining balcony overlooking the Plaza, and the food's fine, too. Salmon, swordfish, lobster, oysters, ceviche, and steaks are all artfully prepared by Chef Isaac Modivah. Margaritas, the house specialty, come in 64 customized flavors. *50 Lincoln Ave., upstairs on the southwest corner of the Plaza, tel. 505/983–8687. Reservations recommended. Dress: informal. AE, DC, MC, V.*

★ **The Palace.** This lively turn-of-the-century saloon-style restaurant—upholstered banquettes and chairs, crystal chandeliers, and red flocked wallpaper—specializes in northern Italian and French cuisine. Diners choose from a large selection of seafood, steak, veal, and pasta entrées. Chef Bruno Pertussini sautés in virgin olive oil only; naturally boiled-down sauces are made without butter or flour. *142 W. Palace Ave., tel. 505/982–9892. Reservations not required. Dress: informal. AE, D, DC, MC, V.*

Plaza Cafe. Can't get into Pasqual's (*see* Inexpensive, *below*) for breakfast? Try this large busy-beehive American-Mexican restaurant only a block away, a fixture on the Santa Fe Plaza since 1918. From all appearances, the decor hasn't changed much since then—there are red leather banquettes, black Formica tables, tile floors, and vintage Santa Fe photos on the walls, topped off by a coffered tin ceiling. A 1940s-style service counter runs along the right wall. There are Greek specialties (kitchen manager Len Razato is the son of a Greek father and a New Mexican mother) along with such Southwestern fare as sizzling enchiladas and cheese, and a nice selection of wine and beer. The Plaza is also open for lunch and dinner. *54 Lincoln Ave., tel. 505/982–1664. No reservations. Dress: informal. MC, V.*

Shohko-Cafe. This popular Japanese-Chinese restaurant across the street from the Eldorado hotel specializes in tempura combinations, sushi, sashimi, sukiyaki, and teriyaki, along with vegetarian and seafood specials. The 36-foot sushi bar offers 300 artfully prepared varieties. A concession to local tastes is green-chile tempura, as well as the handmade Southwestern-style tables and chairs. Dim sum lunches are served on Saturday. *321 Johnson St., at Guadalupe St., tel. 505/983–7288. Reservations required. Dress: casual. AE, MC, V.*

Tecolote Cafe. *Huevos rancheros* (eggs served on a tortilla, with hot sauce and refried beans)—New Mexico's unofficial state breakfast—are fabulous at this easygoing place, as are the biscuits, muffins, and coffee (all you can drink). The shirred eggs Tecolote are a luscious combination of baked eggs, sautéed chicken livers, and salsa. *1203 Cerrillos Rd., tel. 505/988–1362. Reservations not required. Dress: informal. AE, DC, MC, V.*

Vanessie. High beamed ceilings and two massive oak tables with highback chairs set a clubby, lodgelike tone for this longtime local favorite. At the same time, a glassed-in kitchen, contemporary paintings, and a tile floor give the place an open, airy feel. You can catch the strains of wistful tunes from the piano bar as you enjoy such specialties as rack of lamb, fish, and filet mignon. *434 W. San Francisco St., tel. 505/982–9966. Reservations not required. Dress: formal. AE, MC, V.*

Inexpensive **Burrito Company.** For a quick get-up-and-go kind of breakfast or a spicy treat at lunch, run, don't walk, to this great little spot adjacent to the Main Post Office and just off the Plaza. It's an attractive fast-food place with indoor and outdoor sidewalk seating, large and airy with a high ceiling studded with track lights. The food is served on paper plates, and customers order McDonald's-style at the counter, picking up their orders when their name is called. Breakfast burritos are scrambled eggs wrapped in a flour tortilla, doused with chile sauce, and served with a side of potatoes, onions, and peppers. Start there; you'll keep coming back. *111 Washington Ave., tel. 505/982–4453. Dress: informal. No credit cards. Open Mon.–Sat. 7:30–7:30, Sun. 10–5.*

★ **Cafe Pasqual's.** Regional specialties are served at this cheerful, informal place only a block southwest of the Plaza. Forget the pancakes and order a *chorizo burrito* (Mexican sausages, scrambled eggs, home fries, and scallions wrapped in a flour tortilla and doused with red- or green-chile sauce); for dinner there's fresh trout with green-chile sauce and toasted pine nuts. Though the restaurant is small, it seems larger thanks to a high ceiling and huge colorful murals; piñatas, strings of chile peppers, and ceramic pottery add a festive tone. It's open for three meals, with breakfast served all day for sleepyheads. Expect a line outside. *121 Don Gaspar Ave., tel. 505/983–9340. Reservations suggested for dinner. Dress: informal. MC, V.*

★ **Maria's New Mexico Kitchen.** You haven't been to Santa Fe until you've eaten at this landmark restaurant, in business for over 40 years. In addition to such standard fare as ribs, steaks, and burgers, traditional Mexican specialties and typical local favorites are served daily: homemade tamales, rellenos, blue-corn tamales, fajitas, green-chile stew. Women in colorful costumes make the tortillas by hand. Margaritas are created from scratch, hand-shaken and served with silver droplets shimmering on the glass. The decor is Old Mexico, with piñatas, ceramic pottery, wooden tables, and colorful paper flowers. There's a patio for summer dining and fireplaces lit in winter. *555 W. Cordova Rd., just east of St. Francis Dr., tel. 505/983–7929. Reservations strongly advised. Dress: informal. AE, D, MC, V.*

The Shed. Great homemade pies and tasty New Mexican cuisine make this a luncheon favorite of almost everyone in Santa Fe, judging by the lines. Housed in a rambling, historic adobe hacienda dating from 1692, the restaurant is decorated throughout with festive folk art. Specialties include red-chile enchiladas, green chile with potatoes, *posole* (corn chowder), and charbroiled "Shedburgers." *113½ E. Palace Ave., tel. 505/982–9030. Reservations not required. Dress: informal. No credit cards. Lunch only. Closed Sun.*

Tortilla Flats. Between a Taco Bell on one corner and a McDonald's on the other, Tortilla Flats is an oasis of great New Mexican food served in pleasant, informal surroundings. The service is a bit slow, but you'll forget once breakfast arrives—perhaps chorizo Mexicana (spicy red sausage served with a three-egg omelet), a chorizo-and-scrambled-egg burrito, or the traditional huevos rancheros, served with refried beans and good, hot coffee that keeps on coming. *3139 Cerrillos Rd., tel. 505/471–8685. Reservations not necessary. Dress: informal. MC, V. Breakfast and lunch only.*

Lodging

Santa Fe is a hot tourist destination that attracts lots of upscale travelers. As a result, prices have been escalating steadily in recent years and are likely to continue to climb as long as a steady stream of fat cats continues to show up and pay them. Low-season hotel rates, which fluctuate considerably from place to place, are generally in effect from the beginning of November until the end of April (excluding the Thanksgiving and Christmas holidays), and then they soar. But the savings are far from spectacular, even at no-frills hotels.

Highly recommended lodgings in each price category are indicated by a star ★.

Category	Cost*
Very Expensive	over $150
Expensive	$100–$150
Moderate	$65–$100
Inexpensive	under $65

All prices are for a standard double room, excluding tax (5.8% in New Mexico)

Hotels

Very Expensive **Eldorado Hotel.** This is one of the city's newest and most luxurious hotels—a bit too modern for some—located in the heart of downtown, not far from the Plaza. Its rooms are stylishly furnished with carved Southwestern-style desks and chairs, nature prints, and large upholstered club chairs, all in warm, desert colors. Baths are spacious and completely tiled. Many of the rooms have balconies, and all offer views of the Santa Fe mountains. The hotel's Old House restaurant is one of the city's best (*see* Dining, *above*). *309 W. San Francisco St., 87501, tel. 505/988–4455. 218 rooms and minisuites, 5 suites. Facilities: restaurants, bar, rooftop pool, entertainment, shopping arcade. AE, D, DC, MC, V.*

★ **Inn of the Anasazi.** One of Santa Fe's newest showpieces (opened in 1991), in the heart of the historic Plaza district, this hotel was clearly designed with the upscale traveler in mind. Each individually designed room has beamed ceilings; a kiva (beehive-style) fireplace; a handcrafted desk, dresser, and tables; and a four-poster bed. Services include a personal attendant who acts as a concierge, twice-daily maid service, and room delivery of exercise bikes upon request. The restaurant serves good regional fare, and a private wine cellar seats up to 12 guests for dinner. Guests can browse in an in-house library, which focuses on the lore and legends of New Mexico and the Southwest. *113 Washington Ave., 87501, tel. 505/988–3030 or 800/688–8100. 60 rooms and suites. Facilities: TV, VCR, film library, stereo, minibar, safe. AE, DC, MC, V.*

★ **Inn on the Alameda.** Nestled between the Santa Fe Plaza shopping district and gallery-filled Canyon Road is one of the city's most prestigious small hotels. This inn on the Santa Fe River (Alameda means "place by the river"), with its adobe architecture and enclosed courtyards and portals, combines a relaxed New Mexico country atmosphere with

Santa Fe Lodging

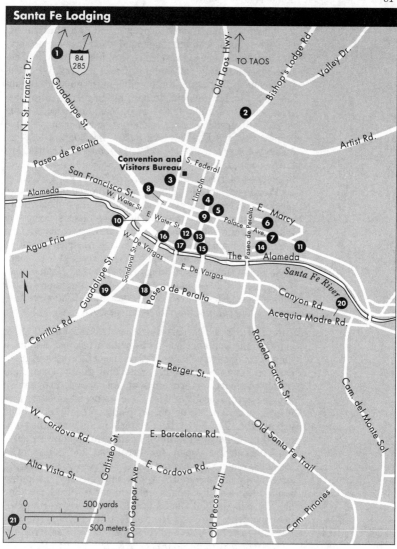

Alexander's Inn, **11**

Antonio and Hank's
Adobe Guest
House, **21**

The Bishop's
Lodge, **2**

Dunshee's, **20**

Eldorado Hotel, **8**

The Grant Corner
Inn, **3**

Hilton of Santa Fe, **10**

Hotel St. Francis, **13**

Hotel Santa Fe, **19**

Inn at Loretto–Best
Western, **15**

Inn of the Anasazi, **5**

Inn of the Animal
Tracks, **6**

Inn of the
Governors, **17**

Inn on the
Alameda, **14**

La Fonda, **12**

La Posada de Santa
Fe, **9**

Preston House, **7**

Pueblo Bonito B&B
Inn, **18**

Rancho Encantado, **1**

Territorial Inn, **4**

Water Street Inn, **16**

the luxury and amenities of a world-class hotel. The Southwest color scheme in the bedrooms carries over into the accessories, beds, wall hangings, and wood-framed mirrors. Handmade armoires, oversize chairs, headboards, and ceramic lamps and tiles all exemplify local artistry. While the inn has no dining room, its complimentary gourmet breakfast is a wonder: homemade muffins, bagels, creamy pastries, cinnamon rolls, fruit, juice, teas, and special Kona coffee, all served up by a friendly team of young Native Americans. *303 E. Alameda, 85701, tel. 505/984-2121 or 800/289-2122, fax 505/986-8325. 47 rooms and suites. Facilities: spa, lobby library, bar, hot tub, room wet bars and refrigerators, free local calls. AE, DC, MC, V.*

La Posada de Santa Fe. This Spanish Colonial inn, only two blocks from the Plaza, is situated on 6 acres of beautifully landscaped gardens and expansive green lawns shaded by giant elms and cottonwoods. The charming rooms all have fireplaces, beamed ceilings, and Native American rugs. In the center of this hotel complex is the excellent Victorian-style Staab House (*see* Dining, *above*). *330 E. Palace Ave., 87501, tel. 505/986-0000 or 800/727-5276 outside NM. 119 rooms, 33 suites. Facilities: restaurant, Victorian bar, swimming pool, health-club privileges. AE, DC, MC, V.*

Expensive **Hilton of Santa Fe.** This downtown establishment has a comfortable and spacious lobby with a beamed ceiling, a huge wrought-iron chandelier, and colorful Native American wall hangings. The large, renovated guest rooms, done in muted Southwestern tones of tan, cream, and golden brown, feature locally crafted table lamps, fine modern furniture, and hanging or potted plants. The hotel is built around the Casa de Ortiz, a historic home whose now-enclosed patio houses the hotel's delightful Chamisa Courtyard restaurant, open for breakfast and lunch. The intimate Piñon Grill serves entrées cooked over crackling fires of piñon, mesquite, apple, and hickory, including grilled Kansas City steaks and wild game selections. (The Tuscan hills around Chef Luca Tossani's native Florence are alive with wildlife.) *100 Sandoval St., 87501, tel. 505/988-2811 or 800/HILTONS. 155 rooms. Facilities: 2 restaurants, bar, heated outdoor pool. AE, D, DC, MC, V.*

Hotel St. Francis. Listed in the National Register of Historic Places, this tan, three-story building, constructed in 1920, has walkways fronted by turn-of-the-century lampposts. In addition to a prime location—one block southwest of the Plaza—the hotel offers small and simple rooms with high ceilings, casement windows, brass-and-iron beds, marble and cherrywood antiques, and original artwork. Bathrooms feature the original hexagonal tile and porcelain pedestal sinks. Afternoon tea, with scones and finger sandwiches, is served daily in the lobby and, weather permitting, on the veranda. Francisco's restaurant, a local favorite, offers Santa Fe grilled entrées and freshly made pastries. *201 Don Gaspar Ave., 87501, tel. 505/983-5700 or*

800/666–5700 outside NM. 81 rooms. Facilities: restaurant, bar, garden patio. AE, MC, V.

Inn at Loretto–Best Western. Built in the traditional Pueblo style, this hotel has been designed with historical accuracy in mind, with such touches as light fixtures custom-made of tinwork or pottery, and Native American Mimbres (drawings of legendary birds and animals), petroglyphs, and other ancient designs on the walls. Rooms are decorated in light colors and feature beds with handmade oak headboards and nightstands inlaid with recessed tilework. The inn is adjacent to the famous Loretto Chapel (*see* Tour 3 in *Exploring Santa Fe, above*). *211 Old Santa Fe Trail, 87501, tel. 505/988–5531 or 800/528–1234 outside NM. 136 rooms. Facilities: restaurant, lounge, pool, shops, galleries, beauty salon. AE, D, DC, MC, V.*

★ **Inn of the Governors.** This hotel, just two blocks from the Plaza, is one of the nicest in town. A small, intimate lobby makes the traveler feel quickly at home. Standard rooms have a Mexican theme, with bright colors, hand-painted folk art, Southwestern fabrics, and handmade furnishings; deluxe rooms are balconied Southwestern-style minisuites with fireplaces. The dining room specializes in native New Mexican dishes and lighter fare. *234 Don Gaspar Ave. (at Alameda), 87501, tel. 505/982–4333 or 800/234–4534 outside NM. 100 rooms. Facilities: restaurant, piano bar, patio dining in summer, ground-level and underground parking, swimming pool. AE, D, DC, MC, V.*

★ **La Fonda.** When Santa Fe was established in 1610, official records show that the town already had an adobe *fonda*, or inn, to accommodate travelers. Two centuries later, the original hotel was still welcoming guests—traders, trappers, mountain men, soldiers, and politicians. The present structure was built on the site of the original inn in 1864 and has been refurbished countless times since. The only lodging directly on the Plaza, it is perhaps also the only hotel in the world that can boast having had both Kit Carson and John F. Kennedy as guests. A spacious tiled lobby is decorated with Spanish Colonial antiques, early Mexican pieces, and classic Native American art. Each room is unique, featuring hand-decorated wooden furniture, wrought-iron light fixtures, beamed ceilings, oak door paneling, and motifs painted by local Pueblo artists; many accommodations have turn-of-the-century pieces, and all the suites have fireplaces. *100 E. San Francisco St., 87501, tel. 505/982–5511 or 800/523–5002 outside NM. 164 rooms, 35 suites. Facilities: enclosed courtyard restaurant, lounge, bar, swimming pool, whirlpool, private dining rooms. AE, D, DC, MC, V.*

Moderate **Hotel Santa Fe.** Controlling interest in this Pueblo-style three-story hotel is owned by the Picuris Pueblo, smallest of the eight northern New Mexico Native American tribes in the Valley of the Sangre de Cristo Mountains. Rooms and suites are decorated in traditional Southwestern style, with locally handmade furniture and Pueblo paintings (*Picuris* means "the painters"), many by well-known artist Gerald Nailor. All suites have microwave ovens, and smaller rooms have access to a common kitchen. The hotel-lobby bar serves a Continental breakfast. The lobby is also decorated with Native American art, including a large hand-loomed rug and the tower bell from the pueblo's 200-year-old mission. The hotel gift shop, the only such tribal-owned store in Santa Fe, has prices lower than most nearby retail stores, and hotel guests receive an additional 25% discount. Most staff members are from the Picuris Pueblo and travel the 60 miles to and from work each day by van. *1501 Paseo de Peralta, 87504, tel. 505/982–1200 or 800/825–9876 outside NM. 40 rooms, 91 suites. Facilities: bar, deli. AE, D, DC, MC, V.*

Bed-and-Breakfasts

Moderate **Alexander's Inn.** This 1903 Victorian house exudes all the charm of an old country inn, with American country-style wooden furnishings, flower arrangements, and lots of open space. A colorful flowered walkway runs alongside the building. In a lovely east-side residential area, only a few blocks from the Plaza and the Canyon Road shops and galleries, Alexander's Inn serves a generous Continental breakfast, including homemade bread and muffins. *529 E. Palace Ave., 87501, tel. 505/986–1431. 5 rooms, 3 with private baths, 2 with shared bath. MC, V.*

Antonio and Hank's Adobe Guest House. Book the Georgia O'Keeffe Room in the main house and you'll be sleeping in the same bed the artist slept in. The ancient adobe farmhouse was originally owned by Berta Dutton, New Mexico's first female archaeologist and a close friend of O'Keeffe's. It's constructed of adobe brick and furnished with hand-crafted Southwestern furniture and family heirlooms, including a vintage Victrola with hundreds of old 78s. The separate two-room guest house was O'Keeffe's studio during her visits; recently remodeled to accommodate guests, it has double beds in both rooms and floor-to-ceiling windows. There's also a full working kitchen with custom pine cabinets and Mexican tile counters. The inn, three miles south of the Plaza and surrounded by five acres of piñon, juniper, peach, and cherry trees, is also a working farm with pigs, turkeys, and more than 300 free-range chickens. *356 W. Zia Rd., 87505, tel. 505/982–9184. 5 rooms, one with bath, plus 2-bedroom guest house. No credit cards.*

Dunshee's. This pretty B&B, set in a quiet neighborhood just a mile from the Plaza, is so romantic that its patio has been used for weddings. Guests have two options. One is a spacious suite in the restored adobe home of artist Susan Dunshee, the proprietor. The suite has its own private entrance and includes a cozy living room, a bedroom with a double bed, and a Mexican tile bath. The rooms have kiva fireplaces and *viga* ceilings (with large timber rafters) and are furnished with antiques, quilts, and folk art, and you get a full gourmet breakfast into the bargain. The other, more expensive choice is an adobe casita with two bedrooms, a living room, a Mexican tile bath, a patio, and a kitchen complete with iron, dishwasher, and a refrigerator amply stocked for a do-it-yourself breakfast. It, too, features vigas, a kiva fireplace, decorative linens, and folk art. All in all, a good buy for upscale Santa Fe. *986 Acequia Madre, 87501, tel. 505/982–0988. Suite and 2-bedroom casita. MC, V.*

The Grant Corner Inn. This delightful Colonial-style lodging, located downtown, but surrounded by a patio and garden, combines antique Spanish and American country furnishings with potted greens and knickknacks. The rooms feature tile stoves, old-fashioned fixtures, quilts, and Native American blankets. The ample breakfast includes home-baked breads and pastries, jellies, and such unique local treats as blue-corn waffles. *122 Grant Ave., 87501, tel. 505/983–6678. 5 rooms with private bath, 6 with shared bath, and 2 with private bath in an adjoining hacienda. MC, V.*

★ **Inn of the Animal Tracks.** Three blocks east of the Plaza is this enchanting 90-year-old restored adobe, with beamed ceilings, hardwood floors, handcrafted furniture, and fireplaces. Each guest room is decorated with an animal theme: Whimsical Rabbit, Gentle Deer, Soaring Eagle, Playful Otter, and Loyal Wolf. Be prepared for cuteness: The Whimsical Rabbit room, for instance, is filled with stuffed and terra-cotta rabbits, rabbit books, rabbit drawings and paintings; bunny-rabbit slippers are tucked under the bed. A full breakfast and high tea are served; high tea is also available by reservation for nonguests. *707 Paseo de Peralta, 87504, tel. 505/988–1546. 5 rooms, all with private bath. AE, D, MC, V.*

Preston House. This 1886 Queen Anne house, the only one of its kind in the city, is tucked away in a quiet garden setting not far from the Plaza. Its pleasant rooms feature period furnishings, Edwardian fireplaces, and stained-glass windows. Fruit bowls and fresh-cut flowers add to the appeal. *106 Faithway St., 87501, tel. 505/982–3465. 15 rooms. AE, MC, V.*

Pueblo Bonito B & B Inn. Minutes from the Plaza is this century-old adobe compound—one of the few bed-and-breakfast inns in Santa Fe that retain the pure Southwest Pueblo design throughout. The handmade and hand-painted furnishings are all in the traditional Old Santa Fe style; works by local Native American and Western artists hang on the walls, and pottery made by New Mexican craftspeople grace the shelves, bookracks, and mantels. All the rooms have fireplaces. A filling breakfast is served in the main dining room (there's also room service), which has French doors that open onto a patio. *138 W. Manhattan Ave., 87501, tel. 505/984–8001. 12 rooms, 3 suites, all with private bath. Facilities: sun deck. MC, V.*

Territorial Inn. Creature comforts are a high priority in this elegant 100-year-old brick structure, nestled amid restaurants and shops; it's now one of Santa Fe's leading bed-and-breakfasts, only one block from the Plaza. The decor is Victorian throughout; among the well-maintained rooms, No. 9 has a canopied bed and a fireplace. A hot tub is also available, with robes provided. In addition to Continental breakfast, the inn offers afternoon treats, and brandy turndowns in the evening. *215 Washington Ave., 87501, tel. 505/989–7737. 10 rooms, all with private bath. MC, V.*

Water Street Inn. This intimate, restored adobe house blends regional Southwestern furnishings with period antiques. All the rooms have fireplaces and private baths. *427 W. Water St., 87501, tel. 505/984–1193. 6 rooms. MC, V.*

Resorts

Very Expensive **The Bishop's Lodge.** This resort sits 3 miles north of downtown Santa Fe, in the rolling foothills of the Sangre de Cristo Mountains. Geared toward families, particularly during the summer, the property offers a variety of outdoor activities, including horseback riding, hiking, skeet shooting, tennis, swimming in an outdoor heated pool, and lawn games. Guest rooms and public spaces in the one- and three-story lodges have old Southwestern furnishings, such as shipping chests, tables, and desks dating from 1917–20, when the hotel was built, along with tinwork from Mexico and original Native American and Western art. The dining room, one of the finest in the Southwest, offers a bountiful luncheon buffet; Sunday's meal draws large crowds of nonguests from town. Jackets are required for dinner. *Bishop's Lodge Rd., 87504, tel. 505/983–6377. 56 rooms, 18 suites. Facilities: restaurant, bar, heated pool, whirlpool, 18-hole golf privileges, available airport and railroad transfers, supervised children's programs. No credit cards. Closed Jan.–Apr.*

Rancho Encantado. This elegantly casual resort offers horseback riding, indoor and outdoor swimming, hiking, jogging, and seasonal skiing in the rolling, piñon-covered hills above the sprawling Rio Grande Valley. The guest rooms have Southwestern-style furniture, handmade and hand-painted by local craftspeople, in addition to fine Spanish and Western antiques from the 1850s and earlier. Some rooms have fireplaces and/or private patios; some are carpeted, while others have tile floors. The acclaimed dining room specializes in rack of lamb and fresh fish. *Located on U.S. 285 near Tesuque, 8 mi north of Santa Fe (Rte. 4, Box 57C), 87504, tel. 505/982–3537. 22 rooms, 10 suites. Facilities: restaurant, 2 pools, heated whirlpool, tennis, golf privileges. AE, DC, MC, V.*

Camping

With its wide, open spaces, good roads, and knock-'em-dead scenery, northern New Mexico draws camping enthusiasts and RV road warriors like teenagers to a rock concert. The Santa Fe National Forest is right in the city's backyard and includes the Dome Wilderness (5,200 acres in the volcanically formed Jemez Mountains) and the Pecos Wilderness (223,333 acres of high mountains, forests, and meadows at the southern end of the Rocky Mountain chain). Administrators of the Santa Fe National Forest have spent $600,000 to open a 14-site campground, 12 shaded picnic units, and a 45-vehicle parking area, and to improve trout habitats along a six-mile stretch of the Jemez River. Public sites remain open from May through October. For specifics, call the **Santa Fe National Forest Office** (1220 South St. Francis Dr., Box 1689, 87504, tel. 505/988–6940). Some private campground operators provide literature at the **La Bajada Welcome Center** (La Bajada Hill, 13 mi southwest of Santa Fe on I–25, tel. 505/471–5242). The following are a few of the main campground and recreational vehicle facilities:

Los Campos Recreational Vehicle Park. The only full-service RV park within the city limits, Los Campos even has a swimming pool. Tucked behind a car dealership on one side, it offers open vistas on the other: poplars and Russian olive trees, a dry riverbed, and mountains rising in the background. *3574 Cerrillos Rd., 87501, tel. 505/473–1949. Facilities: 5 hookups plus assorted tent sites (back-ins $20.75, pull-throughs $22.75), showers, bathrooms, swimming pool, LP gas, picnic tables.*

Rancheros de Santa Fe Camping Park. Located on I–25N (at Exit 290 on the Las Vegas Hwy., 10½ mi from the Santa Fe Plaza), this beautiful camping park is on a hill in the midst of a piñon forest. *Las Vegas Hwy., 87505, tel. 505/983–3482. Facilities: RV and tent sites ($12.50 plus $2 per person for more than 2 people, children $1.50, under-3s free), hookups ($16.50), pull-throughs ($17.50), swimming pool, hot showers, grocery, ice, laundry, bathrooms, LP gas available.*

Santa Fe KOA. Set in the southwestern foothills of the Sangre de Cristo Mountains, this large campground is well treed with piñon, cedar, and juniper. *Rte. 3, Box 95-A, 87501, tel. 505/982–1419. Facilities: full hookups ($17.50), tent sites ($11.50, plus $2 per person for more than 2 people), grocery, laundry, recreation room (video games, pool, ping-pong), bathrooms, showers.*

Tesuque Pueblo RV Campground. This campground, operated by the Tesuque Pueblo, 10 miles north of Santa Fe (St. Francis exit off I–25), is on an open hill with a few cedar trees dotting the landscape; off to the west is the Tesuque

River. *Tesuque 87501, tel. 505/455-2661. Facilities: RV and tent sites ($11 plus $2 per person for more than 2 people), 63 full hookups ($14), toilets, showers, drinking water, security gate, laundry.*

The Arts and Nightlife

Check the entertainment listings in Santa Fe's daily newspaper, the *New Mexican,* or the complimentary *Inside Santa Fe,* available at most hotels and shops, for special performances and events.

The Arts

Music Artistically and visually the city's crowning glory, the famed **Santa Fe Opera** is housed in a strikingly modern structure, a spectacular, 1,173-seat, indoor-outdoor amphitheater carved into the natural curves of a hillside, 7 miles north of the city. It overlooks a vast panorama of mountains, mesas, and sky. Blend in some of the most acclaimed singers, directors, conductors, musicians, designers, and composers from Europe and the United States, and you begin to understand the excitement that explodes each July and August amid the tall pines of the Sangre de Cristo Mountains. Founded in 1957 by John Crosby, who remains its general director, the company offers a blend of seasoned classics, neglected masterpieces, and innovative premieres. For schedules and further information, call 505/982-3855, or write the Santa Fe Opera, Box 2408, 87504.

Under the direction of maestro Stewart Robertson, the **Santa Fe Symphony** (tel. 505/983-3530, Box 9692, 87504) performs seven concerts each season (September through May) to sold-out audiences at Sweeney Center. Also from September through May, regular concerts are given by the professional chamber **Orchestra of Santa Fe** (tel. 505/988-4640, Box 2091, 87504). Its Mozart Festival in February and its annual holiday presentation of Handel's *Messiah* have become local traditions. In addition, **Santa Fe Summerscene** (tel. 505/989-8062) offers a series of free concerts (rhythm and blues, light opera, jazz, Cajun, salsa, folk, and bluegrass), dance performances (modern, folk), lectures, and storytelling sessions staged on the Santa Fe Plaza each Tuesday and Thursday from mid-June through August at noon and 7 PM.

Theater On Friday, Saturday, and Sunday nights during July and August, **Shakespeare in Santa Fe** (tel. 505/982-2910, Box 2188, 87504) presents free performances of the Bard's finest at the courtyard of the John Meem Library at St. John's College (Camino de Cruz Blanca, the next left past the cutoff for the International Folk Art Museum on the Old Santa Fe Trail). The music begins at 6, the show at 7. Picnic baskets are welcome, in the tradition of the Old Vic, but, please, no ripe tomatoes. There's also a concession stand. Seating is limited to 350, so it's best to get tickets in advance.

Staging at least four productions each October through May, the beautiful **Greer Garson Theater** (tel. 505/473–6511 or 505/473–6439, College of Santa Fe, St. Michael's Dr., 87501) is the scene of some of northern New Mexico's most spirited comedies, dramas, and musicals. (The actress after whom it is named is a principal contributor to the college's performing-arts program and a resident of Santa Fe.)

Live theatrical performances are also available throughout the year at the **New Mexico Repertory Theater** (tel. 505/983–2382), which presents original, as well as established, dramas and comedies; the **Santa Fe Actors' Theater** (tel. 505/982–8309), dedicated to fostering the growth of the performing arts in Santa Fe and staging the works of playwrights ranging from Euripides to Sam Shepard; the **Santa Fe Community Theater** (tel. 505/988–4262), with its adventurous mix of avant-garde, established drama, and musical comedy; and the **Santa Fe Performing Arts Company** (tel. 505/984–2003 or 505/989–8008), offering a five-week intensive training program for students 8–19, culminating with a major production at the end of the summer session.

Nightlife

The lounges, hotels, and night spots of Santa Fe offer a wide variety of entertainment options, from lively dancing at a frontier saloon to quiet cocktails beside the flickering embers of a piñon fire. You can throw both your wallet and your hip out of joint at any of the following: **Club Luna** (519 Cerrillos Rd., tel. 505/989–4888) plays "the hottest dance music in town." **Chez What** (213 W. Alameda, tel. 505/982–0099) is a casual French bistro with tie-dyed tablecloths and a spacious U-shaped bar serving patrons on both sides; its ample floor turns to music and dancing after the mesquite-grilled pork chops have been served. **Edge** (135 W. Palace Ave., tel. 505/986–1700) offers mostly DJ-powered music but veers to live sounds on Monday and Tuesday. **Rodeo Nites** (2911 Cerrillos Rd., tel. 505/473–4138) attracts a country-Western crowd. **The Bull Ring** (414 Old Santa Fe Trail, tel. 505/983–3328), one of the better restaurants in town (*see* Dining, *above*), presents a live rock band on weekends. Rock and roll is also the mainstay at **Shooters** (1196 Harrison Rd., tel. 505/438–7777), which offers dance instructions on Wednesday night. **The Red Rooster** (Los Alamos Hwy., tel. 505/455–2724) has a good jukebox.

Excursion 1: Pecos National Historic Park and Las Vegas

A visit to the ancient New Mexican past and to a contemporary town that lives in the past are highlighted in this pleasant excursion to the region south of Santa Fe.

Tourist Information

The **visitor center** of Pecos National Historic Park (Drawer 418, Pecos 87552, tel. 505/757–6032), at the monument entranceway, offers information about the area, including a free brochure, a 10-minute film, and a small exhibit.

Las Vegas Chamber of Commerce (727 Grand Ave., Box 148, Las Vegas 87701, tel. 505/425–8631) provides brochures and other printed matter about the town and its colorful history.

Getting There

Pecos National Historic Park is about 25 miles southeast of Santa Fe via I–25. Continuing another five miles on I–25 in the same direction brings you to Las Vegas.

Exploring Pecos National Historic Park

Pecos National Historic Park is the site of what was perhaps the greatest Native American pueblo. Located in a fertile valley and strategically situated between the buffalo hunters of the Great Plains and the farmers of the Rio Grande Valley, Pecos was an early trading center. It was the largest and easternmost pueblo reached by the Spanish conquistadores, who built two missions here in their zeal to convert the Indians to Catholicism, and it became a major landmark on the Santa Fe Trail.

The ruins of the missions and of the excavated and partially stabilized pueblo may be visited on a self-guided tour, which can be completed in about one hour. Containing more than 1,100 rooms and once the multidwelling home of as many as 2,500 Native Americans, the pueblo was four stories high in places. It was abandoned in 1838, and its 17 surviving occupants moved to the Jemez Pueblo. Today's visitors will find an exhibit and information center at the monument entranceway, where an introductory film is screened. *Pecos National Historic Park, Drawer 418, Pecos 87552, tel. 505/757–6032. Admission: $4 per car, $2 per bus passenger. The Golden Age Passport (issued to U.S. citizens 62 and older) allows free admission to all occupants of the same car, regardless of age.*

Exploring Las Vegas

The antithesis of its Nevada namesake, Las Vegas was once an oasis for stagecoach passengers on the Santa Fe Trail who were seeking refuge from Native Americans and outlaws. And it was once, in the late 19th century, one of the state's major centers of commerce. Now the seat of San Miguel County, Las Vegas lies where the Sangre de Cristo Mountains merge with the high plains of New Mexico. At an altitude of 6,470 feet, its climate is delightful—summer days averaging in the low to mid-80s, winter days rarely below freezing. If you like to go traipsing through the past, back to a time when men were slow on words but fast on the draw, you'll enjoy a day or two in this town.

Sheriff Pat Garrett, who killed Billy the Kid, lived in the building that now houses the **Las Vegas Chamber of Commerce** (727 Grand Ave.). Teddy Roosevelt held a Rough Riders reunion in the Castaneda Hotel—once a crown jewel in the Fred Harvey chain—which has clearly seen better days. And, fresh from his triumph at San Juan Hill, he announced his candidacy for the vice-presidency in the lobby of the Las Vegas Harvey House. **Theodore Roosevelt's Rough Riders Memorial and City Museum** houses Native American artifacts, documents pertaining to the city's history, and memorabilia from the Spanish-American War. *Chamber of Commerce Bldg., 727 Grand Ave., tel. 505/425–8726. Admission free. Open Mon.–Sat. 9–4; closed Sun. and holidays.*

Las Vegas's 15,000 inhabitants unabashedly live in the past. Today's Las Vegas is built around old churches, old salons, old hotels, old houses, and old shops (many selling memorabilia and antiques of the period). Las Vegas has nine historic districts and some interesting lodgings, including the elegant, historic 1882 Plaza Hotel on the Old Town Plaza (tel. 505/425–3591) and the Inn on the Santa Fe Trail, 2 miles away (tel. 505/425–6791).

Time Out   In Old Town, on the Plaza, **Byron T's Lounge** (Plaza Hotel, 230 Old Town Plaza, tel. 505/425–3591) offers American favorites (steaks, chops, and chicken), as well as Southwestern cuisine, including steaming bowls of chili and hearty soups. Half a block away, **El Realto** (141 Bridge St., tel. 505/454–0037) serves seafood and Mexican specialties in a historic 1890s building furnished with Victorian and early West antiques.

Excursion 2:
Around Los Alamos

With the Jemez Mountains on one side and the Sangre de Cristo range on the other, Los Alamos's mesa-top location provides spectacular scenery and clean mountain air that's pleasantly cool in summer and ideal for outdoor pursuits in winter. There are plenty of fine accommodations, good food, convenient shopping, and several excellent museums. Hundreds of archaeological sites dot the Los Alamos area. Many of the best are located in Bandelier National Park— where cave and cliff dwellings, ancient ceremonial kivas, and other stone structures stretch out for more than a mile as the sheer walls of the Frijoles Canyon rise to a tree-fringed rim—and in Jemez State Monument. Nearby Valle Grande and Soda Dam provide insight into the geology of the region.

Los Alamos, birthplace of the atomic bomb, spreads over fingerlike mesas at an altitude of 7,300 feet. While research continues at the Los Alamos National Laboratory (in areas such as lasers, nuclear energy, superconductivity, and medicine), the community now emphasizes its link to the prehistoric past, promoting the more than 7,000 archaeological sites in the area (*see* Bandelier National Monument, *below*).

Tourist Information

Los Alamos County Chamber of Commerce (Fuller Lodge, 2132 Central Ave., Box 460 VG, Los Alamos 87544, tel. 505/662–8105) offers a free *Visitor Guide*, brochures, and other promotional material upon request.

Getting There

Los Alamos is 45 minutes north of Santa Fe, west of U.S. 84–285, on NM 502. **Gray Line of Santa Fe** (tel. 505/983–9491) offers a four-hour tour of Los Alamos and the nearby Bandelier Cliff Dwellings.

Exploring Los Alamos

The community of Los Alamos was founded in absolute secrecy in 1943 as a center of defense research. The disclosure of its existence two years later made international headlines. A visitor today might suspect the place was kept secret because it's so ugly: army barracks and middle-income tract houses that could have been imported from some depressed area of New England.

Bradbury Science Museum offers visitors a chance to experiment with lasers, use advanced computers, and witness research in solar, geothermal, fission, and fusion energy. You can get a glimpse of World War II's historic Project Y, as well as some of today's advanced science and technology, at the Los Alamos National Laboratory. *Los Alamos National Laboratory, Diamond Dr., tel. 505/662–4444. Admission free. Open Tues.–Fri. 9–5, Sat.–Mon. 1–5.*

Housed in a national historic landmark, **Fuller Lodge Art Center** features works of northern New Mexican artists and traveling exhibits of both national and regional importance. The massive log structure, built in 1928, served as the dining and recreation hall for students of the Los Alamos Ranch School before World War II. *Fuller Lodge, 2132 Central Ave., tel. 505/662–9331. Admission free. Open Mon.–Sat. 10–4, Sun. 1–4.*

Also located on the grounds of the former ranch school, **Los Alamos Historical Museum** displays artifacts of early Native American life, as well as photographs and documents of the community's history, before and after World War II. *Fuller Lodge, 2132 Central Ave., tel. 505/662–4493. Admission free. Open Mon.–Sat. 10–4, Sun. 1–4.*

From Los Alamos, take NM 502 (Trinity Dr.) west and then NM 501 (West Jemez Rd.) south until you reach NM 4 at a "T" intersection. Turn left (east) and drive 6 miles to the entrance of **Bandelier National Monument.**

Seven centuries before the Declaration of Independence was signed, egalitarian, compact cities existed in the desert Southwest. Remnants of one of the most impressive of them, the **Anasazi Ruins,** can be seen at Frijoles Canyon in Bandelier National Monument. At the canyon's base, beside a gurgling stream, are the ruins of a three-story-high pueblo, crumbling walls representing an irregular circle of small stone rooms. Visitors using primitive wooden ladders, rungs lashed into place with leather strips, can squeeze through the doorway and get a feel for what it was like to live within the cell-like, four-foot-by-four-foot rooms. As the population expanded, additions were made to the original buildings. Natural caves in the soft volcanic tuff nearby were enlarged, and houses were built out from the cliffs.

For hundreds of years, the Anasazi people, early relatives of today's Rio Grande Pueblo Native Americans, thrived on wild game and crops of corn and beans. Suddenly, for reasons that are still undetermined, the settlements were abandoned. Climatic changes? A great drought? Crop depletion? No one knows for sure what caused the hasty retreat.

Visitors may ponder these and other mysteries while following a paved, self-guided trail through the site. Bandelier National Monument, named after author and ethnologist Adolph Bandelier (his novel, *The Delight Makers,* is set in Frijoles Canyon), contains 37,737 acres of wilderness, waterfalls, and wildlife, traversed by 60 miles of trails. A small museum in the visitor center focuses on Native American culture and artifacts from AD 1200 to modern Pueblo times. Some information about the area's wildlife is also displayed. *Bandelier National Monument, Los Alamos 87544, tel. 505/672–3861. Admission: $5 per car, $3 per bus passenger. The Golden Age Passport (issued to U.S. citizens 62 and older) allows free admission to all occupants of the same car, regardless of age.*

Take a left when you leave the national monument onto NM 4 west and follow the winding, scenic road up through the mountain forest to Jemez Springs; the drive should take about 45 minutes. Between Bandelier and Jemez, you'll pass magnificent **Valle Grande,** the world's largest volcanic caldera, only a fraction of which can be seen from the road. Once a bubbling inferno of lava, it's now a lush green high-mountain valley with herds of grazing cattle. The entire 50-mile Jemez range, formed by cataclysmic upheavals, is now filled with gentle streams, hiking trails, and campgrounds.

Jemez State Monument, on NM 4, 1 mile north of Jemez Springs, contains another impressive Native American ruin. Approximately 600 years ago, ancestors of the people of Jemez Pueblo built several villages in and around the narrow mountain valley. One of the villages was Guisewa, a name that refers to the numerous hot mineral springs in the area. The Spanish colonists discovered it in 1598 and built a mission that was abandoned in 1630. Jemez is a year-round vacation destination, with hiking, cross-country skiing, and camping in nearby U.S. Forest Service areas. *Tel. 505/ 829–3530. Admission: $2.10 adults, children under 15 free. Open May–Sept. 15, daily 9–6; Sept. 16–Apr., daily 8:30– 4:30. Closed for state holidays except July 4, Memorial Day, and Labor Day.*

A mile north of Jemez State Monument, just off NM 4, is a geological wonder known as **Soda Dam.** The so-called dam was created over thousands of years, formed by travertine deposits from mineral precipitation as waters cooled the earth's surface. The site's strange, mushroom-shaped exterior and the natural caves that have formed in and around it create the mystical aura that made it a sacred place to the ancient Native Americans. Numerous artifacts, prayer sticks, and rabbit clubs have been found here, as well as the mummy of a Native American baby wrapped in a blanket. In the warm summer months, the Jemez River at Soda Dam is a popular swimming spot.

Dining and Lodging

Dining **Ashley's.** This handsome restaurant and lounge located in the Los Alamos Inn serves American and Southwest regional specialties for breakfast, lunch, and dinner; the Sunday brunch is a local favorite. The large dining room, decorated in modern Southwestern style, is filled with booths and rows of tables. *2201 Trinity Dr., tel. 505/662–7211. Reservations suggested for dinner. Dress: casual. AE, D, MC, V. Moderate.*

Hill Diner. This large, friendly restaurant used to be called the Good Eats Café; it still boasts the finest gourmet burgers in town ($5.99), along with chicken-fried steaks, chicken-fried chicken, homemade soups, and heaps of fresh vegetables. Hill Diner is a good buy, with generous portions and relatively painless prices. A steak and shrimp dinner tops the menu at $10.99. *1315 Trinity Dr., tel. 505/662–9745. Reservations not required. Dress: casual. D, DC, MC, V. Closed Sun. Inexpensive–Moderate.*

Lodging **Hilltop House Hotel.** Minutes from the Los Alamos National Laboratory, the three-story Hilltop House is geared toward traveling scientists and businesspeople as well as vacationers. Deluxe rooms have kitchenettes, and mini- and executive suites offer full kitchen facilities. All accommodations are furnished with modern Southwestern-style beds, desks, chairs, and tables. Guests get a complimentary cooked-to-order breakfast on weekdays, and the hotel's Trinity Sights restaurant offers good American and Southwestern cuisine in an elegant, white-tablecloth and flickering candlelight setting. *Trinity Dr. at Central Ave., Box 250, Los Alamos 87544, tel. 505/662–2441. 88 rooms. Facilities: restaurant, lounge, indoor pool, self-service laundry, car-rental agency on premises. AE, DC, MC, V. Moderate.*

Los Alamos Inn. Rooms in this sprawling ground-level hotel feature modern Southwestern decor and provide sweeping canyon views. Its dining room, Ashley's Restaurant (*see* Dining, *above*), does a Sunday brunch that's popular with locals as well as vacationing visitors. *2201 Trinity Dr., Los Alamos 87544, tel. 505/662–7211. 114 rooms. Facilities: outdoor pool and spa, restaurant, bar. AE, DC, MC, V. Inexpensive–Moderate.*

Orange Street Inn. Situated in a rather unremarkable 1948 wood-frame house in a quiet residential neighborhood, this B&B offers the usual amenities. Rooms are furnished in Southwest and contemporary styles; the public area has cable TV and a VCR; guests may use the kitchen facilities and the laundry. Breakfast is an ample Continental-plus. In the summer you get afternoon wine and hors d'oeuvres, and pay-as-you-go soft drinks and snacks are always available. *3496 Orange St., Los Alamos 87544, tel. 505/662–2651. 7 rooms, 3 with bath. D, MC, V. Inexpensive–Moderate.*

Excursion 3:
The High Road to Taos

If time isn't important, your drive from Santa Fe to Taos can be far more scenic and memorable if you detour a bit, skip the main highway (NM 68), and take the high road, a route by which you can literally travel back in time. The drive through the rolling hillsides studded with orchards and tiny picturesque villages noted for weavers and wood-carvers, all set against the rugged alpine mountain back-drop, is stunning. A note of caution, however. As pretty as the high-road country is in winter, when the fields turn deep, soft white and the villages, fences, and naked trees are silhouetted like bold pen-and-ink drawings against the sky, the roads can be icy and treacherous. Check on weather conditions before attempting the drive, or stay with the more conventional Santa Fe–Taos route.

Out of Santa Fe past Tesuque on U.S. 84/285, turn north-east at Pojoaque on NM 503 (about 12 mi north of Santa Fe). You'll come first to Nambe Pueblo and the lovely Nambe Falls picnic area. Continue on through the village of Cundiyo to **Chimayo,** sometimes called "the Lourdes of the Southwest." Nestled into the rugged hillsides where gnarled piñons seem to grow from bare bedrock, Chimayo is a town famous for its weaving, regional food, and the **Santuario de Chimayo** (once you reach the village, you can't miss it; signs everywhere point the way). The Santuario is a small, frontier adobe church built on the site where, believ-ers say, a mysterious light came from the ground on Good Friday night in 1810. Some men from the village investi-gated the phenomenon, trying to find its source. Pushing away the earth, they found a large wooden crucifix. Today the chapel sits above a sacred *pozito* (a small well), the mud from which is believed to have miraculous healing proper-ties, as the dozens of abandoned crutches and braces left at the altar—along with many notes, letters, and photos left behind in thanksgiving and prayer—dramatically testify. The Santuario draws a steady stream of worshipers all year long, but during Holy Week as many as 50,000 people visit. The shrine is a National Historic Landmark, but unlike similar holy places, it remains free of hysteria, and the com-mercialism is limited to a small adobe shop nearby that sells brochures, books, and religious articles. *Tel. 505/351–4889. Admission free. Open daily.*

Chimayo is also known for its colorful weaving. At the junc-tion of NM 520 and NM 76, **Ortega's Weaving Shop** offers high quality Rio Grande work by a family whose Spanish ancestors brought the craft to New Mexico in the 1600s. Adjacent to the weaving shop is the **Galeria Ortega,** featur-ing traditional New Mexican Hispanic and contemporary

Native American arts and crafts. The mailing address for both shops is Box 325, Chimayo 87522, tel. 505/351–4215.

About 4 miles east–northeast of Chimayo, just off NM 76 (look for the clearly marked signs), is the town of **Cordova.** Hardly more than a mountain village with a small central plaza, Cordova is the center of the regional wood-carving industry. Craftspeople whose ancestors carved santos and other religious and ornamental figures for church altars and private chapels still fashion them here from local wood. There's not much to see in the village, which consists of a schoolhouse, post office, and a few stores, except for the **St. Anthony of Padua Chapel,** which is filled with beautiful handcrafted statues and retablos.

Cordova supports no fewer than 35 full-time and part-time carvers. The most famous of them is George Lopez, whose house is just south of the plaza. If you visit, you'll see an Ansel Adams portrait of Jose Dolores Lopez, George's father, considered a creative genius of wood carving; it was taken by the photographer in 1928. Most of the santeros in Cordova have signs outside their homes indicating that the statues are for sale. The pieces are expensive, ranging from several hundred dollars for small ones to several thousand for larger figures. Collectors snap them up at any price.

Continuing north on NM 76, about 1½ miles from Cordova, you'll come to **Truchas,** where Robert Redford shot the movie *The Milagro Beanfield War* (based on a novel written by Taos author John Nichols). This breathtakingly beautiful village is perched on the rim of a deep canyon with the towering Truchas Peaks, mountains high enough to be almost perpetually capped with snow, dominating the horizon. The tallest of the Truchas Peaks is 13,102 feet, the second-highest mountain in New Mexico. Truchas (Spanish for "trout") has a colorful array of shops and galleries, the best-known of which is **Cordova's Weaving Shop** (Box 425, Truchas 87579, tel. 505/689–2437). Proprietor Harry Cordova, whose son played a part in the Redford movie, is quick to point out that his shop's back door was also in the film as the front door of the town's newspaper office.

Next is the village of Trampas, founded in 1751. Turn right on winding NM 75, then left on NM 518 to Talpa and on to Rancho de Taos, site of the famous San Francisco de Asis church. Turn right on NM 68 to Taos.

Dining and Lodging

Dining
★
Rancho de Chimayo. Where aficionados of northern New Mexican cooking go to find the best of it. Set in a century-old adobe hacienda tucked into the mountains, with white-washed walls and hand-stripped vigas, cozy dining rooms, and lush, terraced patios, the Rancho de Chimayo is still owned and operated by the family who originally occupied the house. They use locally grown products and recipes that

are generations old. (On sale at the cash register and in bookstores everywhere is the *Rancho de Chimayo Cookbook.)* There's a roaring fireplace in the winter and summer dining alfresco. *NM 520, tel. 505/984–2100. Reservations advised. Jacket and tie advised. AE, MC, V. Moderate.*

Lodging **Hacienda de Chimayo.** Across the street from the Rancho de Chimayo restaurant and owned by the same people is the Hacienda de Chimayo, more of a country inn than a bed-and-breakfast (though a Continental breakfast is served). Its rooms are all decorated with turn-of-the-century antiques, and each has a private bath and a fireplace. The lovely mountain setting and the charming furnishings make this a delightful accommodation. *NM 520, tel. 505/351–2222. 6 rooms, 1 suite. AE, DC, MC, V. Moderate.*

La Posada de Chimayo. This small country inn features two guest houses (one built in 1891) of typical northern New Mexico adobe, with brick floors, viga ceilings, and traditional kiva fireplaces. The cozy rooms have Mexican rugs, handwoven bedspreads, comfortable regional furniture, and some good books. Owner Sue Farrington, an expert on Mexico and Mexican cooking, offers a full gourmet breakfast in a variety of south-of-the-border flavors. *279 Rio Arriba (Box 463), Chimayo 87522, tel. and fax 505/351–4605. 2 rooms with bath, 3 suites. MC, V. Moderate.*

4 Taos

Mysterious, spiritual, and ageless, Taos is an enchanted town of soft lines and delineations that once viewed will remain etched in the mind forever. Romantic courtyards, stately elms and cottonwood trees, narrow streets, and the profusion of adobe all add to its timeless appeal.

Just as layers of history can be read on the rock walls of the 650-foot-deep Rio Grande Gorge, carved into the otherwise table-flat landscape just west of Taos, so, too, are layers of history revealed in the town itself. The tawny-colored one- and two-story adobe buildings that line the two-centuries-old Plaza reveal the influence of Native American and Spanish settlers. Overhanging balconies supported by slender beams were added later by American pioneers who came west after the Mexican War of 1846. Some of the roads extending from the Plaza are still unpaved today; when it rains, they're not unlike the rutted streets of yesteryear. Taos is actually three towns in one.

The first is the community itself, which many compare to Santa Fe before all the glitz and glamour arrived. The second, 3 miles northwest of the commercial center, is the Taos Pueblo, the home of the Taos-Tiwa Indians, whose apartment-house-style pueblo dwelling is one of the oldest continually inhabited communities in the country. The third Taos, 4 miles south of town, is Ranchos de Taos, an adobe-housed farming and ranching community settled by the Spanish centuries ago. A bit scruffy these days, Ranchos de Taos is best known for the San Francisco de Asis Church, with its massive buttressed adobe walls and graceful towers. Generations of painters and photographers—including Georgia O'Keeffe, Paul Strand, and Ansel Adams—have been inspired by its beauty. Its graveyard, or *campo santo*, is one of the most photographed in the country, with a beauty surpassed only by the church's wealth of religious artifacts and paintings. The church is the focal point of St. Francis Plaza and its shops and antiques galleries.

These three distinct faces of Taos merge at the place where the sky meets the mountains, in a magnificent 7,000-foot-high plateau. With a combined population of under 5,000, Taos, the Taos Pueblo, and Ranchos de Taos offer a unique blend of history and culture. Add to this a remarkable literary and artistic heritage, names like D.H. Lawrence, Mabel Dodge Luhan, Frank Waters, Lady Dorothy Brett, and a score of other well-known artists and writers, and the town's appeal is evident.

Life at the Taos Pueblo predates Marco Polo's 13th-century travels in China and the arrival of the Spanish in America in 1540. The northernmost of the 19 Pueblo Native American settlements scattered throughout the Rio Grande Valley, Taos Pueblo is now the home of some 200 of the more than 2,000 members of the reservation (most of whom live in fully modern homes elsewhere on the Pueblo's 95,000 acres). It retains much of its rich cultural heritage, as exemplified by the soft, flowing lines of the dramatic architecture and in the seasonal dances performed on the open plaza. The Taos Pueblo has no electricity, no telephones (except at the visitor center), and no plumbing; water is carried by bucket from the crystal-clear stream that rushes through the pueblo's center. A sign reading "Please, No Wading" warns thoughtless tourists away from this sacred river, the pueblo's only source of drinking water. Unlike many Native American tribes that were forced to relocate to government-designated reservations, the Taos Pueblo Native Americans have resided at the base of the 12,282-foot-high Taos Mountain for centuries, remaining a link between prehistoric inhabitants who originally lived in the Taos Valley and their descendants who reside there now.

In many ways Taos is still very much a frontier town. In the dry summer months, dust covers everything, affording the place a comfortably worn, weathered look.

Essential Information

Important Addresses and Numbers

Tourist Information Brochures, maps, a calendar of events, and general information are available from the **Taos County Chamber of Commerce** (1139 Paseo del Pueblo Sur, Post Office Drawer I, Taos 87571, tel. 505/758–3873 or 800/732–8267). Its Visitor's Information Center, located two blocks south of the Plaza on Paseo del Pueblo Sur, is open 9 AM–6 PM daily during the summer months, 9 AM–5 PM daily during the rest of the year.

Emergencies **Fire, medical,** or **police** (tel. 911). **Taos police** (tel. 505/758–2216), **state police** (tel. 505/758–8878).

Ambulance (tel. 505/758–1911).

Hospital emergency room: Holy Cross Hospital (Paseo del Pueblo Sur, tel. 505/758–8883).

Pharmacies **Taos Pharmacy** (S. Santa Fe Rd., tel. 505/758–3342); **Furr's Pharmacy** (1102 Paseo del Pueblo Sur, tel. 505/758–9891); **Springer's Drug** (825 4th St., Springer, tel. 505/483–2356).

Arriving and Departing by Plane

Airport The closest major airport is in Albuquerque, 2½ hours south of Taos. The **Taos Municipal Airport** (U.S. 64, tel. 505/758–4995), 12 miles west of the city, services only private planes and air charters. For air-charter information, call 505/758–4995.

Between the Airport and Downtown **Pride of Taos** (tel. 505/758–8340) offers daily shuttle service to the Albuquerque Airport ($25 one-way, $45 round-trip). The price for its shuttle service between Taos and Santa Fe—just half the distance—is the same.

Faust's Transportation (Box 1050, in nearby El Prado, tel. 505/758–3410 or 505/758–7359) offers radio-dispatched taxis between the Taos Airport and town. The cost is $12.

Arriving and Departing by Car, Train, and Bus

By Car The main route from Santa Fe to Taos is NM 68. From points north, take NM 522; from points east or west, take NM 64. Roads can be treacherously icy during the winter months; call New Mexico Road Conditions (tel. 800/432–4269) before heading out. The altitude in Taos will affect your car's performance, causing it to "gasp" because it's getting too much gas and not enough air.

By Bus **Texas, New Mexico, Oklahoma Coaches** (a subsidiary of Greyhound/Trailways) runs buses once a day from Albuquerque to the Taos Bus Station (corner of Paseo del Pueblo Sur and Paseo del Cañon, tel. 505/758–1144).

By Train **Amtrak** (tel. 800/872–7245) provides service into Lamy Station (County Rd. 41, Lamy 87500) half an hour outside Santa Fe, the closest train station to Taos. **Faust's Transportation** (Box 1050, in nearby El Prado, tel. 505/758–3410 or 505/758–7359) offers radio-dispatched taxis to the train station.

Getting around Taos

Taos, like Santa Fe, radiates around its famous central Plaza and is easily maneuvered on foot. And, like Santa Fe, it has a La Fonda Hotel directly on the Plaza, although the two hotels have no official affiliation. Since the Plaza is the city's prime location, many of the top restaurants, stores, boutiques, and galleries are either on it or within its immediate vicinity. The main street through town is Paseo del Pueblo Norte, which turns into Paseo del Pueblo Sur. All the major hotels have ample parking space, and parking areas can be easily found just beyond the Plaza (though space may be tight during the peak summer months). To reach many of the sights of interest outside town, transportation will be necessary.

Car Rentals **Hertz Rent-A-Car** is located on Santa Fe Road (tel. 505/758–1668); **Jeep Trailways Rentals** is at Alpine Lodge, Red River (tel. 505/754–6443); and **Rich Ford Rent-A-Car** is located at the Taos Municipal Airport (tel. 505/758–9501).

By Bus **The Pride of Taos** (tel. 505/758–8340) provides pickups and drop-offs to various points within town. The cost is $7 for the first passenger, $2 for each additional passenger.

By Taxi Taxi service is sparse. However, **Faust's Transportation** (Box 1050, El Prado, tel. 505/758–3410 or 505/758–7359), in nearby El Prado, has a fleet of radio-dispatched cabs.

Opening and Closing Times

Banks, weekdays 9–5; museums, daily 9–5; stores, daily 9 or 10–5 or 6; post office, weekdays 9–5.

Guided Tours

Orientation **Pride of Taos Tours** (Box 1192, Taos 87571, tel. 505/758–8340) provides 70-minute narrated trolleylike bus tours of Taos highlights, including the San Francisco de Asis Mission Church that Georgia O'Keeffe painted, the Martinez Hacienda that portrays Spanish Colonial life in the 17th and 18th centuries, and Kit Carson's House and Museum near the Plaza. The cost is $10 for adults, $3 for children under 12. The departure points for tours, shuttles, and pickups is next to the Chamber of Commerce office on Paseo del Pueblo Sur and the Taos Plaza.

Special-Interest **Native Sons Adventures** (813A Paseo del Sur, tel. 505/758–
Tours 9342 or 800/753–7559) organizes biking, backpacking, rafting, and snowmobiling expeditions. **Roadrunner Tours** (Box 274, Angel Fire, tel. 505/377–6416) is run by Nancy and Bill Burch, who offer horseback, Jeep, snowmobile, and ski rentals. **Taos Fitness Adventures** (216-M Paseo del Pueblo Norte, Suite 173, tel. 505/776–1017) provides week-long hiking and fitness programs during the summer and fall, limited to eight persons housed in a luxury mountain lodge. Hikes range from easy to advanced, covering up to 15 miles a day. **Taos Indian Horse Ranch** (Taos Pueblo, tel. 505/758–3212 or 800/659–3210) features two-hour trail rides, as well as old-fashioned horse-drawn sleigh rides through the Taos Pueblo backcountry, winter weather permitting, complete with brass bells, a Native American storyteller, marshmallows, and green chile roasts. Escorted horseback tours and hayrides are run through Native American lands during the remainder of the year. (By reservation only. No liquor permitted.)

Exploring Taos

Taos is a year-round destination. Its fabulous ski slopes beckon in the wintertime, and summer brings a flood of tourists, both longtime regulars and newcomers who have heard or read about the enchanting little town in northern New Mexico and want to see it for themselves. Situated on a rolling mesa at the base of the rugged Sangre de Cristo Mountains, where lofty Wheeler Peak, the state's highest mountain, rises 13,161 feet, Taos has more than enough attractions to stand on its own and is worth more than a day trip out of Santa Fe. The town, with its intrinsically rustic charm, is a world-famous art and literary center, bringing both artists and collectors to the many museums and galleries surrounding the historical Plaza. Another of its primary draws is that it is a tricultural community, with strong Na-

tive American, Spanish, and Anglo influences. A visit to
the Taos Pueblo north of town is a good introduction to the
centuries-old culture of the Pueblo Native Americans. Restored haciendas and the famous San Francisco de Asis
Church to the south of the Plaza reflect Taos's strong Spanish heritage. There are also numerous sights of interest
outside Taos proper, including the Enchanted Circle, the
Rio Grande Gorge, and the haunts of well-known Taos personalities, such as D. H. Lawrence and Georgia O'Keeffe.

Highlights for First-time Visitors

Blumenschein Home (*see* Tour 1)
D. H. Lawrence Shrine (*see* Tour 4)
Historical Plaza Area (*see* Tour 1)
Kit Carson Museum (*see* Tour 1)
Martinez Hacienda (*see* Tour 3)
Millicent Rogers Museum (*see* Tour 4)
Ranchos de Taos and the San Francisco de Asis Church
(*see* Tour 3)
Taos Pueblo (*see* Tour 2)

Tour 1: The Plaza Tour

*Numbers in the margin correspond to points of interest on
the Taos map.*

❶ The **Taos Plaza** bears only a hint of the grace, dignity, and
stateliness of the Plaza in Santa Fe, although its history is
drawn with the same pen. The first Europeans to appear in
the Taos Valley were led by Captain Alvarado, who was exploring the area for the 1540 Coronado Expedition. Don
Juan de Onate, the official colonizer of the province of
Nuevo México, arrived in Taos in July 1598. An established
mission, trading arrangements with the Taos Pueblos, and
abundant water and timber attracted early Spanish settlers. Because of the many fires that plagued the city, none
of the buildings on the Plaza predates the 19th century. At
the center of the Plaza, the U.S. flag flies night and day, as
authorized by a special act of Congress in recognition of Kit
Carson's heroic stand, when he and his men stood guard
over the flag to protect it from Confederate sympathizers
during the Civil War. Next to a covered gazebo, donated by
heiress and longtime Taos resident Mabel Dodge Luhan, is
the Tiovivo, an antique carousel that delights children
when it's put into operation during summer fiestas (only
three days per year, in late July during the Fiestas de Santiago Y Santa Ana; tickets are 50¢ per ride).

A walking tour of historic Taos begins logically enough on
the Plaza, with its many smart shops and galleries. On the
south side of the Plaza, don't miss the extraordinary **La
Fonda de Taos Hotel,** with all its eccentric charm. For an admission fee of $3, you can enter the manager's office and
view the erotic paintings done by D. H. Lawrence. The

105

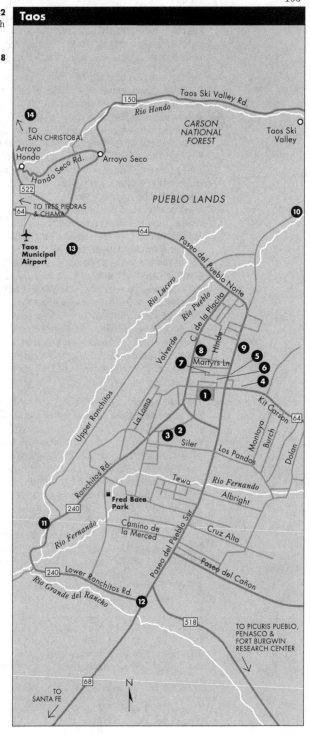

paintings were banned in London, as were many of the author's books. Hardly scandalous by today's standards, the paintings are certainly worth a visit for anyone with more than a passing interest in Lawrence and his work.

Next, take a detour off the southeast corner of the Plaza to Ledoux Street, where a number of historic adobe buildings can be explored. Two blocks from the Plaza is the ❷ **Blumenschein Home,** a fully restored, original adobe masterpiece. Ernest L. Blumenschein was the cofounder of the Taos Society of Artists, an art colony that flourished from 1912 to 1927. His paintings and those of his talented wife, Mary Green Blumenschein, and their daughter, Helen, are on display inside, along with works of other Taos artists. Blending the sophistication of European charm with the beauty of classic adobe, the house is furnished with handmade Taos furniture, as well as with European antiques and artifacts gathered by the artist and his family from all over the world. The house creates a colorful picture of the life of the early Taos Society of Artists. *222 Ledoux St., tel. 505/758-0505. Admission: $3 adults, $2 children and senior citizens. Open daily 9-5. Note: A family ticket is available for $6, admitting parents and three children under 16. Also, special combination tickets can be purchased for $7 adults, $5 for children and senior citizens that permit admission to the Blumenschein Home, as well as to the Kit Carson Home and the Martinez Hacienda, all part of Kit Carson Historic Museums of Taos, a private, nonprofit organization.*

❸ Farther along Ledoux Street is the **Harwood Foundation Library and Museum,** the former home of Burt C. Harwood, a member of the original Taos art colony. On display are more than 100 paintings by early and modern Taos artists, plus rare *santos* (saints) carvings done by early Spanish wood-carvers—almost all from the private collection of Taos art patron Mabel Dodge Luhan. This is where the Museum of Taos Art exhibits and researches the art, artists, and history of Taos County. It's also the site of the Taos Public Library, which houses an excellent collection of volumes on the Southwest, Western and Native American art, and volumes by and about D. H. Lawrence. *238 Ledoux St., tel. 505/758-3063 (library), 505/758-9826 (museum). Admission free. Library open weekdays 10-5 (Mon. and Thurs. 10-8), Sat. 10-4; museum open weekdays noon-5, Sat. 10-4.*

Time Out If you're ready for a break, stop off at **Marciano's Ristorante** in a courtyard at the top of Ledoux (1 Ledoux St., tel. 505/751-0805) for a light repast. If you just want to rest your feet, head for the peaceful garden behind the Harwood Museum.

If you head east from the Plaza across the intersection of Paseo del Pueblo Norte and Paseo del Pueblo Sur, you'll

find more fine shops, some of the best in town. Here, too, is
❹ the **Kit Carson Home and Museum,** once home of the famous
mountain man and scout who left an indelible mark on the
history of Taos. Carson purchased the 12-room adobe home
in 1843 as a wedding gift for his young bride, Josefa
Jaramillo, the beautiful daughter of a powerful and politi-
cally influential Mexican family. Josefa was 14 when Carson, dashing in dun-colored buckskins with long fringes
and colorful beadwork, began courting her; he was 32 and
already twice married to Native American maidens. The
couple lived in the house for more than 25 years. Three of
the rooms are furnished as they were when the Carson family lived here, offering a glimpse of Taos's rich and colorful
history. The rest of the museum is devoted to gun and
mountain-man exhibits, as well as to Native American,
Spanish, and early Taos antiques, artifacts, and manuscripts. In the patio outside, the Carson House Shop has
four rooms filled with gifts and collectibles, Native American art, folk art, jewelry, kachinas, and handcrafted furniture. *Kit Carson Rd., tel. 505/758–0505. Admission: $3
adults, $2 children and senior citizens; family and combi-
nation tickets are available (*see *Blumenschein Home,
above). Open early Oct.–mid-June, daily 9–5; mid-June–
Sept., daily 8–6.*

Back at the intersection of Paseo del Pueblo Norte and
Paseo del Pueblo Sur, turn right and walk to the **Taos Inn,** a
historical landmark and the site of the original town well,
now a fountain in the hotel lobby. Next door to the Taos Inn
❺ is the **Stables Art Center,** the visual arts gallery of the Taos
Art Association. The association purchased the handsome
adobe building, formerly a private home, in 1952. It was in
the stables in back of the house that the association first began exhibiting the work of members and of invited non-
member artists from all over northern New Mexico—thus
the gallery's name. The main building was once the home of
Arthur Manby, a recluse who gained considerable notorie-
ty by securing himself behind barred doors and snarling
guard dogs for most of his 30 years in Taos. The Stables presents changing exhibits almost monthly; all the artwork is
for sale. *133 Paseo del Pueblo Norte, Taos 87571, tel. 505/
758–2036. Admission free. Open daily 10–5. Closed Christmas.*

Leaving the Stables, cross Paseo del Pueblo Norte and
you'll be on Bent Street, one of the town's major shopping
venues, lined with attractive galleries and boutiques. The
❻ **John Dunn House** (124A Bent St., no tel.) was the onetime
homestead of a notorious Taos gambler and entrepreneur,
who founded the town's first transportation company. It
contains a number of interesting shops, including G. Robinson Old Prints and Maps and Moby Dickens, a popular and
eclectic bookstore and prime gathering spot for the local li-
terati (*see* Shopping, *below*). Also on this small street is the
❼ **Governor Bent Museum.** In 1846, when New Mexico became

a United States territory during the Mexican War, Charles Bent, an early trader, trapper, and mountain man, was appointed governor. A year later he was killed in his house by an angry mob protesting New Mexico's annexation by the United States. The well-kept adobe building where Bent lived is filled with his family's possessions, furniture, and Western Americana. Governor Bent was married to Maria Ignacia, older sister of Kit Carson's wife, Josefa Jaramillo. *117 Bent St., tel. 505/758-2376. Admission: $1 adults, 50¢ children. Open daily 10-5.*

Two blocks north of Bent Street on the corner of Armory Street and Placitas Road is the Taos Volunteer Fire Department, home of the **Firehouse Collection.** More than 100 paintings by Taos artists, including some of the town's most famous—Joseph Sharp, Ernest Blumenschein, Bert Phillips, and others—are on display. The paintings are exhibited in the Fire Department's meeting hall, adjoining the station house, where five fire engines are maintained at the ready. An antique fire engine is housed here as well. *323 Placitas Rd., Box 4591, Taos 87571, tel. 505/758-3386. Admission free. Open weekdays 9-4.*

If you head east from the Firehouse back to Paseo del Pueblo Norte, and turn left, you'll come to the wooded, 20-acre **Kit Carson Park,** two blocks farther. Kit Carson's grave is located here, marked with a *cerquita,* a spiked wrought-iron rectangular fence, traditionally used to outline and protect gravesites. Mabel Dodge Luhan, the art patron and longtime guiding light of the Taos social scene, is also buried in the same small graveyard.

A short walk north is the **Fechin Institute,** housed in a traditional Southwestern adobe house with a Russian-style interior. Filled with extraordinary hand-carved doors, windows, and gates, the home was built in 1928 by artist Nicolai Fechin, a Russian émigré who arrived in Taos one year earlier. Fechin designed the extraordinary house, with its exotic hand-carved architectural motifs and Russian furnishings, to showcase his daringly colorful portraits and landscapes. Listed in the National Register of Historic Places, the Fechin Institute hosts annual exhibits and special workshops devoted to the artist's unique approach to learning, teaching, and creativity. *227 Paseo del Pueblo Norte, tel. 505/758-1710. Admission: $3 donation suggested. Open May-Oct., Wed.-Sun. 1-5:30, or by appointment.*

Tour 2: The Taos Pueblo

Three miles north of town, driving on Paseo del Pueblo Norte, you'll come to Taos's number-one tourist attraction, the **Taos Pueblo,** selected in 1993 as a World Heritage Site (the United Nations' world-scale equivalent of a National Historic Landmark). For nearly 1,000 years, the Taos-Tiwa

Native Americans have lived at or near the present pueblo site. The northernmost of New Mexico's 19 Native American pueblos, it is the largest existing multistory pueblo structure in the United States. Continuously inhabited for centuries, it holds within its mud-and-straw adobe walls—frequently several feet thick—a way of life little changed by the passage of time. Two separate buildings rise in earthy magnificence, containing many individual homes built side by side and in layers, with common walls but no connecting doorways. (Because there were neither doors nor windows, access to the dwellings was gained only from the top, via ladders that were retrieved after entering.) Small buildings and corrals are scattered about. The two main buildings, Hlauuma (north house) and Hlaukwima (south house), separated by a creek, are believed to be of a similar age, most likely constructed between AD 1000 and 1450.

The pueblo today appears much as it did when the first Spanish explorers arrived in New Mexico in 1540: Seeing the golden shades of its smooth adobe walls, the conquistadores thought they had discovered one of the fabled Seven Cities of Gold. The outside surfaces are continuously maintained by replastering with thin layers of mud, and the interior walls are frequently coated with thin washes of white earth to keep them clean and bright. The roofs of each of the five stories are supported by large timbers—*vigas*—hauled down from the mountain forests. Rotted vigas are replaced as needed. Smaller pieces of wood—pine or aspen *latillas*—are placed side by side between the vigas; the entire roof is then packed with dirt.

Tribal ritual allows no electricity or running water within the pueblo, where approximately 200 Taos Native Americans live full-time. Some 2,000 others live in conventional homes on the pueblo's land, which extends over 95,000 acres, television antennas poking out from above the roofs. Inside the pueblo, the traditional Native American way of life has endured even after 400 years of Spanish and Anglo presence. The crystal-clear waters of the Rio Pueblo de Taos, originating high above in the mountains at the sacred Blue Lake, still serve as the primary source of drinking water and irrigation. Bread is still baked in outdoor domed ovens, a system unchanged for centuries. Artisans of the Taos Pueblo produce handcrafted wares by using techniques that have been passed down through the generations; the mica-flecked pottery and silver jewelry made in the pueblo are sold at many of the individually owned curio shops within the compound. Great hunters, the Taos Native Americans are also renowned for their work with animal skins, creating excellent moccasins, boots, and drums.

The pueblo dwellers are about 90% Catholic, but they practice their religion alongside ancient Native American religious rites that remain an important part of life in the Taos

Pueblo. This combination derives from a concession often made by the Spanish missionaries, who were anxious to convert the "pagan savages." A costumed Native American Deer dancer in full regalia often comes thumping down the church aisle during or immediately after the celebration of the Catholic mass. The striking adobe Church of San Geronimo (St. Jerome, the patron saint of the Taos Pueblo) on the pueblo grounds was completed in 1850 to replace a church that was destroyed by the U.S. Army in 1847 during the Mexican War. With its graceful flowing lines, arched portal, and twin bell towers, the church is a popular subject of photographers and artists (but, please, no photographs inside).

Although many religious activities are restricted to tribal members, the public is invited to witness certain ceremonial dances. These include the following: January 1, Turtle dance; January 6, Buffalo or Deer dance; May 3, Feast of Santa Cruz–Foot Race and Corn dance; June 13, Feast of San Antonio–Corn dance; June 24, Feast of San Juan–Corn dance; July (2nd weekend), Taos Pueblo Powwow; July 25 and 26, Feast of Santa Ana and Santiago–Corn dance; September 29–30, Feast of San Geronimo–Sunset dance; Christmas Eve, Procession; Christmas Day, Deer dance or Matachines. Although there is no charge for general admission to the Taos Pueblo, certain rules must be observed. These include respecting the "restricted area" signs that protect the privacy of pueblo residents and sites of native religious practices; not entering private homes or opening any doors not clearly labeled as curio shops; not photographing tribal members without asking permission; not entering the cemetery grounds; and not wading in the Rio Pueblo de Taos, the community's sole source of drinking water. *Taos Pueblo, Box 1846, Taos 87571, tel. 505/758–9593. Tourist fees: $5 per vehicle (for parking), $10 for tour buses (plus $1 per passenger, 50¢ for students); $5 for a still-camera permit, $10 for a movie-camera permit, artist's sketching fee $15, and artist's painting fee $35. Open daily 8–5:30, except during funerals or religious ceremonies not open to the public. The pueblo also often closes for a one-month "quiet time" in late winter or early spring; check before planning a visit at this time.*

Time Out When you're ready for a quick snack, look for the "Fry Bread" signs on individual dwellings. You can enter the kitchen and enjoy fresh fry bread—bread dough that is flattened and deep-fried until it's puffy and golden brown and then topped with honey or powdered sugar—and a cup of coffee while watching the Native American women cook.

American Express offers Travelers Cheques built for two.

American Express® Cheques *for Two*. The first Travelers Cheques that allow either of you to use them because both of you have signed them. And only one of you needs to be present to purchase them.

Cheques *for Two* are accepted anywhere regular American Express Travelers Cheques are, which is just about everywhere. So stop by your bank, AAA* or any American Express Travel Service Office and ask for Cheques *for Two*.

©1993 American Express Travel Related Services Company, Inc. *Available at participating clubs.

Rediscover
the most exciting
and exotic country
in the world...
America.

From Fodor's — Comprehensive, literate, and beautifully illustrated guides to the individual cities and states of the United States and Canada, Compass American Guides are unparalleled in their cultural, historical, and informational scope.

"Wickedly stylish writing." — *Chicago Sun-Times*
"Exceptional color photos." — *Atlanta Constitution*

Guides also available to Las Vegas, Los Angeles, New Orleans, Oregon, Utah, and Canada.
Available Spring 1994: Maine, South Dakota, Virginia, and Wisconsin

$16.95, at bookstores now, or call 1-800-533-6478 (and please mention #019-01-23)

COMPASS AMERICAN GUIDES
Fodor's

Tour 3: The Spanish Colonial Heritage

In Taos, one quickly steps into the town's rich Spanish past with a visit to the outstanding Martinez Hacienda Museum and the cherished, oft-photographed and -painted Ranchos de Taos.

Two miles south of Taos Plaza, on Ranchitos Road (NM 240), is **La Hacienda de Don Antonio Severino Martinez,** one of the only fully restored Spanish Colonial adobe haciendas open to the public in New Mexico. The fortlike building, on the banks of the Rio Pueblo, served as the Martinez family's home and a community refuge against Comanche and Apache raids. With massive adobe walls and no exterior windows, the hacienda has 21 rooms surrounding two courtyards. Magnificently restored period rooms illustrate the lifestyle of the Spanish Colonial era, when the only supplies to Taos came by oxcart on the Camino Real over the "Journey of Death." Built in progressive additions between 1804 and 1827 by Severino Martinez, the house gives testimony to the pure, rich Spanish heritage that survived the rugged colonial conditions and remains to this day. Padre Antonio José Martinez, Severino's son, became a famous leader of his people and founder of *El Crepúsculo* (The Dawn), possibly the first newspaper published west of the Mississippi.

Along with the room exhibits, the fortresslike house is also used for changing exhibits on Spanish culture and history and photography shows. In addition, there's a working blacksmith's shop, and other living-history demonstrations. On the last weekend in September, the hacienda hosts the annual Old Taos Trade Fair, which reenacts the fall trading fairs of the 1820s, when Plains Native Americans and trappers came to trade with Spanish and Pueblo Native Americans in Taos. The two-day event includes traditional crafts demonstrations, native foods, entertainment, traditional-style caravans, and music. *Ranchitos Rd. (NM 240), tel. 505/758–0505. Admission: $3 adults, $2 children and senior citizens. Family and combination tickets are available (see Blumenschein Home, above). Open daily 9–5.*

Four miles east of the Martinez Hacienda on Ranchitos Road (NM 240) is **Ranchos de Taos** (on NM 68), an adobe-house Spanish Colonial ranching and farming community. An early home of Taos Native Americans, it was settled by Spaniards in 1716. The centerpiece of Ranchos de Taos is the monumental adobe masterpiece, the **San Francisco de Asis Church,** first built in the 18th century as a spiritual and physical refuge from raiding Apaches, Utes, and Comanches. In a state of deterioration, the church was rebuilt by community volunteers in 1979, using traditional adobe bricks. It's a spectacular example of adobe Mission architecture, and the shapes and shadows of the walls and supporting bulwarks have inspired generations of painters and photographers, including Georgia O'Keeffe, Paul Strand, and Ansel Adams. If you've got a camera handy and want to try it yourself, late afternoon offers the best exposure of the heavily buttressed rear of the church, while morning is best for the front. Bells in the church's twin belfries call faithful Taoseños to services on Sunday and holidays, when worshipers fill the church to overflowing.

In the parish hall nearby, a 15-minute slide presentation explains the history and restoration of the church, and the famous mystery painting, *Shadow of the Cross,* may be seen throughout the day. In the evening, as well as in total darkness, the shadow of a cross, which isn't there during the daylight hours, appears over Christ's shoulder. Scientific studies made on the canvas and the paint pigments cannot explain the phenomenon. *Ranchos de Taos, tel. 505/758–2754. Admission free. Open Mon.–Sat. 9–4, on Sun. and holy days during church services: Sun. Mass 7 AM (in Spanish), 9 AM, and 11:30 AM.*

Many of the old adobe homes around Ranchos Plaza now house shops, restaurants, and galleries, including the **Hacienda de San Francisco Galeria** (4 St. Francis Plaza, tel. 505/758–0477), with its collection of fine Spanish Colonial antiques and sculptured bronzes by such masters as Mexico's Francisco Zúñiga.

Time Out   **Ranchos Plaza Grill** (tel. 505/758–1120), on the historic church plaza, is a good place to cool your heels.

Tour 4: Artistic and Literary Taos

If you have time to visit only one museum in Taos, make it
⑬ the **Millicent Rogers Museum,** 4 miles northwest of the Plaza, just off NM 522 (turn left at the blinking light and follow the signs to the museum). Founded in 1953, it contains more than 5,000 pieces of Native American and Hispanic art, the core of Standard Oil heiress Millicent Rogers's private lifetime collection. The granddaughter of Henry Huddleson Rogers, one of John D. Rockefeller's partners in the Standard Oil Company and founder of Anaconda Copper and U.S. Steel, she visited New Mexico in 1947 and, like many others, fell in love with the country and its people. A woman of keen intellect and artistic talent, she became intently interested in the area's culture and art. She gathered baskets, blankets, rugs, jewelry, kachina dolls, santos, carvings, and paintings—a collection that remains unsurpassed to this day. A recent acquisition of major importance is the pottery and ceramics of Maria Martinez and members of the famous San Ildefonso family of potters. The museum's Hispanic collection, including recently acquired rare pieces of religious and secular artifacts, is equally impressive. Missing, of course, is the presence of Millicent

Rogers herself, a striking beauty with a flair for fashion and a love of costumes. A debutante in the heyday of the Jazz Age, she was tall, with a perfectly proportioned figure, a born "clotheshorse" with long, painted nails, wide-set eyes, and alabaster skin. Married three times, she numbered among her suitors Clark Gable, Serge Obolensky, Ian Fleming, and James Forrestal. Many of her costumes and jewelry designs are included in the museum's holdings. The Millicent Rogers Museum features permanent and changing exhibits, guided tours on request, and a gift shop, as well as educational activities such as field trips, lectures, films, workshops, and demonstrations. *Box A, Taos 87571, tel. 505/758–2462, fax 505/758–5751. Admission: $4 adults, $3 senior citizens and students, $2 children (6–16), $8 family groups. Open daily 9–5, except major holidays.*

⑭ Leaving the Millicent Rogers Museum, follow NM 522 north for 10 miles, and you'll reach the **D. H. Lawrence Ranch** and the **D. H. Lawrence Shrine.** The noted British author lived in Taos only briefly, about 22 months over a three-year period between 1922 and 1925. He and his wife, Frieda, arrived in Taos at the behest of Mabel Dodge Luhan, who collected famous writers and artists the way some people collect butterflies. Luhan provided them with a place to live, Kiowa Ranch, on 160 acres in the mountains north of Taos. Rustic and remote, it's now known as the D. H. Lawrence Ranch, although Lawrence never actually owned it. Nearby is the smaller cabin where Dorothy Brett, the tag-along companion of the Lawrences, stayed while traveling with the couple. The houses, now owned by the University of New Mexico, are not open to the public. The D. H. Lawrence Shrine, nearby at the end of a step walk on wooded Lobo Mountain, can be visited, however. A small white shedlike structure, it is simple and unimposing. The writer fell ill while visiting France and died in a sanatorium there in 1930. Five years later, his wife, subsequently married in Italy to Angelo Ravagli, had Lawrence's body disinterred, cremated, and brought back to Taos. Frieda Lawrence is buried, as was her wish, in front of the shrine. *Hwy. 522, Box 190, San Cristobal 87564, tel. 505/776–2245. Admission free. The D. H. Lawrence Shrine is open daily.*

Tour 5: The Enchanted Circle

Numbers in the margin correspond to points of interest on the Taos Environs: The Enchanted Circle map.

No visit to northern New Mexico is complete without experiencing the 84-mile day trip through the Enchanted Circle, a breathtaking panorama of deep canyons, passes, alpine valleys, and towering mountains of the verdant Carson National Forest. It's a journey that in many ways will take you into another century. This tour can easily be combined with Tour 4, *above.* Both the D. H. Lawrence Ranch and the Millicent Rogers Museum are on the loop.

Traveling east from Taos along U.S. 64, you'll soon be winding your way through Taos Canyon, climbing toward 9,000-foot-high Palo Flechado Pass (Pass of the Arrow). On the opposite side of the pass are stunning vistas—Moreno Valley, and the towns of Angel Fire and Eagle Nest. Now

❶ known primarily as a ski resort, **Angel Fire** was for hundreds of years little more than a long, empty valley, the fall meeting grounds of the Ute Indians. The name derives from the glow that covers the mountain in the late autumn and early winter. Angel Fire started getting developed in the early 1970s and is fast becoming one of the most comprehensive resort areas in New Mexico. Here you'll find the stunning Vietnam Veterans Memorial, a 50-foot-high gull wing–shaped monument built in 1971 by D. Victor Westphall, whose son David was killed in that war. The memorial's textured surface captures the constantly changing sunlight of the New Mexican mountains, vividly changing their colors throughout the daylight hours as the sun moves across the sky. It's on the north side of U.S. 64, 8½ miles southwest of Eagle Nest.

❷ At **Eagle Nest,** a tiny village surrounded by thousands of acres of national forest, you'll get on to U.S. 38 and head over

❸ Bobcat Pass (just under 10,000 ft elevation) to **Red River,** another major ski resort, with 33 trails and a bustling little downtown community filled with shops and sportswear boutiques. Red River came into being as a miners' boom town in the last century, taking its name from the river whose mineral content gave it a rich, rosy color. When the gold petered out, Red River died, only to be rediscovered in the 1920s by migrants who were escaping the dust bowl. Situated at 8,750 feet above sea level at the base of Wheeler Peak (New Mexico's tallest mountain), Red River is the highest, if not the loftiest, town in the state. Much of the Old West flavor remains in Red River, with Main Street shoot-outs, a genuine melodrama, and plenty of square dancing and two-stepping. In fact, because of its many country dances and festivals, Red River is affectionately called "The New Mexico Home of the Texas Two-Step."

From Red River, the Enchanted Circle heads west to
❹ **Questa** ("hill" in Spanish), a town settled in the 1840s with considerable difficulty because of Indian raids. In 1870, it was officially established—as were many Western towns—with the opening of its first post office; to date, Questa has had only six postmasters. Don't miss St. Anthony's Church, built of adobe with 5-foot-thick walls and viga ceilings. The Red River Trout Hatchery (*see* Taos for Free, *below*) is also worth a visit. Known as the "Heart of the Sangre de Cristo Mountains," Questa is a small, quiet village, nestled between Taos and the Red River amid some of the most beautiful mountain country in New Mexico. Turning left at downtown Questa's main intersection, you're on your way back to Taos on NM 522, passing through the picturesque communities of San Cristobal and Arroyo Hondo. It's on

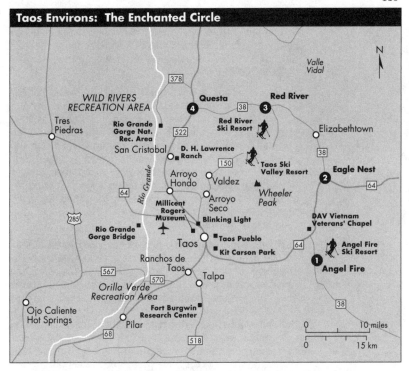

Taos Environs: The Enchanted Circle

this last stretch that you can stop and visit the D. H. Lawrence Ranch or the Millicent Rogers Museum, both off NM 522.

Time Out In Red River, stop by the **Sundance** (High St., tel. 505/754–2971) for Mexican food or **Texas Red's Steakhouse** (Main St., tel. 505/754–2964) for steaks, chops, burgers, or chicken. If you want to stay overnight, try the **Red River Lodge** (Box 818, Red River 87558, tel. 505/754–6280), which has 20 moderately priced rooms, hot tubs in the winter, and picnic tables in the summer.

Taos for Free

Taos is a major art center, so it's not surprising that many of the town's major free attractions involve, and evolve from, an appreciation of art. Visitors are welcome to browse through more than 80 art galleries (indeed, in some cases they may even be pulled in off the street to do so) and to enjoy a number of major museum exhibits free of charge. These exhibits include the Harwood Foundation, the Firehouse Collection, and the Stables Art Center (*see* Tours 1 and 2 *above*). The Taos Inn (tel. 505/758–2233) sponsors a free Meet the Artist Series in spring (mid-May–mid-June) and again in fall (mid-Oct.–mid-Dec.) every Tuesday and

Thursday evening at 8. This is a unique opportunity to have one-on-one contact with nationally known artists who are residing in Taos. Another major free attraction is the magnificent San Francisco de Asis Mission Church in Ranchos de Taos (*see* Tour 3, *above*).

In Questa, about 20 miles north of Taos (at the end of NM 515), the **Red River Trout Hatchery** offers a fascinating look at how the king of freshwater fish is hatched, reared, stocked, and controlled. There's a visitor center with displays and exhibits, a show pond, and a machine that dispenses fish food, so you can feed the trout yourself. Self-guided tours last anywhere from 20 to 90 minutes, depending on how enraptured visitors become. Guided tours are available for groups upon request. Parking space and a picnic area are on the grounds. *Box 410, Questa 87556, tel. 505/586–0222. Open daily 9–5.*

Fort Burgwin Research Center, 10 miles southeast of Taos on NM 518, is a restored fort that once housed the First Dragoons of the United States Cavalry (1852–60). Their function was to protect the citizens of Taos and the travelers coming from and going to Santa Fe, the territorial capital, from renegade Native Americans. Operated by the Southern Methodist University of Dallas, Texas, the center now conducts extension courses for its university students, particularly in theater, music, and the arts. Summer concerts, plays, and lectures are presented to the public free of charge. Call for a schedule (tel. 505/758–8322). *Box 300, Ranchos de Taos 87557, tel. 505/758–0322. Admission free. Open daily 9–5.*

What to See and Do with Children

Anyone who has children and goes to Taos without them is bound to regret it. Almost everywhere they turn, parents will find something they wish their children were there to see. The **Taos Pueblo** (*see* Tour 2, *above*) offers insights into a way of life that has remained virtually unchanged over the centuries. The **Kit Carson Home and Museum** and **Kit Carson Park** (*see* Tour 1, *above*), where Carson's grave is located, are bound to be spellbinders. In Kit Carson Park there's a playground for youngsters, picnic tables and grills, an ice-skating rink in winter, and bicycle and walking paths. **Fred Baca Park,** 2 miles west, also has tennis courts, a playground, a baseball field, and basketball hoops. The **Red River Trout Hatchery** in Questa (*see* Taos for Free, *above*) will fascinate the younger set. And if your child is one that has to be bribed, bound, and chained before being dragged screaming and kicking into an art gallery, you may find the **Firehouse Collection** (*see* Tour 1, *above*) a painless introduction. After all, there are all those beautiful fire engines to ogle.

Off the Beaten Track

Of **Ghost Ranch/Abiquiu,** Georgia O'Keeffe wrote, "When I first saw the Abiquiu house it was a ruin with an adobe wall around the garden broken in a couple of places by fallen trees. As I climbed and walked about in the ruin I found a patio with a very pretty well house and a bucket to draw up water. It was a good-sized patio with a long wall with a door on one side. That wall with a door in it was something I had to have. It took me 10 years to get it—three more years to fix the house up so I could live in it—and after that the wall with the door was painted many times." After a long history of regular visits to New Mexico and the Southwest, the artist moved permanently to Abiquiu, New Mexico, in 1949. The rocky desert vistas between Ghost Ranch, where O'Keeffe purchased her first home in New Mexico, and Abiquiu, 20 miles to the south, where she had her second home, are all that remain open to public scrutiny; both homes are in private hands.

Before her death in 1986 at the age of 98, O'Keeffe added special provisions in her will to ensure that the houses would never be turned into public monuments, in order to protect the land she loved so much from an onslaught of tourists. Thus a pilgrimage to O'Keeffe country, a good 60 miles east of Taos (NM 68 south of Espanola, U.S. 84 to Albiquiu; look for a dirt road off 84 marked with a cattle-skull highway sign), is purely what the visitor makes of it. Ghost Ranch was originally called El Rancho de los Brujos, the Ranch of the Witches. A Spanish rancher was murdered in the sprawling adobe homestead, and the villagers believed that the voices of the female spirits who roamed there could be heard howling through the nearby canyons. Anglos shortened the name to Ghost Ranch. Possessed or not, the area remains hauntingly beautiful.

Rio Grande Gorge Bridge (west of Taos on U.S. 64) is the second highest expansion bridge in the country. Viewing the dramatic gorge, with the Rio Grande River 650 feet below, is a breathtaking experience. Hold on to your camera and eyeglasses when looking down, and watch out for low-flying planes. The Taos Municipal Airport is close by, and daredevil private pilots have been known to challenge one another to fly *under* the bridge.

Camposantos means "holy fields," as the Spanish-speaking New Mexicans call their parish and community graveyards. More than 400 such graveyards can be found in New Mexico, usually next to a church or off on a country road. Numerous crosses, some made of wood, others of iron or even welded pipes, dot the lonely gravesites. Anonymous graves are marked with the same devotional images. Paper flowers, hand-carved angels, wrought-iron rectangular fences (*cerquitas*) used for defining and protecting gravesites, and candles whose flames have long since burned away com-

memorate the dead while recalling the living who so loving-
ly tend and care for them.

Shopping

When it comes to shopping, Taos is basically an extension of
Santa Fe, with many of the same shops and galleries (as well
as some restaurants) represented in both cities. If Taos has
any edge over the capital in this regard, it's in the crafts-
manship of its Spanish carvers and carpenters, whose techniques have been handed down from father to son for nearly
300 years. Complementing such skills is the work of talented young artists, who have been drawn to the town's
legendary reputation as an art center and as a place of spiritual fulfillment. This energy can be seen everywhere in
Taos, in the decor of buildings, in the presentation of food in
restaurants and dining rooms, in the attitude and enthusiasm of the people, and in the wares that fill the galleries and
showcases.

Shopping Districts

The main concentration of shops in Taos is directly on or
just off the historic central Plaza. That area includes the
John Dunn Boardwalk and Bent Street, running parallel to
the Plaza on the north, and Kit Carson Road, extending
east off the northeast corner. With plenty of municipal
parking just beyond Bent Street, these shopping districts,
concentrated as they are, are easy to maneuver on foot. Except for its broad open space in the center, there isn't a
spare niche anywhere along the Plaza that isn't a shop or
restaurant of some kind or another, from Charley's North
and West, two large gift shops on the northwest corner, to
the Clothes Horse on the southeast corner. It's pockets of
unrelieved commercialism such as these, as appealing as
they may be to some, that have critics complaining that
Taos is going the way of tourist centers everywhere and is
quickly losing its distinctive charm. Cheap souvenir stores
and fast-food outlets are popping up everywhere, and the
downtown traffic bottleneck is at times beyond comprehen-
sion.

Bent Street, happily, seems less overdone. Named in honor
of New Mexico's first governor, Bent Street was long home
to mountain men, traders, and artists of the Old West. The
street now houses some of the finest galleries and shops in
town. Kit Carson Road, named in honor of the legendary
scout, also hosts top art galleries, as well as El Rincon, the
oldest trading post in Taos. In addition, the Ranchos de
Taos area, 4 miles south of the Plaza, contains a number of
fine shops, including some of the town's priciest.

Galleries

Bert Geer Phillips and Ernest Blumenschein, traveling from Denver on a planned painting trip into Mexico in 1898, stopped in Taos to have a broken wagon wheel repaired—a chance occurrence that led to the development of Taos as a major art center. Enthralled with the dramatic Taos landscape, earth-hued adobe buildings, thin, piercing light, and clean mountain air, they decided to stay. Word of their discovery soon spread to fellow artists. In 1912, the Taos Society of Artists was formed. At its nucleus were Blumenschein, Phillips, Joseph Henry Sharp, and Eanger Irving Coue, all graduates of the celebrated Parisian art school Académie Julian. Members of the society painted in Taos but shipped their work to art markets on the East Coast and in Europe.

Most of the early Taos artists spent their winters in New York or Chicago teaching, painting, or illustrating to earn enough money to free them for their summers in New Mexico, where they worked under difficult conditions at best, often without running water or electricity. Most were fascinated with Native Americans, their customs, modes of dress, and ceremonies, feeling—rather romantically—a spiritual kinship with them. The society was disbanded in the late 1920s, but Taos continued to attract artists. Several galleries opened, and in 1952 local painters joined to form the Taos Artists' Association, forerunner to today's highly active Taos Art Association. At present, more than 80 galleries and shops display original art, sculpture, and crafts.

Clay and Fiber Gallery (126 W. Plaza Dr., tel. 505/758–8093), located on the southwest corner of the Plaza, emphasizes ceramics and cloth work such as hand-painted silks and traditional and contemporary weavings.

El Taller Taos Gallery (119A Kit Carson Rd., tel. 505/758–4887) is the exclusive Taos representative of original works by Amado Pena. It also handles sculpture, jewelry, weavings, glass, and clay.

Gallery Elena (119 Bent St., tel. 505/758–9094) has watercolors by Keith Crown and bronze sculpture by Veloy Vigil, and the works of other artists of regional and national importance. Although relatively new, the gallery's growing reputation continues to attract sophisticated art buyers.

E. S. Lawrence (132 E. Kit Carson Rd., tel. 505/758–8229) shows both traditional and contemporary paintings, as well as Santa Fe–style furnishings.

Mission Gallery (138 E. Kit Carson Rd., tel. 505/758–2861), now in its 31st year, features early Taos artists, early modernists, and important contemporary artists. The gallery is located in the former home of early Taos painter Joseph H. Sharp.

Navajo Gallery (210 Ledoux St., tel. 505/758–3250) offers the varied works of Navajo artist R. C. Gorman, widely considered the best Native American artist and probably the best known of all the modern Southwestern artists. Dubbed "the Picasso of Indian Art" by the *New York Times*, Gorman opened the Navajo Gallery in 1968, becoming the first Native American artist to operate his own gallery. A branch of the Navajo Gallery was opened in Albuquerque's historic Old Town district in 1989.

R. B. Ravens (St. Francis Plaza, Ranchos de Taos, tel. 505/758–7322) presents paintings by the founding artists of Taos, weavings, ceramics, and sketches by famous Native American painter Elbridge Ayer Burbank. It also features Navajo textiles—both blankets and rugs—pottery, regalia, and pawn jewelry.

The Shriver Gallery (401 Paseo del Pueblo Norte, tel. 505/758–4994) handles traditional bronze sculpture and paintings, including oils, watercolors, and pastels, as well as drawings and etchings.

Stewart's Fine Art (108 Kit Carson Rd., in the Cabot Plaza Mall, tel. 505/758–0049), the largest gallery in Taos, specializes in Southwestern realism, from the 17th century to today. Work by Dorothy Brett, longtime companion to Frieda and D. H. Lawrence, can be found here.

Taos Traditions Gallery (221 Paseo del Pueblo Norte, tel. 505/758–0016), located next to the Fechin Institute, mainly showcases the works of contemporary artists, including oils, pastels, and watercolors.

The Taos Gallery (403 Paseo del Pueblo Norte, tel. 505/758–2475) features Western and Southwestern impressionism and an exclusive collection of bronzes.

Western Heritage Art (110 S. Plaza, tel. 505/758–4376), established in 1985, handles paintings, alabaster and bronze sculpture, Navajo rugs, and Native American artifacts and pottery. Bill Rabbit and Robert Redbird are among the artists represented here.

Specialty Stores

Home Furnishings **Casa Cristal Pottery** (on Hwy. 3 in El Prado, tel. 505/758–1530), 2½ miles north of the Taos Plaza, has it all: stoneware, serapes, clay pots, Native American ironwood carvings, ceramic sunbursts, straw and tin ornaments, *ristras* (strings of chile peppers), fountains, sweaters, ponchos, clay fireplaces, Mexican blankets, clay churches, birdbaths, baskets, tile, piñatas, and blue glassware from Guadalajara. Also featured are antique reproductions of park benches, street lamps, mailboxes, bakers' racks, and other wrought-iron products. Casa Cristal has outlets in Colorado Springs, Colorado, and Velarde, New Mexico.

Dwellings Revisited (10 Bent St., tel. 505/758–3377) offers time-worn, authentic primitive pine furniture, architecturals, and other antique treasures from New Mexico.

At **Hacienda de San Francisco** (4 St. Francis Plaza, Ranchos de Taos, tel. 505/758–0477), you'll find an exceptional collection of Spanish Colonial antiques.

Greg Flores (120 Bent St., tel. 505/758–8010), located in the Dunn House Building, offers quintessential Taos furnishings. Much in demand, the distinctive, versatile line of young designer Greg Flores includes small stools, sofas, occasional tables and chairs, benches, *trasteros* (cupboards), and dining sets. Each piece is signed and dated.

High Mesa Furniture (S. Hwy. 68, Ranchos de Taos, tel. 505/758–4253) offers handcrafted ranch-style log furniture. You can visit their workshop, across the highway from the Taos Drum factory.

Lo Fino (201 Paseo del Pueblo Sur, tel. 505/758–0298), in a contemporary adobe, provides one of the largest selections of handcrafted furniture in New Mexico, with the works of 10 top Southwestern furniture and lighting designers featured in one large showroom. Hand-carved beds, tables, chairs, cupboards, chests, lamps, and doors are all on display, along with Native American alabaster sculptures, basketry, and pottery.

Taos Blue (101A Bent St., tel. 505/758–3561) specializes in Taos-style interior furnishings and just about everything else you might need to beautify your space. Behind the blue door on the corner of Bent Street and Paseo del Pueblo Norte is an extensive collection of one-of-a-kind accessories. On display are Pawnee/Sioux magical masks, decorated with feathers, horsehair, and scarves; "storyteller figures" from the Taos Pueblo; ceramic dogs baying at the moon; and Native American shields and rattles, sculptures, leather hassocks, and painted buckskin pillows.

Native American Arts and Crafts

Broken Arrow (222 N. Plaza, tel. 505/758–4304) specializes in collector-quality Native American arts and crafts, including sand paintings, rugs, prints, jewelry, pottery, artifacts, and Hopi kachina dolls.

Buffalo Dancer (103 E. Plaza, tel. 505/758–8718) buys, sells, and trades Southwestern Native American arts and crafts, including pottery, concho belts, kachina dolls, hides, and silver-coin jewelry.

Don Fernando Curio and Gift Shop (104 W. Plaza, tel. 505/758–3791) is the oldest Native American arts shop on the Taos Plaza. It opened in 1938, hoping to catch some business from the newly opened La Fonda Hotel across the Plaza. Guests from La Fonda still wander in to pick out a turquoise bracelet, a kachina mud man, a woven straw basket, or some colorful beads.

El Rincon (114 E. Kit Carson Rd., tel. 505/758–9188), housed in a traditional adobe from the turn of the century, was and still is a trading post, the oldest in Taos. Native American items of all kinds are bought and sold here: drums, feathered headdresses, Navajo rugs, beads, bowls, baskets, shields, beaded moccasins, jewelry, arrows, and spearheads. A free museum of Native American and early Spanish American artifacts is located off the main room of the shop. One of its most prized acquisitions is a pair of Kit Carson's buckskin pants. In back of the shop is the El Rincon Bed and Breakfast, reminiscent of the era when Native Americans often traveled for days on horseback to visit the reservation trading post and were invited to spend the night.

R. B. Ravens (St. Francis Plaza, Ranchos de Taos, tel. 505/758–7322) features the best in Navajo blankets and rugs, historical pots, regalia, pawn jewelry, and fine paintings, many from the founding artists' group of Taos painters.

Southwest Moccasin & Drum (803 Paseo del Pueblo Norte, tel. 505/758–9332 or 800/447–3630) has one of the country's largest selections: 716 native moccasin styles and 72 sizes of drums, many painted by local artists.

Taos Drums (Santa Fe Hwy., NM 68, tel. 505/758–3796 or 800/424–DRUM) is the factory outlet for the Taos Drum Factory (5 miles south of the Taos Plaza on NM 68; look for the large tepee). For sale are authentic handmade Pueblo log drums, leather lampshades, and wrought-iron and Southwest furniture.

Tony Reyna's Indian Shops (Kachina Lodge, Paseo del Pueblo Norte, tel. 505/758–2142; on Taos Pueblo Rd., tel. 505/758–3835) are Pueblo-owned and -operated and offer authentic Native American jewelry, paintings, and kachina dolls.

Clothing   **Mariposa Boutique** (John Dunn House, 120 Bent St., tel. 505/758–9028) features original contemporary Southwestern clothing and accessories by leading Taos designers. Handcrafted jewelry is also featured.

Martha of Taos (121 Paseo del Pueblo Norte, tel. 505/758–3102), next to the Taos Inn, specializes in Southwestern-style dresses, pleated Navajo "broomstick" skirts, Navajo blouses, and velvet Navajo dresses with silver.

Overland Sheepskin Company (NM 522, tel. 505/758–8822) has a huge selection of high-quality sheepskin coats, hats, mittens, and slippers, many using Taos beadwork, Navajo rug insets, and buffalo hides for exotic new styles. There are branches in Santa Fe, San Francisco, and the Napa Valley area of California.

The Outfitter (127 Paseo del Pueblo Sur, tel. 505/758–2966) is a one-of-a-kind shop offering made-to-order custom leather moccasins, cowboy and mountain-man gear, and women's clothing, along with Native American trade beads, walking sticks, skulls, antiques, and collectibles.

Books   **The Brodsky Bookshop** (218 Paseo del Pueblo Norte, tel. 505/758–9468) has a fine selection of contemporary books and Southwestern classics. If you don't see what you want, Brodsky's will order it on the spot.

Fernandez de Taos Book Store (N. Plaza, tel. 505/758–4391), located right on the Plaza, has books, art magazines, and major out-of-town newspapers, such as the *New York Times* and the *Washington Post*.

G. Robinson Old Prints and Maps (124 Bent St., tel. 505/758–2278), located in the John Dunn House, has a wide selection of original antique maps and prints (16th–19th century), Edward Curtis Native American photographs, and rare books.

Moby Dickens (No. 6, John Dunn House, 124A Bent St., tel. 505/758–3050) is roomy and well lighted, with lots of windows that let in the bright Taos sun. A bookstore for all ages, it has a good selection of contemporary best-sellers, as well as an outstanding selection of books on the Southwest.

Taos Book Shop (122D Kit Carson Rd., tel. 505/758–3733), a half block west of the Taos Plaza in a lovely walled adobe building, is the oldest bookshop in New Mexico. It was founded in 1947 by Genevieve Janssen and Claire Morrill, whose recollections of their years in Taos, *A Taos Mosaic* (University of New Mexico Press), remains by far the best local history of the Taos area. Frequent book signings and receptions for authors are held in the shop, which specializes in out-of-print and Southwestern selections. The shop has a second location in the Taos Ski Valley (tel. 505/776–2506), open only during the season.

Ten Directions Books (228C Paseo del Pueblo Norte, tel. 505/758–2725) buys and sells new and used books. It welcomes book searches, locating out-of-print and hard-to-find volumes.

Sports and the Outdoors

Whether you're going to be pumping iron or jogging along Paseo del Pueblo Norte, the altitude in Taos (over 7,000 ft) takes a toll. Even your car will be gasping, getting too much gas and not enough air. Your body works almost the same way at high altitudes, with decreased oxygen content and decreased humidity. You may experience symptoms of nausea, insomnia, shortness of breath, diarrhea, sleeplessness, and tension. Eat lightly during the first few days and try to avoid alcohol, which aggravates "high-altitude syndrome." Keep physical exertion to a minimum. And, voilà! After a few days you should be your old self again and ready to hit the road running.

Participant Sports

Bicycling   **"Gearing Up" Bicycle Shop** (129 Paseo del Pueblo Sur, tel. 505/751–0365), a full-service bike shop that also offers tours and guides, and **Taos Mountain Outfitters** (114 S. Plaza, tel. 505/758–9292), an outdoor sporting-equipment store, both have bicycles to rent. The Taos-area roads are steep and hilly, and none have marked bicycle lanes. Be cautious; drivers, many from out of state, may be as unfamiliar with a passing bicycle as they are with a passing deer. Serious bikers may want to participate in the annual autumn **Enchanted Circle Wheeler Peak Bicycle Rally** and the **Aspencade,** both held in late September: Hundreds of cyclists challenge the 100-mile route through Red River, Taos, Angel Fire, Eagle Nest, and Questa, past a brilliant blaze of fall color.

Golf If golf's your game, take your clubs to Angel Fire's 18-hole PGA mountain course, one of the highest in the nation. Contact the **Angel Fire Pro Shop** (Drawer B, Angel Fire 87710, tel. 505/377-3055 or 800/633-7463) for tee times and greens fees. The new **Taos Country Club** (south of Taos at NM 240, tel. 505/758-7300), an 18-hole championship course with separate practice facility, opened in August 1992. Greens fees for 18 holes are $20 on weekdays, $22 on weekends.

Health Clubs The **Taos Spa and Court Club** (111 Doña Ana Dr., tel. 505/758-1980) has indoor and outdoor pools, a sauna, a Jacuzzi, tennis and racquetball courts, and aerobics classes. All are open to nonmembers for fees ranging from $8 to $10. Hotel health facilities are generally reserved only for the use of guests.

Jogging The Taos mountain roads are challenging to a jogger, to say the least. You might try the running track that rings the football field at Taos High School (134 Cervantes St., tel. 505/758-5230). It isn't open to the public, but no one seems to object if nonstudents, within reasonable numbers, jog there. The paths through Kit Carson Park are also suitable.

River Rafting White-water rafting through the Taos Box section of the Rio Grande Wild and Scenic River is a growing sport in the region. **Native Sons Adventures** (tel. 800/753-7559) and **Native Sons Tours** (tel. 505/986-0804 or 800/5-PUEBLO) offer full- and half-day rafting trips. Contact the **Bureau of Land Management** (tel. 505/758-8851) for a list of other registered river guides or for information on running the river on your own.

Skiing Resorts In winter, within a 90-mile radius, Taos offers five ski resorts with beginning, intermediate, and advanced slopes, as well as snowmobile and cross-country skiing trails. These resorts include the **Angel Fire Resort** (Drawer B, Angel Fire 87710, tel. 505/377-6401 or 800/633-7463 outside NM), open from December 15 through the first week in April; the **Red River Ski Area** (Box 900, Red River 87558, tel. 505/754-2382), open from Thanksgiving to Easter; the **Sipapu Lodge and Ski Area** (Rte. Box 29, Vadito 87579, tel. 505/587-2240), open from mid-December to the end of March; and the **Taos Ski Valley** (Box 90, Taos Ski Valley 87525, tel. 505/776-2291), open from November 22 through the first week in April.

Cross-Country At the **Enchanted Forest Cross-Country Ski Area** (Box 521, Red River 87558, tel. 505/754-2374), the season runs from

December 1 to April 7. The **Carson National Forest Service** (Box 558, Taos 87571, tel. 505/758–6200) can provide a good self-guide map of cross-country trails throughout the park.

Swimming The **Don Fernando Municipal Swimming Pool** (124 Civic Plaza Dr., tel. 505/758–9171) is open for recreational swimming from 1 PM to 5 PM daily. The charge is $1.25 for adults, 75¢ for children.

Tennis Kit Carson Park and Fred Baca Park both have free public tennis courts, available on a first-come, first-served basis. For information, call the Taos Department of Parks and Recreation (tel. 505/758–4160). The **Quail Ridge Inn and Tennis Ranch** (Taos Ski Valley Rd., tel. 505/776–2211) has eight Laykold tennis courts (2 indoors), which are free to guests. Nonguests can play on the two indoor courts for $35 an hour.

Spectator Sports

Spectator sports include the annual **Rodeo de Taos,** held at the Taos County Fairgrounds in mid-June, and the **Taos Mountain Balloon Rally,** held in a field south of downtown during the last week in October in conjunction with the "Taste of Taos" food and wine tasting.

Dining

For a city with a population of fewer than 5,000, Taos has an extraordinary number of fine restaurants. As in Santa Fe, many of the restaurants rely heavily on northern New Mexico–style cooking, offering flavorful dishes that are rooted deep in the Spanish culture, with recipes that, for the most part, have been handed down for generations. (*See* Dining in Chapter 1 for an explanation of Mexican food terms.) The clientele at all these establishments is a cross section of locals and seasonal tourists, skiers in the winter and art and nature lovers in the summer.

Highly recommended restaurants in each price category are indicated by a star ★.

Category	Cost*
Expensive	over $15
Moderate	$10–$15
Inexpensive	under $10

per person, excluding drinks, service, and sales tax (6.75% in the town of Taos, 6.25% in the county)

Expensive **Apple Tree.** Located in a historic adobe Territorial house on
★ Bent Street, only a block from the Plaza, this cozy and casual restaurant is a popular luncheon and early dinner spot for locals as well as visitors. A series of intimate dining rooms

Abe's Cantina and Cocina, **5**

Amigos Natural Grocery and Juice Bar, **16**

Apple Tree, **11**

Bent Street Deli and Cafe, **10**

Brett House, **1**

Carl's French Quarter, **3**

Casa Cordova, **6**

Casa de Valdez, **19**

Chile Connection, **2**

Doc Martin's, **9**

Don Fernando's, **18**

Double AA Grill, **17**

El Patio de Taos, **12**

Lambert's of Taos, **15**

Michael's Kitchen, Coffee Shop, and Bakery, **8**

Ogelvie's Bar and Grill, **13**

Rhoda's Restaurant, **7**

Roberto's, **14**

The Stakeout Grill and Bar, **20**

Villa Fontana, **4**

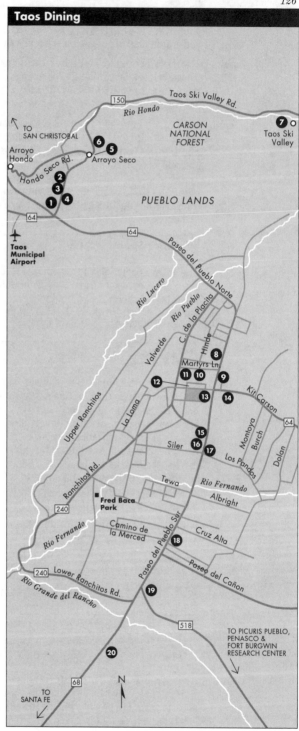

Taos Dining

divided by open archways have pastel walls and wooden tables flanked with straw chairs. Kiva (beehive) fireplaces burn brightly in winter, and there's patio dining in summer; the large tree in the courtyard gives the restaurant its name. Among the excellent dinner entrées are mango chicken, enchiladas, shrimp quesadillas, filet mignon with shiitake mushrooms, and lamb steak (made from organically raised local lambs). Two hot homemade soups are prepared daily, and Sunday brunch, served from 10 to 3, is a Taos tradition. *123 Bent St., tel. 505/758–1900. Reservations advised. Dress: casual. AE, DC, MC, V.*

★ **Brett House.** Four miles north of Taos is the former home and literary salon of Lady Dorothy Brett, friend and frequent traveling companion of Frieda and D. H. Lawrence. Opened in 1983 as a restaurant, the Brett House is now one of the finest in Taos. Chef-owner Chuck Lamendola offers a wide selection of Southwestern and international dishes, including veal scaloppine; rack of lamb; roast duckling in ginger sauce; medallions of veal; fresh fish; and, on Wednesday, ethnic specialties (often Greek or French). Service is impeccable and the views of the Sangre de Cristo Mountains are superb. Set in a traditional old Taos adobe, painted white, are four small rooms with half fireplaces, wood floors, and viga ceilings. Several articles about Lady Brett are framed on the wall, along with photos taken when she still lived in the house, and a large pastel portrait by R.C. Gorman, completed just before she died in 1977. One of the dining rooms is called the R.C. Gorman Room, and a table there is reserved for the artist. His graceful portraits of Indian maidens line the wall, and two bronze sculptures outside can be seen from the window tables. *Rte. 7 and Hwy. 150, tel. 505/776–8545. Reservations recommended. Jacket and tie advised. AE, MC, V.*

Carl's French Quarter. The decor of Carl's French Quarter, where New Orleans cuisine tops the menu, is more reminiscent of Santa Fe than of Bourbon Street: a large stone fireplace, wooden tables and chairs, and a few unimpressive Western paintings on the walls. Owner-chef Carl Fritz features nightly pasta specials, as well as aged Angus beef, quail, and duck. Also recommended are the grilled swordfish with spicy Oriental glaze and fettuccine with lobster cream sauce, topped with shrimp and snow crab. *Quail Ridge Inn, Ski Valley Rd., 5 mi north of the Taos Plaza, tel. 505/776–8319. Reservations recommended. Jacket and tie advised. D, DC, MC, V.*

Casa Cordova. The domain of Johnny Montano, who meets and greets, this L-shaped adobe building with a wooden portal, in a woodsy setting at Arroyo Seco, is the place where chefs go when their own restaurants are closed. A separate lounge and large dining area with two fireplaces form a cozy place for a meal. Menu highlights include escargots à la bourguignonne and homemade pâté among the appetizers, and fresh trout, steak au poivre, quail, and sweetbreads among the entrées. *NM 150 at Arroyo Seco,* *tel. 505/776–2500. Reservations advised. Jacket and tie advised. AE, D, MC, V.*

Casa de Valdez. A large A-frame building with wood-paneled walls and beamed ceilings, Casa de Valdez has a rustic, mountain-lodge feeling. The tables and chairs are handmade, as are the colorful drapes on the windows. Owner-chef Peter Valdez specializes in hickory-smoked barbecues, charcoal-grilled steaks, and regional New Mexican cuisine. *Paseo del Pueblo Sur, 2½ mi south of the Taos Plaza, 505/ 758–8777. Reservations suggested. Dress: casual. AE, MC, V.*

Doc Martin's. The Taos Inn's restaurant, long a popular gathering place for locals, is known for traditional and contemporary Southwestern cuisine, fresh seafood, distinctive game specialties, and Taos's only *Wine Spectator* award-winning wine list. Doc Martin's takes its name from the building's original owner, a local physician who performed operations and delivered babies in the rooms that now make up the dining areas. The decor is the epitome of Southwestern: viga and latilla ceilings (beams and small strips of wood arranged to create a herringbone effect); *nichos* (wall niches) containing pottery and carved wooden santos; fireplaces; balconies with intricately carved railings draped with Native American saddle blankets; and handcrafted wooden tables and chairs. Breakfast and lunch menus are predominantly New Mexican. Favorites here include the shrimp burrito smothered in vegetarian chile verde for lunch and pepper-crusted loin of lamb with rosemary-mint demiglace for dinner. *Taos Inn, 125 Paseo del Pueblo Norte, tel. 505/758–1977. Reservations suggested. Dress: casual. DC, MC, V.*

Don Fernando's. The dining room at the Holiday Inn, 1 mile south of the Taos Plaza, is modern in concept, with Taos flourishes—kiva fireplaces, Indian art, and handcrafted tables and lamps. Out of its busy kitchen comes a wide selection of authentic Southwestern dishes, including enchiladas Puerto Vallarta (stuffed with crab and baby shrimp), shrimp Veracruz (marinated and grilled), and *carne asada* (broiled steak fillet). The adjoining lounge, Fernando's Hideaway (*see* Nightlife, *below*), features live entertainment, with intimate seating around a large adobe fireplace. *1005 Paseo del Pueblo Sur, tel. 505/758–4444. Reservations suggested. Jacket and tie advised. AE, D, DC, MC, V.*

Double AA Grill. Organic buffalo burgers are the specialty of the house at this rustic, unpretentious new Taos hot spot on the west side of Paseo del Pueblo Sur. Chef/owner Adrian Cannon opened his first restaurant in his native England when he was 16; since then he's owned a restaurant in Spain and done a stint as an actor in Hollywood. Eventually he arrived in Taos with his partner, Alison Belanger; thus the double A's—Adrian and Alison. Menu specials include roast wild boar, sautéed quail, medallions of venison, and sirloin of bison. *332 Paseo del Pueblo Sur, tel. 505/758– 1319. Reservations advised. Dress: casual. AE, D, MC.*

★ **El Patio de Taos.** A Taos favorite for over 40 years, El Patio is set in a traditional adobe touted as the oldest structure in Taos (actually, only one of the standing patio walls can truthfully claim that distinction). The main dining room has a skylight and flagstone floors, and a fountain covered by a small green sea of potted plants. A second, smaller dining room, which seats 30, has viga ceilings and Western and Native American paintings on the walls. The restaurant offers classic New Mexican, French, and northern Italian cuisines. Chef Yvon's house specialties include enchiladas con patos (duck), fettuccine Alfredo, New York steak, and blue-corn enchiladas. The Caesar salad is probably the best in town. El Patio has drawn many visiting celebrities over the years. *Teresins La., northwest corner of Taos Plaza, tel. 505/758–2121. Reservations suggested. Jacket and tie advised. AE, D, DC, MC, V.*

Lambert's of Taos. One of the classier spots in town, in the historic Randall House two and a half blocks south of the Plaza. Lambert's is the culinary province of chef/proprietors Zeke and Tina Lambert, whose specialties include pepper-crusted lamb, fresh grilled salmon, and other contemporary American dishes. For dessert, try the chocolate mousse with raspberry sauce. The atmosphere is laid-back and intimate. *309 Paseo del Pueblo Sur, tel. 505/758–1009. Reservations advised. Jacket advised (tie optional). AE, D, MC, V.*

Ogelvie's Bar and Grill. Occupying the second floor of an old two-story adobe building on the east side of the Taos Plaza, Ogelvie's is the perfect spot for people-watching from on high, especially from the outdoor patio in summer. Inside, the restaurant's two adjoining dining rooms and full-service lounge are decorated in what has been described as "early Taos thriftshop": assorted paintings, balloons, vintage black-and-white photos, musical instruments, antique lamps, you name it. Draped tapestries hang from the ceilings, and blue tablecloths cover the handcrafted tables and chairs. The chef and kitchen staff seem far more in control than the decorators, offering prime Angus beef, seafood, and traditional Southwestern and regional specialties that keep people waiting in line to get in. *103 E. Plaza, tel. 505/758–8866. Reservations suggested. Dress: casual. AE, MC, V.*

The Stakeout Grill and Bar. Tucked into the foothills of the Sangre de Cristo Mountains, 8 miles south of Taos, at a place called Outlaw Hill, this old adobe homestead offers views that stretch for hundreds of miles and sunsets that dazzle. Clearly marked by a huge cowboy hat out front, the restaurant has rustic decor, with wood-paneled walls, viga ceilings, hardwood floors, wooden tables and chairs, and muted-glass wall lamps. Changing exhibits of locally produced Western art and handcrafted silver—all of which is for sale—are displayed throughout. But the main attraction is the food—New York strip steaks, filet mignon, roast prime rib, shrimp scampi, swordfish steak, baked Brie, escargots, French onion soup, Caesar salad. *Stakeout Dr. (NM 68), tel. 505/758–2042. Reservations suggested. Dress: casual. MC, V.*

★ **Villa Fontana.** This restaurant is a two-story adobe with a Continental ambience, all aglow with newness and candle-light. Its two intimate dining rooms, with gleaming hard-wood floors and well-appointed tables, starched linens and sparkling crystal, set a classic tone found in many of Europe's finest restaurants. Master chef Carlo Gislimberti and his wife, Siobhan, offer authentic northern Italian cui-sine, including the house specialty of locally picked wild mushrooms and a variety of seasonal game, such as veni-son, duck, and pheasant. *Taos Ski Valley Rd., ⁹⁄₁₀ of a mi north of the blinking light, tel. 505/758–5800. Reservations recommended. Jacket and tie advised. D, DC, MC, V.*

Moderate **Chile Connection.** Six minutes north of the Taos Plaza on
★ Ski Valley Road, Chile Connection is housed in a sprawling ranch-style adobe building with a large patio offering spec-tacular mountain views. The patio is open for dining in sum-mer and on mild sunny winter days; otherwise, meals are served in three separate dining rooms, each with a kiva fireplace, handcrafted tables and chairs, Western art, and decorations from south of the border. Specialties of the house include blue-corn tortillas, homemade salsa, buffalo burgers and steaks, and fajitas. The large-screen TV in the bar is annoying, but after one of the great margaritas served there, you almost don't mind. *Ski Valley Rd., tel. 505/776–8787. Reservations suggested. Dress: casual. AE, D, DC, MC, V.*

Rhoda's Restaurant. Nestled at the base of famed Al's Run in the Taos Ski Valley, Rhoda's is a haven for hungry skiers who can dine while watching fellow enthusiasts lift off to the snowy summits. This sunny, pleasant restaurant, set in a wood-frame building with lots of windows, has hand-crafted pine tables and chairs, peach-colored tablecloths and napkins, and fresh floral bouquets on the tables. You can also dine outdoors on the sun deck. Chef Richard Reyes's daily specials include pasta selections, seafood and poultry, and traditional New Mexican specialties, plus such unusual regional dishes as elk and buffalo brochette. Espe-cially good is *pollo Monterrey*, chicken breast with cheese and chili. Full bar service is available. *Resort Center, Taos Ski Valley, tel. 505/776–2005. Reservations sug-gested. Dress: casual. AE, MC, V. Closed Apr. 8–Thanks-giving.*

Inexpensive **Abe's Cantina and Cocina.** Cocina means "kitchen," and you know what cantina means. This roadside bar and grill in Ar-royo Seco is run by a retired postal worker, Abel Garcia. (Abe's wife, Grace, is the local Avon lady.) There's a bar on one side with a pool table, jukebox, and TV (the satellite dish is out back). A newly added small dining room in the rear has natural wood tables and chairs. In the adjoining kitchen, Abe's daughter turns out hamburgers, fries, menudo, burritos, and other good things to be eaten in the bar or the dining room or to take out. *Ski Valley Road at Arroyo Seco, tel. 505/776–2960. Dress: informal. MC, V.*

Amigos Natural Grocery and Juice Bar. In front of a building that looks like ancient adobe—it's actually composed of railroad ties with adobe plastering—is the grocery store, which stocks a wide assortment of health foods, organic eggs, honey, and fresh local fruit and produce. In back is the natural-food café and juice bar, where blenders purr away, turning carrots, apples, berries, and giant stalks of celery into nectar. Home-baked breads and rolls go well with the juices and fresh daily selections of vegetarian entrées. The bare-bones café section seats 40 on tables and benches. There's also outside seating, weather permitting. *325 Paseo del Pueblo Sur, tel. 505/758–8493. No reservations. Dress: casual. No credit cards. Open daily 11–5.*

Bent Street Deli and Cafe. It's simple and unpretentious, but the place to go if you're dying for a Reuben sandwich. An extensive selection of deli-style food is offered, along with croissants, cappuccino, soups, salads, sandwiches, and desserts. Beer and wine are available, and there's patio dining in the summer. *120 Bent St., tel. 505/758–5787. No reservations. Dress: casual. No credit cards.*

★ **Michael's Kitchen, Coffee Shop, and Bakery.** It seems almost required by law that all Western communities have one top spot for breakfast; in Taos, this is it. Housed in a traditional old adobe, four blocks north of the Plaza, Michael's has been turning out huevos rancheros, tortilla *renadas* (diced ham and scrambled eggs wrapped in a tortilla), and other good things to get the day going for over 15 years. The restaurant's unique decor reflects its past as a curio shop—an antique washing machine, a wood-burning stove, vintage picture frames and mirrors, a turn-of-the-century coat rack, 10-gallon hats, Native American pottery, and a pitcher and commode. The ceilings are beamed, the floors are polished hardwood, and the tables and chairs are all handcrafted. Chef-owner Michael Ninneman also serves lunch and dinner, but it's breakfast that brings the faithful back for more. *304 Paseo de Pueblo Norte, tel. 505/758–4178. Reservations not required. Dress: casual. MC, V. Open 7 AM–8 PM.*

Roberto's. Housed in a 150-year-old adobe, across from the Kit Carson Museum, this New Mexican restaurant affords an ambience of rustic elegance and grace. Owners Bobby and Patsy Garcia reveal a deep-rooted love for their native heritage, using prized recipes handed down through the Garcia family for generations to create authentic native dishes from scratch. Three intimate dining rooms are decorated in Southwestern style throughout, with art and cherished family antiques, including handcrafted lamps and furniture. The margaritas and chile rellenos are particularly good. *E. Kit Carson Rd., tel. 505/758–2434. Reservations suggested for dinner. Dress: casual. MC, V. Closed Tues.*

Lodging

Taos is a tourist town, and it offers a broad range of accommodations from which to choose. There are hotels and motels to suit every need and budget, from big-name chains with all the extra amenities to smaller roadside establishments offering basic accommodations. There's no drastic variation in hotel rates from season to season, but you'll find more rooms available in the spring and late fall.

Most of the art and social events take place May through October; lodging rates are about 20% higher during the peak summer period (July and August) and reservations are highly recommended during this time.

With the development of the Taos Ski Valley and several other nearby ski resorts in the mid-1950s, Taos, long a virtual ghost town in winter, blossomed into one of the premier ski destinations in the country. Depending on snow conditions, the season generally runs from about the third week in November through the first week in April. Skiers now have many deluxe resorts to choose from for comfortable and convenient accommodations.

In order to accommodate the large influx of visitors into their small town, many Taos residents decided to open up their homes. Bed-and-breakfast Taos style means traditional adobe houses and haciendas, some 200 years old, and special Southwestern-flavor breakfasts—blue-corn pancakes and huevos rancheros. Innkeepers often act as concierges, directing guests to specialty shops, arranging river rafting or hot-air balloon excursions, or suggesting the perfect place for dining. For information, contact **Bed and Breakfast of New Mexico** (Box 2805, Santa Fe 87504, tel. 505/982–3332) or the **Taos Bed and Breakfast Association** (Box 2772, Taos 87571, tel. 800/876–7857).

Highly recommended lodgings in each price category are indicated by a star ★ .

Category	Cost*
Expensive	over $95
Moderate	$50–$95
Inexpensive	under $50

All prices are for a standard double room, excluding 3.5% city room tax or 3% county room tax; 6.75% city sales tax or 6.25% county sales tax; and service charges.

Hotels/Motels **Taos Inn.** This sprawling hotel, only steps from the Taos
Expensive Plaza, is a prized local landmark, exemplifying Southwest-
★ ern rustic charm with its adobe walls, wood-burning fireplaces, hand-stripped viga ceilings, hand-loomed rugs, and
wrought-iron fixtures. It's listed in the National Register
of Historic Places; parts of the structure date from the

Taos Lodging

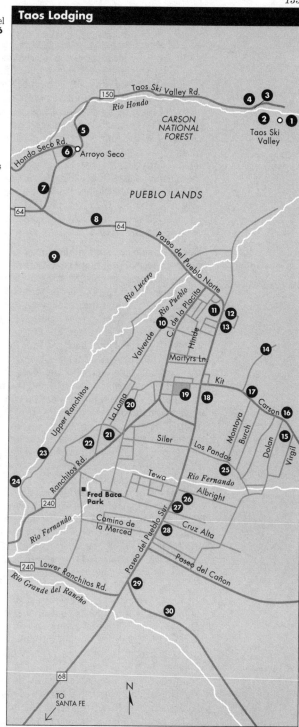

1600s. The guest rooms, all individually furnished in warm Southwestern style, are filled with antiques; handmade Native American bedspreads; custom-made Taos-style furniture built by local artists; and fireplaces created by Carman Velarde, the local Michelangelo of fireplace design. In summer there's dining alfresco on the patio. Paintings on the walls of the dining rooms, as well as in the dramatic two-story lobby, are by Native American and Southwestern artists. The comfortable, inviting lobby is built around an old town well, from which a fountain now bubbles forth; nearby is a sunken fireplace, rimmed with *bancos* (cushioned adobe seating areas). Most of the town's shops and restaurants are within walking distance of the hotel, which is adjacent to the Stables Art Center and the Taos Community Auditorium. *125 Paseo del Pueblo Norte, Taos 87571, tel. 505/758–2233 or 800/TAOS–INN. 39 rooms. Facilities: restaurant, bar, lounge, library, wine shop. DC, MC, V.*

Moderate   **Don Fernando de Taos Holiday Inn.** This is one of the newest hotels in Taos, but it has a venerable past. The original Don Fernando, built in the 1920s by a German entrepreneur, was considered one of the most charming hotels in the Southwest. At the time, Taos was populated by a colorful assortment of Native Americans, trappers, miners, and desperadoes. Hotel guests were met at the train depot in Lamy by guides from the Fred Harvey Company and then endured an arduous 12-hour journey by Model-T Ford to the hotel, 1 mile south of the Taos Plaza. The old Don burned to the ground in 1933, and the new one rose in its place in 1989. It's built in a distinct Pueblo-style design, with rooms grouped around central courtyards and connected by meandering walkways. Accommodations are tastefully appointed with hand-carved New Mexican furnishings, accented with specially designed fabrics in rich Southwestern colors. Many of the rooms have kiva fireplaces. Suites named after D. H. Lawrence, Lady Brett, and others of the charmed literary circle miss a bet by not including a memento or two—not even a photograph—of their celebrated namesakes. Because of its amenities, including the lounge, this is probably the best choice for single travelers. *1005 Paseo del Pueblo Sur, Drawer V, Taos 87571, tel. 505/758–4444 or 800/HOLIDAY, fax 505/758–0055. 126 rooms. Facilities: restaurant, lounge, bar, pool, Jacuzzi. AE, MC, V.*

El Monte Lodge. Nestled among cottonwoods in a quiet residential area four blocks east of the Taos Plaza is the El Monte Lodge, in business for over 50 years. It consists of several one-story white-painted adobe buildings, similar to guest-house cottages in the privacy of their arrangement among the trees. Local color is afforded by beamed viga ceilings, corner fireplaces, bright Native American rugs, and tinwork mirrors and frames. All rooms have refrigerators; some have kiva fireplaces and kitchenettes. A laundry on the premises is available for the guests' use, as are picnic tables outside. Owners George and Pat Schumacher know all the ins and outs of Taos life and are happy to help guests plan their vacation schedules. *317 Kit Carson Rd., Box 22, Taos 87571, tel. 505/758-3171 or 800/828-TAOS. 9 rooms, 4 2-bedroom suites. Facilities: cable TV and refrigerators in rooms, laundry facilities, picnic tables. AE, DC, MC, V.*

El Pueblo Lodge. This low-to-the-ground Pueblo-style adobe, only blocks north of the Taos Plaza, is as practical as it is charming. In-room refrigerators, kitchenettes, and the use of a complimentary guest laundry room make it an ideal home away from home for traveling families. There's even cable TV. The lodge is located on the Ski Valley side of Taos, pointing skiers in the right direction. Room appointments include pale desert colors and traditional Southwestern furnishings—handmade furniture, lamps, and mirrors and Native American and Western art throughout. Many of the rooms have fireplaces. Free Continental breakfast is served in the lobby. *418 Paseo del Pueblo Norte, Box 92, Taos 87571, tel. 505/758-8700 or 800/433-9612. 46 rooms. Facilities: heated pool and hot tub. MC, V.*

Hotel La Fonda de Taos. Tourists on the trail of D.H. Lawrence should make this their first stop. The novelist often took to the easel as a form of relaxation, and for $3 you can enter the manager's office and view Lawrence's erotic paintings. Saki Karavas, the hotel's owner, bought the 11 paintings from Lawrence's widow. They had been banned in London (as were many of Lawrence's books); by today's standards, however, they seem about as offensive as the White Rock fairy. James Karavas, father of the present owner, built the hotel in 1937, and early on it catered to European and American celebrities (Tyrone Power honeymooned here). Karavas's son, the present owner, is, at 72, every bit as gregarious and as sentimental. Although the hotel has been spruced up considerably of late, with new Turkish bedspreads in the rooms, new paint on the handmade wooden furniture, and more lighting in the lobby, it has seen better days. Showcased everywhere are framed newspaper and magazine stories from the old days—as well as photos, posters, Western paintings, Hopi Indian shields, portraits, busts, Pueblo pottery, and Mexican paintings and artifacts. Near the reception desk, two "suits of lights" have been mounted: bullfighters' costumes, in full pose, frequently mistaken by older guests for bellhops. *Taos Plaza, Box 1447, Taos 87571, tel. 505/758-2211 or 800/833-2211. 24 rooms with bath. Facilities: TV in second-floor lounge only. MC, V.*

★ **Kachina Lodge de Taos–Best Western.** Just down the road from the historic Taos Pueblo and only minutes from the Taos Plaza is this large, comfortable lodge, built in a two-story adobe Pueblo style. A kachina theme runs throughout the hotel, with rare and historic kachina dolls, carved from the root of cottonwood trees, decorating many of the hotel's public areas and others—newer, and somewhat more commercial—offered for sale in the hotel shops and lobby area. Chairs and couches, upholstered in fabrics inspired by Southwest Native American designs and colors, rim the large lobby fireplace. Hopi and Pueblo art hangs on the walls. In the hotel's Kiva Coffee Shop (there's also a Hopi Dining Room and Zuni Cocktail Lounge), a huge hand-carved totem pole behind the counter dominates the room. The recently refurbished guest rooms continue the Southwestern Native American theme, with handmade, hand-painted furnishings, colorful fabric bedspreads, and decorative lamps. Every night from Memorial Day through Labor Day, a troupe from the nearby Taos Pueblo performs ritual dances outside by firelight. During the day, the hotel's 7 acres of wooded landscape invite picnics and quiet walks. *N. Pueblo Rd., Box NN, Taos 87571, tel. 505/758–2275 or 800/522–4462, fax 505/758–9207. 122 rooms. Facilities: restaurant, bar, coffee shop, heated pool, hot tub, shopping arcade. AE, D, DC, MC, V.*

★ **Koshari Inn.** Nestled under centuries-old silver aspens in the foothills of Taos Canyon is the Koshari Inn—a former motel that has been painstakingly converted into a traditional Southwestern inn, in the Taos mold. New furnishings include the handmade wooden chairs, desks, end tables, and headboards painted in the pale colors so popular in northern New Mexico. Framed posters by favorite regional artists, including Georgia O'Keeffe and R. C. Gorman, hang on the walls, and the Native American motif is everywhere. Beyond the inn, which is part adobe, part cement block, is the Rio Fernando, more a trickling stream than a mighty river. The inn offers its guests free use of 10-speed all-terrain bicycles for touring the countryside or for trips into town, 2 miles to the west. There's also a small swimming pool on the property for guests' use. Rooms are spacious, and each has a motel-style private entrance. There's no restaurant, but there's a Continental breakfast in the lobby. *910 E. Kit Carson Rd., Box 6612, Taos 87571, tel. 505/758–7199. 12 units. Facilities: pool. MC, V.*

Ramada Inn. The two-story adobe-style Ramada Inn, located 1 mile south of the Taos Plaza, recently underwent a transformation of sorts, putting more of a Taos stamp on the familiar Ramada mold. The remodeled dining room now features desert colors, Western art, and Native American pottery. The lobby has a fireplace. Even the guest-room furnishings have been modified to reflect a Southwestern flavor. The hotel's Cafe Fennell has always specialized in Southwestern and American favorites, but now even the cuisine seems spicier. You can enjoy hors d'oeuvres and sit by a cozy fireplace in the Hearthside Lounge, where guitarist Rufus Perry plays during the week and on weekends during the peak summer months. *Santa Fe Hwy. and Frontier Rd., Box 6257, Taos 87571, tel. 505/758–2900 or 800/272–6232; fax 505/758–1662. 124 rooms. Facilities: indoor heated pool, whirlpool spa with sun deck, dining room, lounge, conference rooms. AE, D, DC, V.*

★ **Sagebrush Inn.** With its graceful portals, enchanting patios, and charming adobe architecture, the two- and three-story Sagebrush Inn is one of the prettiest hotels in town. Built in adobe Pueblo-Mission style in 1929, the inn is furnished with authentic Navajo rugs, rare pottery, Southwestern and Spanish antiques, fine carved pieces, and paintings from many of the old Southwestern masters. Georgia O'Keeffe once lived and painted in one of the third-story rooms. The two large dining rooms (specializing in prime rib and New Mexican cuisine) are decorated in the Southwestern mode, as are rooms and suites, which feature wall niches containing antique religious figures, Native American wall hangings, and Native American–design rugs and bed coverings. Many have kiva fireplaces; some have balconies looking out onto the magnificent Sangre de Cristo Mountains. The Sagebrush Village, a recent addition to the Sagebrush Inn, offers alternative family lodging, condominium style. *1508 Paseo del Pueblo Sur, 3 mi south of the Plaza, Box 557, Taos 87571, tel. 505/758–2254 or 800/428–3626; fax 505/758–9009. 83 rooms. Facilities: 2 restaurants, lounge, nightly entertainment, pool, 2 hot tubs, 2 tennis courts. AE, DC, MC, V.*

Resorts and Ski Lodges
Expensive

Hotel Edelweiss. This quiet, elegant resort hotel, directly on the ski slopes, offers a touch of European alpine flavor, complete with floral arrangements on the dining tables and fresh-baked breads and rolls at the hotel's La Croissanterie restaurant. The large lobby is dominated by a gigantic fireplace, where après-ski coffee and pastries are served; it's the place to meet and socialize. Owners Ilse and Bernard Mayer make their own hearty soups, sandwiches, and desserts. Rooms are more practical than posh, offering just the basics. *Taos Ski Valley 87525, tel. 505/776–2301. 20 rooms. Facilities: Jacuzzi, sauna, massages. MC, V. Closed mid-Apr.–Memorial Day.*

★ **Quail Ridge Inn and Tennis Ranch.** The 20th century comes to sleepy Taos with this all-things-to-all-people family resort and conference center. One- and two-story modern would-be adobe bungalows offer a variety of room choices—plain rooms, studios with kitchen, one- and two-bedroom suites, and rooms with balconies or patios, all decorated in Southwestern contemporary, with viga ceilings and kiva fireplaces. Carl's French Quarter has excellent food (*see* Dining, *above*). Five miles north of Taos Plaza, the Quail Ridge offers a touch of modern elegance set against the magnificent natural backdrop of northern New Mexico. What it lacks in rustic charm it makes up for in a host of recreational amenities, from organized trail rides to hot-tub soaks. A free Continental breakfast is included in the room rate. *Ski Valley Rd. (NM 150), Box 707, Taos 87571, tel. 505/776–2211 or 800/624–4448; fax 505/776–2949. 110 rooms and suites. Facilities: restaurant, lounge, 4 racquetball courts, 8 Laykold tennis courts (2 inside), heated pool, hot tub, fitness center, squash, volleyball. Complete ski, tennis, rafting, mountain-bike, and fly-fish-*

ing packages are available for groups or individuals. D, DC, MC, V.

Thunderbird Lodge and Chalets. Only 150 yards from the main lifts, on the sunny side of the valley, this large, two-story wood-frame inn is the ultimate ski-lodge resort, owned and managed by live-in residents Elizabeth and Tom Brownell. Its dining room is one of the most popular in the valley, with all breads, soups, salads, entrées, pastries, and ice cream made on the premises. A large conference room also serves as a game room, with TV, board games, and a library. Guest rooms are small and functional, typical of ski-resort accommodations. Supervised children's activities include early dinners, movies, and games. *Box 87, Taos Ski Valley 87525, tel. 505/776-2280 or 505/776-2238. 32 rooms. Facilities: whirlpool, sauna, massage, bar, restaurant. MC, V.*

Moderate **Amizette Inn & Restaurant.** A small, wood-frame mountain inn on the banks of the Rio Hondo, 1½ miles from the ski lifts, the Amizette offers all the amenities (as well as the decor) of a traditional alpine chalet—hot tub, redwood sauna, sun deck, trout stream and hiking trails, and comfortable rooms with queen-size beds, private baths, and color TV. The decor, as you might expect, is alpine. *Taos Ski Valley Rd., Box 756, Taos Ski Valley 87525, tel. 505/776-2451. 12 rooms. Facilities: hot tub, sauna. AE, MC, V.*

★ **Austing Haus.** Billed as the largest and tallest timber-frame building in the United States, the Austing Haus is made of over 70,000 board feet of heavy timbers, with more than 3,000 interlocking joints—held together by wooden pegs. The beams are exposed inside and out, providing structural stability and a pleasantly aesthetic design. All the furniture is handmade as well: Owner Paul Austing, an award-winning chef, is as handy with a mallet and saw as he is with his sauces and soufflés. The full front exterior of the building is paneled glass, offering stunning views of the valley from inside and a glimpse of the cozy interior from outside. The hotel's aptly named Glass Dining Room has a Native American loom with a partially completed blanket mounted on the wall; a fireplace; stained-glass paneling; and large picture windows. House specialties are veal Oscar and steak au poivre. Guest rooms are sparse and functional, not unlike those of ski lodges all over the world. The ski lifts are just 1½ miles away. *Taos Ski Valley Rd. (Hwy. 150), Box 8, Taos 87525, tel. 505/776-2649, 505/776-2629, or 800/748-2932. 26 rooms with bath. Facilities: restaurant, hot tub, satellite TV. Converts to bed-and-breakfast inn during the summer. DC, MC, V.*

Inexpensive **Abominable Snow-Mansion Skiers' Hostel and Summer Center.** This large old adobe building, midway between Taos and the Ski Valley (15 minutes either way), is designed for the budget-minded who don't mind bedding down in bunks, dormitory style. You can't miss the garish lettering out front, painted directly on the adobe facade. Inside, the front part of the two-story building is a large general room where everything happens; there are video games, a piano, a fireplace, chairs, couches, and books. Meals are served here buffet style during the ski season. No food is offered during the summer, but kitchen facilities are available to guests. In back and upstairs are six dormitory rooms with bunk beds, mostly five beds to a room; each room has its own bath. During the summer, three of the rooms are offered as private accommodations. There are two cabin units out back and an area set aside for tent camping (conventional and tepee). It's all clean, comfortable, and fun, and a great way to meet people. *Taos Ski Valley Rd. (Hwy. 150), in Arroyo Seco, Box 3271, Taos 87571, tel. 505/776–8298; fax 505/776–8746. 96 beds. No liquor permitted during the summer months. MC, V.*

Bed-and-
Breakfasts
Expensive
★

Casa de las Chimeneas. Just 2½ blocks from the Plaza, secluded behind thick adobe walls, the "House of Chimneys," with its formal gardens and cool, stately entranceway, could serve as the approach to a castle. The interior of this Spanish-style hacienda, originally built in 1912 and renovated a decade ago, is equally grand. The living room features regional art, tiled hearths, French doors, and traditional viga ceilings. Each guest room has its own private entrance and fireplace and each is individually furnished with hand-carved, hand-painted traditional New Mexican chests, tables, chairs, and headboards. Rooms also have tiled bar areas with mini-fridges stocked with complimentary juices, sodas, and mineral waters; there are also Hobbes–Russell tea kettles with tea and coffee setups. A special two-room suite includes a large sitting room with a sofa bed. All rooms overlook the inn's formal gardens and fountains. Large common areas contain cozy nooks for reading or relaxing. The Taos Plaza is just a short walk away, two blocks southeast of the inn. Innkeeper Susan Vernon and her artist husband, Ron Rencher, share the stage with two resident cats. Full complimentary breakfasts—served in the guest rooms, on the terrace, or in the dining room—feature huevos rancheros, blue-corn pancakes with fresh berries and maple syrup, and the like. Nobody goes away hungry. Hors d'oeuvres are served in the late afternoon. *405 Cordoba Rd., Box 5303, Taos 87571, tel. 505/758–4777. 3 rooms, 1 suite, all with bath and cable TV. No smoking. Facilities: outdoor hot tub. MC, V.*

★ **Casa Europa.** There's a marvelously ornate 200-year-old bed in the French Room at the Casa Europa that must take an army of maids to keep polished. But gleaming and polished it is, and you'll feel a little like Louis XIV as you drift off to sleep, with sounds of crickets and field frogs wafting in through the partially open French windows above the courtyard of this two-century-old adobe farmhouse. The inn is run with care and precision by German-born Rudi Zwicker (former owner of the popular Greenbriar Restaurant in Boulder, Colorado) and his wife, Marcia. It was restored in 1983 with its adobe bricks and wood vigas intact. The rooms, whose whitewashed walls are splashed with sunlight, are furnished with an eclectic collection of European antiques and treasured Southwest pieces—including the oldest door in Taos, discovered years ago in the basement of the Guadalupe Church. Breakfasts are elaborate. *157 Upper Ranchitos Rd., Los Cardovas Rte., Taos 87571. 6 double rooms with bath. Facilities: cable TV, Swedish sauna and hot tub. MC, V.*

Salsa del Salto. Seven miles from the Taos Plaza, on the way to the Taos Ski Valley, is this large Western ranch–style home featuring a two-story common room with a massive stone fireplace, heated outdoor pool, hot tub, and tennis court. Located at the edge of the Sangre de Cristo Mountains, overlooking the Taos mesa, it was designed for owners Mary Hockett and Dadou Mayer by well-known architect Antoine Predock. Each of the guest rooms is furnished with handcrafted, hand-painted New Mexican furniture. All have king-size beds with goose-down comforters and tiled bathrooms, and all have spectacular views. The Master/Honeymoon Suite has a fireplace with copper detailing. Full gourmet breakfasts are served each morning. During the summer, the gentle clack of croquet balls can be heard on the front lawn; everyone dresses in white to play. In the winter, Mayer, a renowned French chef, doubles as a ski instructor at Taos Ski Valley. *Hwy. 150, Box 453, El Prado 87529, tel. 505/776–2422. 6 rooms with bath. Facilities: heated pool, hot tub, tennis court. MC, V.*

Taos Country Inn at Rancho Rio Pueblo. The aroma of strong coffee and good things to eat floats through the rooms and hallways of this sprawling hacienda, parts of it built nearly two centuries ago by settlers named Rivera. Yolanda Deveaux, the current owner, comes from an old Taos family; her father, Dr. Reynoldo Deveaux, "delivered half the people in Taos," she says. The inn stands amid 22 acres of pastureland, gardens, and orchards, graced with olive trees, cottonwoods, and willows, a brook here, a sturdy wooden fence there. The guest rooms, with white plaster fireplaces and sitting areas, are spacious and sunny; they all have king- or queen-size beds, leather sofas, and local artifacts and artwork. The public rooms are filled with handcrafted furniture and, owing to their large windows, with plenty of light. Breakfast entrées include cream-cheese-and-salmon omelets and such regional specialties as butter crunch eggs and eggs rancheros. *Box 2331, Upper Ranchitos and Karavas Rds., Taos 87571, tel. 505/758–4900 or 800/866–6548. 9 suites. Facilities: cable TV/VCR on request, massage ($45/hr). MC, V.*

Moderate **American Artists Gallery House.** The 7-foot-tall flat black iron sculpture in front isn't Kokopelli (whose fluty tunes can be heard in every gift shop between San Diego and Santa Fe) but the *God of Bed and Breakfasts*, a special creation of artist Pozani Flanzelli. (And it may be the only piece among the 500 or so works at the inn that doesn't have a price tag on it.) Works by local, regional, and nationally known artists, including such Native American and Southwestern favorites as R. C. Gorman, Amado Pena, and Veloy Virgil, are featured at this bed-and-breakfast art gallery. Each of the guest rooms has a gallery name, and each is individually furnished in charming Southwestern style. For example, the Garden Gallery room is set in a courtyard with brick and fieldstone areas abundant with flowers, while the Gallery Lilac room is in a separate guest house with high wood ceilings, a kiva fireplace, and a kitchen. There's a "honeymoon cottage" in a separate casita. Guests may also enjoy the main living room with its large fireplace, as well as a brick portico and side gardens. Taos Plaza is only minutes away, and owners Judie and Elliot Framan are on hand to offer travel advice and information about the city. Full breakfasts include such specialties as French toast stuffed with nuts and soft cheese, along with fresh fruit, coffee, and bagels. *132 Frontier Rd., Box 584, Taos 87571, tel. 505/ 758-4446 or 800/532-2041. 6 rooms, all with private bath. Facilities: hot tub. MC, V.*

Brooks Street Inn. A large, rambling adobe house with a circular drive and an adjoining guest house comprise the Brooks Street Inn, at one time an artist's residence. Although constructed in 1956, the house was built in the traditional manner with adobe bricks made on the property, beamed ceilings, polished wood floors, and a large stone fireplace. An elaborately carved corbel arch (the handiwork of Japanese carpenter Yaichikido) spans the entranceway, and alongside is a shaded, walled garden. The guest rooms show great attention to detail—the perfect basket; fresh-cut flowers; a decanter of sherry; plump, fluffy pillows. In the large living room, paintings by local artists share wall space with family photographs. The full breakfast features handed-down family recipes, such as Lithuanian bacon buns and Czech coffee cakes, along with muffins, breads, and other home-baked delights. When the weather is warm, breakfast is served at umbrella tables on the patio; in the winter, it's served by the fireplace. *119 Brooks St., Box 4954, Taos 87571, tel. 505/758-1489. 6 rooms with bath. No smoking. AE, MC, V.*

★ **Blue Door.** Located in the foothills between Taos and Ranchos de Taos, the Blue Door is a 100-year-old adobe farmhouse situated amid orchids, flower gardens, lawns, and patios. Nearby is the famous San Francisco de Asis Church, surrounded by colorful shops. Each of the bedrooms is decorated in country style, with viga ceilings, wood floors, hand-carved beds, and Native American–drum end tables. Owner Bruce Allen makes and markets traditional Taos drums, crafted from carved tree trunks and covered with tautly stretched leather. (His **Taos Drums** factory outlet is on NM 68 on the outskirts of town.) His wife, Pat, runs the inn and also raises Arabian horses. Breakfast at the Blue Door is a particular treat—green-chile quiche, juice, fresh fruit, muffins, blueberry pancakes, bacon, waffles, coffee, and homemade jams from the orchard. *La Mirada Rd., Talpa, Box 1168, Taos 87571, tel. 505/758–8360. 2 rooms with bath. MC, V.*

Casa de Milagros. A single-story, turn-of-the-century adobe house, a half-mile east of the Taos Plaza, Casa de Milagros (House of Miracles) offers the texture and flavor of the Taos of long ago, with all the conveniences of today, from hot tub to cable TV. The inn, actually two buildings connected by a portal (where the hot tub is located), is furnished in an eclectic style. Southwestern decor predominates—viga ceilings; Mexican tiled bathrooms; custom cabinets; and lots of pottery, tapestry, and weavings. Native American art, particularly the works of Taos Pueblo artist Jonathan Warmday, hangs on the walls, along with the works of other local artists. Much of it is for sale, and some is commissionable—a portrait, a landscape, if you like. When available from local Native Americans, breakfast includes breads baked in traditional Pueblo *hornos* (ovens), as it has been baked for centuries. There are also fresh fruit, muffins, bread pudding, and homemade granola. *321 Kit Carson Rd., Box 2983, Taos 87571, tel. 505/ 758–8001. 5 rooms, plus a 2-bedroom suite, all with bath. No smoking indoors. MC, V.*

Hacienda del Sol. This is a house with a history. Bordering the Taos Pueblo, it was acquired in the 1920s by art patron Mabel Dodge Luhan. She and her fourth husband, Pueblo Tony Luhan, lived here while building their main house, Las Palomas. After moving, they kept Hacienda del Sol as a private retreat and as a guest house for visiting notables; author Frank Waters wrote *People of the Valley* while staying here. Overlooking 95,000 acres of pueblo land and shaded by huge cottonwood, ponderosa pine, blue spruce, and willow trees, the site offers a majestic, uninterrupted view of the Taos mountains, one particularly enjoyed by today's guests while soaking in the secluded outdoor hot tub. Most of the rooms feature kiva fireplaces, Spanish antiques, Southwestern-style handcrafted furniture, and original artwork, much of it for sale. (The inn has a complete gift shop, just off the reception area.) The Los Amantes Room has a large bedroom with seating area adjoining a room with a double-size black Jacuzzi on a mahogany platform amid a jungle of potted plants. There's a skylight for stargazing while you soak, and the attached bathroom, with its jet-black sink, tub, shower, and toilet— all with gleaming gold fixtures—is a celebration of decadence. A full gourmet breakfast is served. *Box 177, 109 Mabel Dodge La., Taos 87571, tel. 505/758–0287. 8 rooms with bath, 1 suite. Facilities: cable TV, outdoor hot tub. MC, V.*

Mabel Dodge Luhan House. The home of the heiress and longtime Taos resident, now a bed-and-breakfast inn and conference center, was recently declared a National Historic Landmark. Luhan bought the 200-year-old three-room adobe structure, along with the 12 acres surrounding it, in 1915. Then, with the determination of the pharaohs building the pyramids, she enlarged and expanded it, with the intention, some say, of duplicating her palatial villa in Italy. The three rooms grew to 17; the house rose from one story to three. What it resembled, though, was not an Italian villa but a pueblo—and indeed it was built for and with her fourth husband, Tony Luhan, a full-blooded Taos Pueblo Indian. (Originally the only way to enter was pueblo fashion—by ladder. The ladders are still there, but today's guests can use the front door.) Past guests, from pre-bed-and-breakfast days, included D.H. and Frieda Lawrence, Georgia O'Keeffe, Willa Cather, Mary Austin, John Collier, and John Marin. Mabel Dodge Luhan herself died there in 1962 at the age of 83. Today's owners, George Otero and Susan Chambers-Cooke, bought the house 15 years ago from actor Dennis Hopper. There are 10 guest rooms in the main house, 10 more in a separate guest house. The inn is frequently used for literary workshops and artistic, cultural, and educational meetings and workshops. A full Southwest-style buffet breakfast is served. Don't go if you're looking for crisp linen, designer soaps, and a lot of pampering; the buildings are rumpled and frayed, the stairs creak. Ah, but if you want to soak up some of the magic that made Taos what it is today, this is the place. *Box 3400, 240 Morada La., Taos 87571, tel. 505/758–9456 or 800/846–2235, fax 505/751–0431. 18 rooms, 16 with bath; 2 suites. Facilities: meeting rooms, meal service available. Public tennis courts nearby. MC, V.*

★ **La Posada de Taos.** Within walking distance of the Taos Plaza is this provincial adobe with beamed ceilings, a portal, kiva fireplaces, and the intimacy of a private hacienda. Four of its five guest rooms are in the main house; the fifth is a separate cottage with a sky-lit double loft bed, its own sitting room, and a fireplace—all cozy and pretty enough to be dubbed *La Casa de la Luna de Miel* (The Honeymoon House). Wood-burning stoves or adobe fireplaces can be found in all of the guest rooms, which have either mountain or flowered courtyard views. Innkeeper Sue Smoot, who proudly boasts of the Posada (which means "inn") as the first bed-and-breakfast in Taos, offers a full, hearty breakfast, from traditional ham and country eggs to a spicy burrito. *309 Juanita La., Box 1118, Taos 87571, tel. 505/758–8164 or 800/645–4803. 5 rooms with private bath. No credit cards.*

Orinda. Surrounded by open meadows and tall trees, Orinda, built in 1947, is a dramatic adobe estate with spectacular views and country privacy, and it's within walking distance of the Taos Plaza. Even getting there is fun: It's off bustling Placitas Road, down a drive flanked by pastures with grazing horses and groves of cottonwoods and elms. The spacious one- and two-bedroom suites have separate entrances, kiva fireplaces, traditional viga ceilings, and Mexican tile baths. The thick adobe walls ensure peace and quiet. Wisconsinites George and Cary Pratt, the owners since 1992, have remodeled and enlarged the original adobe structure. The main house has a library—media room with a fireplace and a picture window looking onto the Taos Mountains. A hearty breakfast is served in the two-story sun atrium amid a gallery of art and Navajo blankets, all for sale. *461 Orinda La., Box 4451, Taos 87571, tel. 505/758–8581 or 800/847–1837. 2 rooms with bath, 1 suite. No smoking. MC, V.*

Ruby Slipper. This 1930s farmhouse is one of the few adobe structures in Taos with a gabled roof. The inn includes five guest rooms in the main house and two more in an adjoining building, also styled in adobe. All the rooms have private entrances and include kiva fireplaces, Mexican tile baths, and locally crafted furniture—simple and practical, handmade and hand-painted in the brighter colors of the Santa Fe school. Owners Diane Fichtelbert and Beth Goldman envision Taos as a mythical land and have themed all their guest rooms after characters from *The Wizard of Oz.* As innkeepers they are environmentally conscious (only natural foods are served) and spiritualy aware (God's-Eye symbols are used for do-not-disturb signs, and the Neem Karoli Baba Ashram Hindu Temple is just down the road). The inn reaches out to the gay community as well as to honeymooners from Iowa. There's a full breakfast during ski season; the rest of the year, a gourmet basket is delivered to each room. The owners blend their own fine Ruby Slipper coffee. *416 La Lomita Rd., Box 2069, Taos 87571, tel. 505/758–0613. 7 rooms with bath. Facilities: 4-person hot tub and Jacuzzi. No smoking. MC, V.*

Suite Retreat. In historic La Loma Plaza, which predates the Taos Plaza 2½ blocks away, the Suite Retreat is an art-filled adobe that was once the home of Buck Dunton, one of the founders of the Taos Society of Artists. (Unwilling to take his turn at being secretary and arranging shows for the group, he was expelled from the society and left for Texas to pursue his favorite subject, cowboys). Current owners Greg Payton and Diane Enright restored the studio and home. The entrance sign is carved on the back of Dunton's old studio sign, which was uncovered during remodeling. The two bedrooms in the upstairs guest suite are decorated with regional Southwestern furniture, and each has a bedside kiva fireplace. The adjoining living room is filled with Mexican antiques and artwork (Greg Payton is a sculptor of note). An old-fashioned Victrola plays vintage 78s, including one called "Santa Fe Is a Long, Long Way from Broadway." Breakfast is served in the guest rooms or, weather permitting, on the walled garden patio. *110 La Loma Plaza, Box 85, Taos 87571, tel. 505/758–3960. 2-bedroom suite (accommodates 2–6) with bath. No credit cards.*

Inexpensive **Harrison's Bed and Breakfast.** In a rural setting 2½ miles north of the Taos Plaza, this large adobe home is convenient for trips to the Taos Ski Area. It is the domain of Bob and

Jean Harrison, who have lived in Taos for 25 years. The house overlooks a wooded area and the town from the foot of the west mesa and is beautifully set off by trees and bushes. The guest rooms are furnished with handmade and hand-painted desks, tables, and headboards crafted in northern New Mexico, less ornate than their Santa Fe–style counterparts. Breakfast—tailored to guests' preference—is served in the rooms or, weather permitting, on the flower-bedecked patio. *Box 242, Taos 87571, tel. 505/758–2630. 3 rooms, 1 with private bath. No credit cards.*

Camping Thousands of miles of unspoiled wilderness await campers in and around the Taos area. The **Orilla Verde Recreation Area** (Bureau of Land Management, Cruz Alta Rd., Taos 87571, tel. 505/758–8851), located 10 miles south of Taos along the banks of the Rio Grande, offers opportunities for camping, hiking, fishing, and picnicking. It's open year-round; camping fees are $7 per night, $3 per vehicle for day use. The **Carson National Forest** (Box 558, Taos 87571, tel. 505/758–6200) has more than 30 campgrounds (and 400 miles of cool mountain trout streams), including those of the Wheeler Peak Recreational Area, the highest point in New Mexico at 13,161 feet. Most campgrounds are free; some charge a $5–$8 camping fee.

A number of commercial campgrounds can be found as well, among them the **Taos RV Park** (Hwy. 68, Paseo del Pueblo Sur, Ranchos de Taos 87557, tel. 505/758–1667 or 800/323–6009), located next to the Taos Motel just off the intersection of NM 518. The park has 29 spaces: 22 full hookups with cable TV capacity, and 7 tent sites with water and electricity. Hot showers are available. The trailer sites are $15 per night for two; the tent sites are $12 for two. Located in the Sangre de Cristo Mountains, 5 miles from the Rio Grande Gorge, the area is grassy, with a few small trees. Open year-round.

Taos Valley RV Park (120 Estes Rd., Box 200, Ranchos de Taos 87557, tel. 505/758–4469), a former Campgrounds of America (KOA) franchise, has complete campground facilities, with 60-foot pull-throughs and full hookups. Facilities for tenters are also available. In the Rio Grande Valley, 2½ miles south of the Taos Plaza, the campground is at an elevation of 7,000 feet and has been in operation for over 20 years. It has 92 sites, with prices ranging from $12.25 to $17.75, depending on size and requirements. Local TV signals come in sharp and clear. Open March 1–November 1.

Questa Lodge (Questa, Box 155, Questa 87556, tel. 505/586–0300) has 24 units on the banks of the Red River, two blocks from NM 522. Fees are $6 for the tent sites, $12 for full hookups. Open May–mid-October.

The Roadrunner Campground (Red River, Box 588, Red River 87558, tel. 505/754–2286 or 800/243–2286) has 155 units located at the end of Red River–NM 578 in a spectacular wooded mountain setting, with the Red River running right through the campground. Fees are $18 ($20 for a river site), which includes water and electrical hookup, cable TV, and sewer. Open year-round.

The Arts and Nightlife

Taos Magazine (Whitney Publishing, Box 1236, Santa Fe 87504, tel. 505/989–7603), published eight times a year, covers events, fashion, arts, and the general cultural beat in town.

The Arts

The **Taos Community Auditorium** (133 Paseo del Pueblo Norte, tel. 505/758–4677) offers performances of modern dance groups and the local theater group, concerts, movies, and even the sounds of Andean folk music. For a weekly entertainment listing, check the "Tempo" section of the *Taos News*. Contact the **Taos Art Association** (tel. 505/758–2052), which owns and operates the Taos Community Auditorium, for ticket information. The **Taos Spring Arts Celebration** (May) and the **Taos Arts Festival** (Sept. 18–Oct. 4) are the major arts gatherings in Taos. Both events highlight the visual, performing, and literary arts of the community and allow visitors to rub elbows with the many artists who call Taos home. For information, call Taos Arts Celebration (tel. 505/758–3873) and the Taos County Chamber of Commerce (tel. 505/758–3873 or 800/732–8267). The **Wool Festival** (late Sept. or early Oct.), held in Kit Carson Park, features everything from sheep to shawl, with demonstrations of shearing, spinning, and weaving, handmade woolen items for sale, and tastings of favorite lamb dishes.

Music From mid-June through early August, the Taos School of Music and the International Institute of Music fill the evenings with the sounds of chamber and symphonic orchestras at the **Taos Chamber Music Festival.** This is the oldest summer music program in America and possibly the largest enclave of professional musicians in the Southwest. It has been furthering the artistic growth of young string and piano students for over 30 years. Concerts are presented every Saturday evening from June 21 through August at the Taos School of Music, Taos Community Auditorium (tel. 505/776–2388). The tickets are $12. Concerts and recitals are also presented at the **Hotel Saint Bernard** (tel. 505/776–2251) in the Taos Ski Valley. Admission is free. **Music from Angel Fire** is a series of classical and jazz concerts presented at the Community Auditorium from the middle of August to early September. Tickets cost around $12 per concert. For information, call 505/758–4667. *See also* Jazz Clubs, *below.*

Nightlife

Bars and Lounges   **Carl's French Quarter** (Quail Ridge Inn and Tennis Ranch, Ski Valley Rd., tel. 505/776–8319) has classical music on Thursdays. **Fernando's Hideaway** (Holiday Inn, Paseo del Pueblo Norte, tel. 505/758–4444) presents live entertainment nightly, alternating rock, jazz, vocals, and country music. Lavish complimentary Happy Hour buffets are offered on weekday evenings. The **Taos Park Inn International** (Paseo del Pueblo Sur, tel. 505/758–8610) features dancing and live entertainment nightly, usually of the rock or country variety. The **Adobe Bar** (Taos Inn, 125 Paseo del Pueblo Norte, tel. 505/758–2233), Taos's local meet-and-greet spot, offers talented local live acts, from a flute choir to individual guitarists and small jazz, folk, and country bands.

Cabaret   The **Kachina Lodge Cabaret** (413 Paseo del Pueblo Norte, tel. 505/758–2275) brings in headline acts, such as Arlo Guthrie and the Kingston Trio, on a regular basis and is open for dancing.

Country-and-Western Clubs   The **Sagebrush Inn** (Paseo del Pueblo Sur, tel. 505/758–2254) offers live entertainment—mostly of the country-Western variety—nightly in its spacious lobby lounge. There's no cover charge.

Jazz Clubs   Each January, **Thunderbird Lodge** in the Taos Ski Valley (3 Thunderbird Rd., tel. 505/776–2280) presents Jazz Legends, an annual series of concerts that bring world-famous jazz musicians to the intimate setting of the Thunderbird Bar. The concerts are popular and seating is limited, so early reservations are recommended.

5 Albuquerque

A large city—its population is nearing the half-million mark—Albuquerque spreads out in all directions, with no apparent ground rules. No cohesive pattern, either architecturally or geographically, seems to hold it together; the city seems as free and free-spirited as all those hot-air balloons that take part in the Kodak Balloon Festival every October. Even residents seem confused by the street system that, like the city itself, goes this way and that. Each main street and boulevard has a direction designation after it, NE, SW, or what have you, so people can find out where they are.

Once the code is broken, however, it's a marvelous city. Like all of New Mexico, it blends its cultures well; its citizens are descendants of the Native Americans who first inhabited the land and defended it bravely, of the Spanish who came on horseback to conquer and settle, and of the Anglos who were trappers and hunters and traders and pioneers in a new and often inhospitable land. From the beginning, Albuquerque was a trade and transportation center. It was an important station on the Old Chihuahua Trail, an extension of the Santa Fe Trail winding down into Mexico.

Albuquerque's incredible sprawl can be explained in a number of ways. The city was founded in 1706 on the banks of the Rio Grande, near a bend in the river, an ideal location for crop irrigation, transportation, and protection. The settlement prospered, thanks to its strategic trade-route location and its proximity to several Indian pueblos that offered mutual support and commerce. The settlers built a chapel and then a church, the Church of San Felipe de Neri (named after the patron saint of King Philip V of Spain). Their homes were built close together around a central plaza for protection, as were those in other early Spanish settlements in the hostile new land. Entrance to the fortresslike community could be gained only at the four corners, making it easier to defend.

That original four-block downtown area is now known as Old Town, the city's tourist hub, with all its galleries and trendy Mexican and New Mexican restaurants. Had the city simply continued to grow, progressively expanding from its central hub, that would have made sense. But something happened. First the Rio Grande gradually changed its course, moving farther and farther west. That caused a shift in the population. Then, in 1880, the railroad came to Albuquerque, its tracks skirting Old Town by a good two miles. The result was another population shift. Old Town wasn't exactly abandoned, but "New Town" began to sprout up along the train depot, and it grew until it eventually enveloped Old Town. Finally, there was Route 66. Designated in 1926, called the "Mother Road" by John Steinbeck, it sparked much of Albuquerque's early economic development. During the '30s and '40s it surged through town with as much impact as the railroad and the river combined, and the burgeoning city swelled around the asphalt pavement—motels, gas stations, diners, and truck stops, a sea of neon that celebrated America's new independent mobility.

Today Albuquerque is a thriving arts center, as are many other areas of New Mexico. From the moment visitors step off a plane at Albuquerque International Airport, they're surrounded by art. Throughout the terminal building, special display areas are devoted to the works of New Mexican artists—a collection assembled by the Albuquerque Arts Board as part of the city's 1% Art Program, in which 1% of Albuquerque's municipal budget is devoted to public art projects. In addition, the city has numerous privately funded museums and galleries and is a growing center for artists, writers, poets, filmmakers, and musicians.

Essential Information

Important Addresses and Numbers

Tourist Information The **Albuquerque Convention and Visitors Bureau** (Springer Bldg., 121 Tijeras Ave. NE, Box 26866, Albuquerque 87125, tel. 505/842–9918 or 800/284–2282) publishes a variety of informative materials, including quarterly calendars of events and brochures describing local and out-of-town driving tours. An after-hours tape-recorded bulletin on current local events in Albuquerque can be reached after 5 PM on weekdays and all day Saturday and Sunday by phoning 505/243–3696 or 800/284–2282; the same numbers can be used to request an information packet. The bureau also maintains an information center on the lower level of the airport at the bottom of the escalator; it is open daily from 9:30 to 8.

Emergencies **Fire, medical, or police** (tel. 911; police nonemergency tel. 505/768–1986).

Hospital emergency rooms. University Hospital (2211 Lomas NE, tel. 505/843–2411), Presbyterian Hospital (1100 Central Ave. SE, tel. 505/841–1234). Call either for locations of Urgent Care Centers around the city.

Dentist referrals (tel. 505/292–2620).

Late-Night Pharmacies Walgreen's offers a 24-hour prescription-refill service at two locations (2950 Central Ave. SE, tel. 505/262–1743, and 5001 Montgomery NE, tel. 505/881–5050).

Other Numbers **Time and temperature** (tel. 505/247–1611).

Road conditions (tel. 505/827–5213 or 800/432–4269).

Arriving and Departing by Plane

Airport and Airlines **Albuquerque International Airport** (tel. 505/842–4366), 5 miles south of downtown Albuquerque, is the gateway to

New Mexico. Car rentals, air taxis, and bus shuttles are readily available at the airport, which is 65 miles southwest of Santa Fe and 130 miles south of Taos.

Airlines serving Albuquerque International Airport are **America West** (tel. 800/247–5692), **American** (tel. 800/433–7300), **Continental** (tel. 800/525–0280), **Delta** (tel. 800/221–1212), **Mesa Air** (tel. 800/637–2247), **Southwest** (tel. 800/531–5601), **TWA** (tel. 800/221–2000), **United** (tel. 800/241–6522), and **USAir** (tel. 800/428–4322).

Air-shuttle service between Albuquerque and Santa Fe via **Mesa Airlines** operates four times a day; the flying time is approximately 25 minutes.

Between the Airport and Downtown The trip into town from the airport takes about 10–15 minutes, and there is a variety of ground transportation to choose from. Taxis, available at clearly marked stands, charge about $7 (plus 35¢ for each additional rider); *see* the By Taxi section, *below.* Sun Tran buses pick up at the sunburst signs every 15 minutes; the fare is 75¢; *see* the By Bus section in Getting around Albuquerque, *below.* Most major hotels provide shuttle service to and from the airport, including Hilton, La Posada de Albuquerque, Marriott, Ramada, and Sheraton. If you like to go in high style, *see* the By Limousine section, *below.* For car-rental companies that operate out of Albuquerque, *see* Chapter 1, Essential Information.

Arriving and Departing by Car, Train, and Bus

By Car The main routes into Albuquerque are I–25 from points north and south and I–40 from points east and west.

By Train **Amtrak's** (tel. 800/872–7245) Southwest Chief services Albuquerque daily from Los Angeles and Chicago. The Albuquerque Station, built by the Santa Fe Railroad in 1901 and famous for its grand Spanish-style architecture and graceful domes and archways, burned to the ground in January, 1993. A temporary station (214 First St., tel. 505/842–9650), literally in the former station's ashes, now services the line.

By Bus **Greyhound/Trailways** offers comprehensive daily service into **Albuquerque's Transportation Center** (300 Second St. SW, tel. 505/243–4435 or 800/531–5332).

Getting around Albuquerque

Unlike more compact Taos and Santa Fe, Albuquerque sprawls out in all directions, so you'll need transportation to get wherever you're going.

By Bus The **Sun Tran** buses blanket the city with frequent connections (about every 30 minutes, less frequently in the more remote areas of the city and on weekends). The fare is 75¢. Bus stops are well marked with the line's sunburst signs.

For information, call 505/843–9200, or write Sun Tran (City of Albuquerque, 601 Yale SE, Albuquerque 87106).

By Taxi Taxis are metered in Albuquerque, service is around the clock, and rates run about $2.90 for the first mile and $1.40 for each additional mile. Contact **Albuquerque Cab** (tel. 505/883–4888), **Checker Cab** (tel. 505/243–7777), or **Yellow Cab** (tel. 505/247–8888) for service.

By Limousine Albuquerque has several limousine companies offering pampered service for those who require the best. Rates start at $35–$45 per hour for standard limousines and range up to $145 per hour for stretch limos comfortably seating 14; there is usually a two-hour minimum. Call for special airport shuttle rates. Companies include: **At Last, The Past,** Antique Limousine Service (tel. 505/298–9944), **Classic Limousine** (tel. 505/247–4000), **Dream Limousine** (tel. 505/884–6464), **Lucky's Limousine Service** (tel. 505/836–4035), **Luxury First Class Limousines** (tel. 505/269–5049 or 505/836–8007), **VIP Limousine Service** (tel. 505/883–4888).

Opening and Closing Times

General business hours in Albuquerque are 9–5; most shops, galleries, and museums are open 10–5 or 6, with limited hours on weekends. Banking hours are weekdays 9–4, and, in some cases, Saturday 10–2.

Guided Tours

Orientation **Gray Line of Albuquerque** offers several seasonal tours (May–Oct.). Among them is a three-hour Albuquerque city tour, including the University of New Mexico campus, historic landmarks, and Old Town. The tours, departing at 9, are given on Monday, Wednesday, and Friday. For reservations and information, call 505/764–9464.

Special-Interest Gray Line has a three-hour **Indian Heritage Tour,** including a visit to the Indian Pueblo Cultural Center in Albuquerque and to a living pueblo. This tour, departing at 1 PM, is offered on Monday, Wednesday, and Friday.

Tres Vistas (4010 Carlisle NE, tel. 505/888–3466) takes visitors to a variety of retailers in Albuquerque and nearby Santa Fe; tours include discounts, special fashion shows, and lunch.

There are also many operators offering early morning **hot-air balloon tours** of Albuquerque (*see* Ballooning in Sports and the Outdoors, *below*).

Walking Tours The **Albuquerque Museum** (tel. 505/243–7255) leads hour-long historical walks through **Old Town** at 11 AM Tuesday through Sunday. There is no charge for the tour, which is available on a first-come basis and meets in the lobby of the

Albuquerque Museum before setting out for Old Town. Tours do not run in winter.

A 30-minute walking tour of the **University of New Mexico's** campus, available through the Public Affairs office (tel. 505/277–5813), emphasizes the university's cohesive Pueblo-style architecture. Designed for small groups, the tour has no set time and is available only on request. **Student Outreach** (tel. 505/277–5161) offers daily campus tours (9 AM and 1:30 PM), designed primarily for prospective students.

Exploring Albuquerque

Historic and colorful Route 66 is Albuquerque's Central Avenue, unifying, as nothing else, the diverse areas of the city—Old Town cradled at the bend of the Rio Grande, the University of New Mexico to the east, and Nob Hill (a lively strip of restaurants, boutiques, galleries, and shops farther east along Central Avenue). The railroad tracks and Central Avenue/Route 66 divide the city into quadrants, or quarters—SW, NW, SE, NE.

Because Albuquerque covers such a large geographical area, its terrain is rather diverse. Along the river in the north and south valleys, elevations hover at around 4,800 feet. To the northeast, land rises over mesas to the foothills of the Sandia Mountains at an elevation of 6,500 feet; the Sandia Crest is a grand spot from which to view the city spread below and get a feel for its layout. West of the Rio Grande, where much of Albuquerque's growth is taking place, the mesa rises more abruptly than it does in the east—with a difference in elevation of 1,700 feet in the lowlands and highlands of the city. There are corresponding changes in temperature, as much as 10°F at any time; it's even been known to snow or rain in one part of town while remaining dry and sunny in another.

Highlights for First-time Visitors

Indian Pueblo Cultural Center (*see* Tour 1)
New Mexico Museum of Natural History (*see* Tour 1)
Old Town (*see* Tour 1)
Petroglyph National Monument (*see* Parks and Monuments)
Sandia Peak Aerial Tramway (*see* Tour 3)
University of New Mexico Galleries (*see* Tour 2)

Tour 1: Old Town

Numbers in the margin correspond to points of interest on the Albuquerque and Albuquerque Old Town maps.

An exploration of Albuquerque begins where the city began, in Old Town. It was here on the Plaza in 1706 that Don Francisco Cuervo y Valdez, a New Mexico provincial gover-

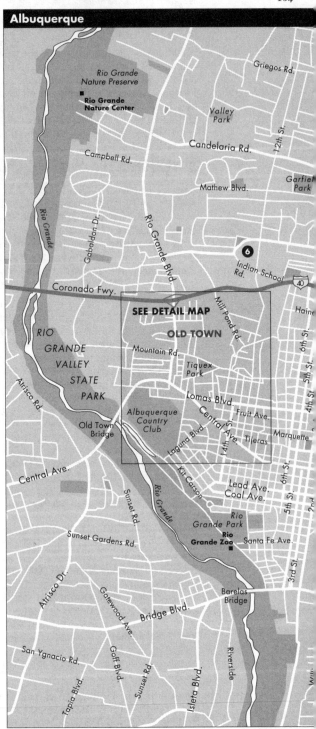

Albuquerque

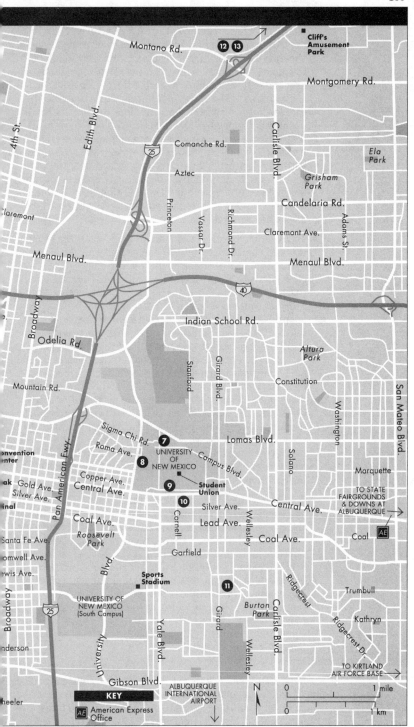

Montano Rd.

Cliff's Amusement Park

Montgomery Rd.

4th St.

Edith Blvd.

I-25

Comanche Rd.

Aztec

Princeton

Carlisle Blvd.

Ela Park

Claremont

Grisham Park

Candelaria Rd.

Vassar Dr.

Richmond Dr.

Claremont Ave.

Adams St.

Menaul Blvd.

Menaul Blvd.

I-40

Broadway

Odelia Rd.

Indian School Rd.

Altura Park

Mountain Rd.

Stanford

Girard Blvd.

Constitution

Washington

San Mateo Blvd.

onvention nter

Sigma Chi Rd.

Roma Ave.

7

8

UNIVERSITY OF NEW MEXICO

Lomas Blvd.

Campus Blvd.

ak

Gold Ave.

Silver Ave.

inal

Pan American Fwy.

Copper Ave.

Central Ave.

9

10

Student Union

Cornell

Silver Ave.

Wellesley

Solano

Marquette

TO STATE FAIRGROUNDS & DOWNS AT ALBUQUERQUE →

Central Ave.

Santa Fe Ave.

omwell Ave.

ewis Ave.

Coal Ave.

Roosevelt Park

Lead Ave.

Coal Ave.

AE Coal

Garfield

Broadway

I-25

Sports Stadium

11

Girard

Burton Park

Ridgecrest

Carlisle Blvd.

Trumbull

Kathryn

nderson

University Blvd.

UNIVERSITY OF NEW MEXICO (South Campus)

Yale Blvd.

Wellesley

Ridgecrest Dr.

TO KIRTLAND AIR FORCE BASE →

heeler

Gibson Blvd.

ALBUQUERQUE INTERNATIONAL AIRPORT

N

12 **13**

KEY

AE American Express Office

0 ——— 1 mile

0 ——— 1 km

nor, decided to seal his mark in history by founding a town. No slouch when it came to political maneuvering, he named the new town, or *villa*, after the Duke of Alburquerque, Viceroy of New Spain, hoping that the flattery would cause the duke to overlook the fact that the newly formed community had only 15 families instead of the required 30 needed for a charter. The Duke of Alburquerque acquiesced, of course, but somewhere down the line the first "r" in his name was dropped. Don Francisco couldn't have made a better choice for the town's location. The new settlement was on the banks of the Rio Grande where the river made a wide curve, providing good irrigation for crops, and where several Native American pueblos already existed, meaning mutual aid, protection, and trade. The nearby mountains and the "bosque" offered ample wood—cottonwoods, willows, and olive trees. The weather was ideal.

❶ Today, Albuquerque's **Old Town Plaza** remains the heart of the city's heritage. While the modern city of 500,000 grew up all around it, the four-square-block area of Old Town clings fiercely to the past, at least in spirit. The tree-shaded Plaza of today is much the Plaza of then, except that a graceful white gazebo and lacy wrought-iron benches have **❷** been added. The **San Felipe de Neri Church** (2005 Plaza NW, tel. 505/243–4628), enlarged and expanded several times over the years, still stands facing the Plaza, its massive adobe walls and other original sections intact. Most of the old adobe homes surrounding the church and the Plaza have been converted into shops, galleries, and restaurants, and many of the hidden *placitas*, or little plazas, offer more of the same. The best time to visit Old Town is early in the morning before the stores have opened and the daily rush of activity begins. In the defused light of morning, you can almost hear the strum of a Spanish guitar and the click of heels, possibly a dancer, a conquistador, or a woman opening her shop.

Old Town, which is one block north of Central Avenue (the city's main street) at Rio Grande Boulevard, is a beehive of activity, with over 150 shops, restaurants, cafés, and delis. The scent of bubbling vats of green chile, enchiladas, and burritos hangs in the air. Gunfights are staged on Romero Street on Sunday afternoons, and during times of fiesta Old Town is alive with mariachi bands and dancing señoritas. You can pick up schedules of events and maps, which contain a list of public rest rooms, at the **Old Town Information Center** across the street from the San Felipe de Neri Church. *305 Romero St., tel. 505/243–3215. Open Mon.– Sat. 10–5, Sun. 11–5.*

Adjacent to Old Town, just off the northeast corner on Mountain Road, are two of the city's major museums. The **❸** solar-heated **Albuquerque Museum** enshrines relics of the city's birth and development and is home to the largest collection of Spanish Colonial artifacts in the nation. The cen-

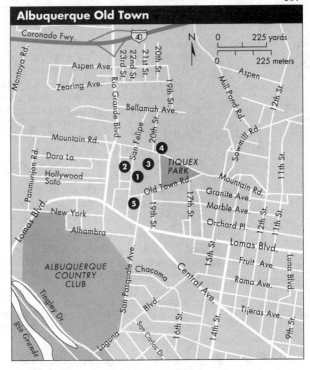

Albuquerque Old Town

terpiece of the exhibit is two life-size models of Spanish conquistadores in chain mail and armor, one on horseback, representing the arrival of Francisco Vásquez de Coronado and his soldiers on their quest for gold in 1540, the turning point of New Mexico's history. Among the museum's attractions are early maps (some from the 15th century showing California as an island and the Rio Grande spilling into the Pacific), treasure chests once filled with pearls and gold coins, colonial and contemporary paintings, and religious artifacts. A multimedia audiovisual presentation chronicles the development of the city since 1875. *2000 Mountain Rd. SW, tel. 505/243–7255. Admission free. Open Tues.–Sun. 9–5.*

The **New Mexico Museum of Natural History,** across the street from the Albuquerque Museum, is the city's newest showpiece. The striking glass and sand-colored building with slanted roofs opened in 1986. Its spectacular world of wonders, rumored to have been mounted, in part, with the help of Disney experts, includes an active volcano (its river of bubbling hot lava flows beneath museum visitors under a see-through glass floor), a frigid Ice Age cave, dinosaurs, and an Evolator (short for Evolution Elevator), a six-minute high-tech ride through 35 million years of New Mexico's geological history via a mountain of video wizardry. An on-board video host on the large elevator escorts 25 passengers per ride, during which the floors and video-screen walls move, simulating a ride through the dimensions. The Dynamax Theater makes viewers feel equally involved. An 85-foot-long replica of the Rio Grande flows from its source in Colorado, all the way down through Texas. A full-size replica of a 100-million-year-old Quetzalcoatlus, with a wingspan of 38 feet, hovers over the museum's central atrium, while visitors arriving via the front walkway outside share space with a giant brontosaurus. The museum has a Fossil Hot Line (call the main number) to assist amateurs in identifying paleontological finds. *1801 Mountain Rd. NW, tel. 505/841–8837. Admission: $4.20 adults, $3.15 senior citizens and students, $1.05 children 3–11, toddlers free. Combination tickets for museum and Dynamax Theater: $7.35 adults, $5.25 senior citizens and students, $3.15 children 3–11. Open daily 9–5.*

For some more specialized natural history, go back down to Old Town, at the corner of San Felipe and Old Town Road:

⑤ In the **American International Rattlesnake Museum,** the largest exhibit of rattlesnakes and rattlesnake memorabilia ever mounted can be viewed. Included are rare and unusual specimens, such as an albino rattlesnake. There are also rattlesnake artifacts, videos, and a Southwestern gift shop. *202 San Felipe NW, tel. 505/242–6569. Admission: $1. Open daily 9–9.*

⑥ A short drive north of Old Town brings you to the **Indian Pueblo Cultural Center.** Its unique multilevel semicircular design was inspired by that of Pueblo Bonito, the famous prehistoric ruin in Chaco Canyon in the northwestern section of New Mexico. The cultural center is owned and operated by the 19 Pueblo tribes of New Mexico, each of which has an upper-level alcove devoted to its particular arts and crafts. Lower-level exhibits trace the history of the Pueblo Native Americans from prehistoric times to the present. Original paintings and sculpture of the highest quality, jewelry, leather crafts, rugs, souvenir items, drums, beaded necklaces, painted bowls, and fetishes on display are for sale. It's the largest collection of Native American arts and crafts in the Southwest and the richest resource for the study of America's first inhabitants of the region. Native American ceremonial dances are performed during the summer and on special holidays, free to the public. *2401 12th St. NW, tel. 505/843–7270. Admission: $2.50 adults, $1.50 senior citizens, $1 students. Open daily 9–5:30; restaurant open 7:30–3:30. Closed major holidays.*

Time Out The Indian Pueblo Cultural Center has a restaurant, open for lunch, that serves Native American food exclusively, including blue-corn enchiladas, posole, Native American bread pudding, and, of course, fry bread—that addictive popoverlike creation topped with honey, beans, chili, or powdered sugar or gobbled up plain. In Old Town, **Zane Graze Cafe & News** (308 San Felipe NW, tel. 505/243–4377) is delightful for lunch or refreshments. A good alternative is the **Owl Cafe** (800 Eubank Blvd. NE, tel. 505/291–4900), a nostalgic 1950s-style diner with a soda fountain, jukebox, pictures of Marilyn Monroe, and milkshakes and green-chile cheeseburgers.

Tour 2: The University of New Mexico

Just east of I–25 on Central Avenue is Albuquerque's 103-year-old **University of New Mexico,** the state's largest university, internationally recognized for its programs in anthropology, biology, Latin American studies, and medicine. It's also noted for its Pueblo-style architecture and superb landscaping. A central oasis within its 700 acres contains knolls, a duck pond, fountains, waterfalls, and benches. Throughout the campus are large-scale sculptures by internationally known artists and murals by famous New Mexican painters. The central information number for the university is 505/277–0111.

The university is a mainstay of Albuquerque's cultural and educational life, and its many outstanding galleries and museums, open to the public free of charge, shouldn't be

7 missed. Included among them is the **Jonson Gallery,** containing the works of the late modernistic painter Raymond Jonson (1891–1982), as well as those of contemporary artists. This intimate gallery is Jonson's former home and studio. A special retrospective exhibit of his work is presented each summer. *1909 Las Lomas NE (University of New Mexico campus), tel. 505/277–4967. Admission free. Open Tues. 9–4 and 5–9, Wed.–Fri. 9–4; closed Sat.–Mon. and all major holidays.*

8 The **Maxwell Museum of Anthropology,** in the university's Anthropology Building, one block north of Grand Avenue on University Boulevard, has two permanent galleries. In one, the "Ancestors" exhibit chronicles 4 million years of human emergence. In the other, "Peoples of the Southwest" explores the lifeways, art, and cultures of 11,000 years of human occupation in the Southwest. The museum shop offers a wide selection of traditional and contemporary Southwestern Native American jewelry, rugs, pottery, basketry, beadwork, and folk art from around the world. It also has a children's section with inexpensive books, kits, and handmade tribal artifacts. *Maxwell Museum of Anthropology (University of New Mexico campus), tel. 505/277–4404. Admission free. Open weekdays 9–4, Sat. 10–4, Sun. noon–4.*

9 The **University Art Museum,** located in the Fine Arts Center just northwest of the entrance on Stanford Drive and Central Avenue, features permanent and changing displays of contemporary and historical art. Its fine-art collection is the largest in the state and includes the work of such

Old Masters as Rembrandt and such newer ones as Picasso and (of course) Georgia O'Keeffe. The museum also has one of the largest holdings of prints and photographs in the country, including contemporary leaders and early pioneers in the field. *Fine Arts Center (University of New Mexico campus), tel. 505/277–4001. Admission free. Open Tues. 9–4 and 5–9, Wed.–Fri. 9–4, Sun. 1–4; closed Mon. and Sat.*

At the corner of Central and Cornell avenues is the sales and exhibit gallery of the **Tamarind Institute,** an internationally renowned school and workshop for lithographers, where fine-art prints pulled from stones and metal plates are created. A Tamarind Master Printer certification is to an artist what a degree from Juilliard is to a musician. Tamarind maintains a gallery where prints and lithographs done by professionals, as well as those recently produced by students, are on display. Special guided tours are conducted on the first Friday of each month at 1 PM. *108 Cornell Ave. SE, tel. 505/277–3901. Admission free. Open weekdays 9–5 and by appointment.*

Two blocks south of the university on Girard Boulevard SE, you'll find the **Ernie Pyle Memorial Library,** the memorabilia-filled home of the beloved Pulitzer Prize–winning war correspondent, now the smallest branch of the Albuquerque Public Library. Pyle bought the house in 1940 after several visits to New Mexico with his wife, Jerry. On display are photos, handwritten articles by Pyle, and news clippings of his career and of his death by a sniper's bullet on April 18, 1945, on the tiny Pacific island of Ie Shima; he's buried in the National Cemetery of the Pacific in Punchbowl Crater, near Honolulu. "There are really two wars," wrote John Steinbeck. "One is the war of maps, logistics, campaigns, ballistics, divisions. . . . Then there is the war of the homesick, the weary, the wounded and dying, the common man . . . that is Ernie Pyle's war." *900 Girard Blvd. SE, tel. 505/256–2065. Admission free. Open Tues. and Thurs. 12:30–8, Wed., Fri., and Sat. 9–5:30. Closed Sun. and Mon.*

Time Out   The university's **Student Union Building** (tel. 505/277–2331) on Central Avenue, just north of the visitors parking area, is a good spot to grab a burger or just rest your feet for a while. Here you'll also find changing exhibits and students' showings in three exhibit spaces—the Centennial (on the main level), Union (north end, lower level), and ASA (south end, lower level) galleries.

Tour 3: Sandia

For a view of Albuquerque on high—and of half of New Mexico for that matter—head for **Sandia Crest,** the 10,678-foot summit of the Sandia Mountains. The road to the

Crest, the Sandia Crest National Scenic Highway (east on I–40 to NM 14, north to NM 536), is well paved and carefully maintained year-round. Of course, there's more than one way to get to the top. The **Sandia Peak Aerial Tramway,** the world's longest single-span tramway, takes visitors from a point outside Albuquerque's city limits on an awesome 2.7-mile climb to the top of Sandia Peak, where at sunset the desert skies produce a kaleidoscope of changing colors. From its lower terminal the tram car glides across a terrain of jagged boulders and clawing peaks, causing deer or perhaps a family of Rocky Mountain bighorn sheep to scamper away from the strange sight. The tram cars were custom-made in Switzerland with plenty of window space. From the sky-top observation deck at the summit, you can see Santa Fe to the northeast and Los Alamos to the northwest. And isn't that Tucson over there? Heading back, you can go the way you came or take the double-chair skiers' chair lift 7,500 feet down the other side. To reach the tramway's base, take I–25 north to the Tramway Road exit, then east on Tramway Road, or take Tramway Boulevard north from I–40 and Central Avenue for 8.5 miles to the stop sign, then head right on Tramway Road. *Sandia Peak Tramway, 10 Tramway Loop NE, tel. 505/298–8518. Open Memorial Day–Labor Day, daily 9–10; Labor Day–Memorial Day, Sun.–Thurs. 9–9 (opens later on Wed.), Fri.–Sat. 9–10. Weekends only during the 2nd and 4th weeks of April. Tickets for the 90-minute round-trip are $12 adults, $9 senior citizens and children 5–12.*

Time Out   There's a pricey restaurant atop the tramway called, appropriately, **High Finance** (Sandia Peak, tel. 505/243–9742). Needless to say, the view is outstanding. An alternative is the **Firehouse Restaurant** (tel. 505/292–3473), at the base of the tram. If you choose to drive to Sandia Crest, try **Sandia Crest House Gift Shop and Restaurant** (Sandia Crest, tel. 505/243–0605), which provides family dining and more spectacular views.

A few miles farther north, the **Sandia Pueblo** is one of the most industrious of the Rio Grande Pueblos. *See* Pueblos Near Albuquerque in Chapter 7.

Albuquerque for Free

Among the city's free attractions are the **Albuquerque Museum** (*see* Tour 1, *above*), the numerous galleries at the **University of New Mexico** (*see* Tour 2, *above*), and the **National Atomic Museum** (Kirtland Air Force Base, Wyoming Gate, tel. 505/845–6670), which is devoted to an exploration of atomic energy and the role New Mexico played in nuclear technology. Exhibits include replicas of Little Boy and Fat Man, the atomic bombs dropped on Japan. In the Missile Park section you can examine a B-52 bomber and an F-105D fighter bomber, touch the rocket that was used to boost

Alan Shepard into space, and see an array of historic flying machines with names like *Hound Dog*, *Bomarc*, *Mace*, and *Snark*. David Wolper's film *Ten Seconds That Shook the World* can also be seen here; call ahead for movie times. The charming **Old Town** area (*see* Tour 1, *above*), marking the site of Albuquerque's original Spanish settlement, is filled with colorful shops, galleries, and restaurants. It's ideal for browsing, shopping, or relaxing over coffee or a cool drink in the shade of a cottonwood tree that has stood tall since before the time of the conquistadores.

What to See and Do with Children

Cliff's Amusement Park, on Osuna Road at San Mateo Boulevard, includes 23 thrill rides, live entertainment, games, an arcade room, and private picnic areas. *4800 Osuna Rd., tel. 505/881–9373. Admission including unlimited rides: Tues.–Thurs. $8.95, Fri.–Sun. $10.95. Admission without rides: $3.50. Open Apr. 3–Oct. 14.*

The Hands-on Corner at the **Indian Pueblo Cultural Center** (*see* Tour 1, *above*) allows youngsters to touch Native American pottery, jewelry, dried corn, weaving, and tools. Children can draw their own petroglyphs or design pots. Colorful Native American dances in the museum's courtyard will impress the entire family.

Go about 30 miles north of Albuquerque on NM 14, which runs between Albuquerque and Santa Fe, where you can visit the **Old Coal Mine Museum** in the quasi ghost town of **Madrid,** now populated with writers, artists, potters, and poets, and home to a sprinkling of unusual shops and galleries. Children love exploring the old coal mine tunnel, with its vein of coal; climbing aboard a 1906 steam train; and nosing through a variety of antique buildings full of marvelous old relics, including 1920s movie projectors, early hospital and dental equipment, antique cars, and even a 1928 International dump truck. Tickets for the museum are available at the Mine Shaft Tavern out front. If you're there on a weekend between Memorial Day and Labor Day, catch the museum's old-fashioned melodrama, staged in a former roundhouse machine shop that's been converted into the **Engine House Theater.** It's probably the only theater anywhere with a full-size steam train that comes chugging onto the stage; the rear of the theater opens onto the tracks. In this production, when the pretty heroine gets tied onto the tracks, she's really got something to worry about. *Old Coal Mine Museum, Madrid, tel. 505/473–0743. Admission: $2.50 adults, $1 children under 6. Melodrama tickets: $8 adults, $6.50 senior citizens, $4 children under 12. Open daily 9:30–dusk, weather permitting.*

New Mexico Museum of Natural History (*see* Tour 1, *above*) is particularly appealing to children, since a number of interesting programs and exhibits have been designed just for them. A big favorite is the Evolator, which takes visitors through 35 million years, back to a seacoast where dinosaurs roamed. The naturalist center lets children touch snakes and frogs, see objects through microscopes, and make animal tracks in a sand box. The museum also arranges camp-ins in which groups of children can sleep overnight—if they dare close their eyes—with dinosaurs, giant flying reptiles, and an active volcano.

What child doesn't love the zoo? Albuquerque's **Rio Grande Zoological Park** is home to more than 1,000 animals from around the world, from pink flamingos to chest-thumping gorillas. Don't miss Moonshadow, the snow leopard, one of the rarest of its kind. Sprawled over 60 acres, the zoo is especially well known for its spacious naturalistic exhibits and lush landscaping, including a half-dozen waterfalls. *903 10th St. SW, tel. 505/843–7413. Admission: $4.25 adults (ages 16–64), $2.25 senior citizens and children. Open daily 9–4:30.*

While in the Sandia Mountains, you'll find lots to do with the children. A quick stop at the **Sandia Ranger Station** (tel. 505/281–3304), off NM 14 South, will provide you with pamphlets, maps, and a fire-prevention program with a *Smokey the Bear* movie and occasional tours to the nearby fire station; call to reserve a time. You might also take a couple of hours to see **Sierra Goat Farms,** 15 miles south of NM 14. Here you and your little ones will meet Carmen Sanchez, the Goat Lady, who owns the farm and delights in teaching children. Ms. Sanchez shows children how to milk the animals and care for them. The baby goats are the biggest attraction, blurting a nasal "wa, wa, wa, wa" in unison. The farm has plenty of outdoor grills and picnic tables, and a variety of goat cheeses, cheesecakes, and chocolates are for sale. *Sierra Goat Farms, Hwy. NM 40, Tijeras, tel. 505/ 281–5061. Admission free. Open Tues.–Sun. 10–6.*

There are plenty of interesting attractions for small-fry travelers in Albuquerque, but perhaps none more so than the **Tinkertown Museum** in Sandia Park on the way to Sandia Crest. Run by Ross and Carla Ward, the museum houses a world of miniature carved-wood characters. It contains the results of more than 30 years of carving and collecting by its owners, including an animated miniature Western village. The latest addition is a circus exhibit with wooden merry-go-round horses from the 1940s and original circus emblems. Tiny vendors sell cotton candy, pink lemonade, and popcorn; other figures include trapeze artists, a bear act, a fire eater, a tiger trainer, and an animated fat lady. Visitors entering the roadside attraction, passing through the building's colorful glass-bottle facade, are greeted by ragtime piano music. There's a life-size general store, where deliveries arrive by horse-drawn wagon. Put a quarter in a slot and Boot Hill Cemetery comes to life, as lightning crackles and the devil and an angel do battle over a poor lost soul. Tinkertown and most of its delightful creations represent a lifetime of carving for Ross Ward, whose dream was hatched in the late 1950s. Today, more than 900 figures populate the tiny village. *Tinkertown Museum, Hwy. 536, Sandia Park, tel. 505/281–5233. Admission: $2 adults, 50¢ children 16 and under. Open Apr. 1–Oct. 31, daily 9–6.*

Off the Beaten Track

A scenic drive initiated nearly a quarter-century ago and still popular, the **Turquoise Trail** departs from freeway travel and ventures into backroad country, where the pace is slow, talk is all about weather and crops, donkeys have the right of way, and Albuquerque seems like another planet. It's the old route between Albuquerque and Santa Fe, now full of ghost towns that are being restored, thanks to writers, artists, and travelers who come through.

Heading east on I–40, the NM 14 North exit takes you to the back road of Sandia Crest (NM 536), snaking up through a portion of Cibola National Forest and on to the 10,678-foot crest. Stop to enjoy the view. Back on NM 14, again heading north, you'll hit **Golden,** site of the first gold rush (1825) west of the Mississippi. Golden has a rock shop and a mercantile store, and its rustic adobe church and graveyard send photographers into a state of euphoria. La Casita, a shop at the north end of the village, serves as a kind of unofficial Chamber of Commerce, in case you've got any questions.

Ten miles past Golden, you'll come to **Madrid** (*see* What to See and Do with Children, *above*), where coal was once king. Long abandoned, Madrid has been rebuilding, but slowly. Weathered old houses have been repaired and a shop opens here, and another one there, mostly converted company stores or old homes. Some of the shops are definitely worth a visit—**Carmen's Purple Palace** (tel. 505/471–8393), for Southwestern fashions, blankets, coats, and such; **Madrid Earthenware Pottery** (tel. 505/471–3450); the **Turquoise Trail Trading Post** (tel. 505/471–3450); the **Tapestry Gallery** (tel. 505/471–0194), for hand-loomed knits and rugs; and **Maya Jones** (tel. 505/473–3641), for Guatemalan imports. You'll probably also want to visit the **Old Coal Mine Museum** and its **Engine House Theater,** remnants of a once-flourishing coal mining business. During melodramas staged here on weekends during the summer, you can cheer the hero and hiss the villain.

A few miles farther north on NM 14, **Cerrillos** comes into view, yet another echo of bygone days. A boomtown in the 1880s, its mines brimmed with gold, silver, and turquoise; it had eight newspapers, four hotels, and 21 taverns flourishing. Then the mines went dry, and the town went bust. More recently, Cerrillos has been the location site for a number of television and Hollywood Westerns (*Young Guns, Lonesome Dove*). The town has a number of interesting shops along its tree-shaded streets, including **What Not Shop** (tel. 505/471–2744), which carries a little bit of just about everything. The **Casa Grand** (tel. 505/438–3008), a sprawling 21-room adobe, offers early mining exhibits, a gift shop, a petting zoo, and a scenic overlook.

When you're ready to return to Albuquerque, you can turn around and drive back the way you came, or head west when you reach NM 22 and drive to the **Santo Domingo Reservation and Trading Post** (*see* Pueblos Near Albuquerque in Chapter 7), then drive south to town.

Parks and Monuments

Aztec Ruins National Monument So named because early 19th-century settlers believed they had stumbled upon the Halls of Montezuma, Aztec contains 500 rooms laid out in an E-shaped plan around a plaza. Archaeologists recently restored the kiva here to mint condition, complete with a timbered roof packed with mud. The site even offers mood music; stereophonic Navajo chants can be summoned by the mere push of a button. There's a visitor center and a museum (ancient pottery, clothes, tools, and artifacts). A complete tour of the site takes about 90 minutes. *Aztec Ruins National Monument, Box 640, Aztec 87410, tel. 505/334–6174. I–25 north from Albuquerque to Bernalillo, NM 44 north another 140 mi to Aztec. Total driving time is 3½–4 hours one-way. Admission: $2 per person. The Golden Age Passport, issued to U.S. citizens 62 or older, allows free admission to all occupants of the same car, regardless of age. Open Memorial Day weekend–Labor Day weekend, daily 8–6:30; rest of the year, daily 8–5; closed Christmas and New Year's Day.*

Coronado State Monument Coronado State Monument is named in honor of the first Spanish expedition into the Southwest (1540–42). This prehistoric Kuaua pueblo, on a bluff overlooking the Rio Grande, is believed to have been the headquarters of Francisco Vasquez de Coronado's army of 1,200, who came seeking the legendary Seven Cities of Gold. The pueblo's restored kiva contains copies of magnificent frescoes done in black, yellow, red, blue, green, and white, depicting fertility rites, Rain dances, and hunting rituals; the original frescoes are preserved in a small, nearby museum next to the visitor center. The area is lovely. The Sandia Mountains rise abruptly from 5,280 to 10,678 feet a mere 6 miles away. The small community of Bernalillo, settled by Spanish colonists before Albuquerque was founded in 1706, is nearby. In the autumn, the views are especially breathtaking, with the trees turning russet and gold. Coronado State Monument is part of Coronado State Park, which has campsites and picnic grounds. *Coronado State Park, Box 853, Bernalillo 87004, tel. 505/867–5351. 1 mi northeast of Bernalillo on NM 44, off I–25. From Albuquerque's Old*

Town, travel 20 mi north on I–25 and take either the first turnoff (Bernalillo) or the second directly to the monument on NM 44. Admission: $2 adults, children 17 and under free. Open daily 9–6 except holidays.

Fort Sumner State Monument Established in 1862, Fort Sumner is located in De Baca County, 2 miles east of the town of Fort Sumner and 4 miles south of U.S. 60 on Billy the Kid Road along the east bank of the Pecos River. Artifacts and photographs on display—the Soldiers, the Native Americans, and Billy—relate to Fort Sumner and the Bosque Redondo Reservation, where 9,000 Navajos were interred from 1863 to 1868. Forced to make the infamous "Long Walk," they were brought to the site by Colonel Kit Carson from their original homeland in Canyon de Chelly, Arizona. The land was far from hospitable. Natural disasters destroyed crops, wood was scarce, and even the water from the Pecos proved unhealthy. Those who survived the harsh treatment and wretched living conditions (3,000 didn't) were allowed to return to Arizona in 1868. When the garrison left, the post was sold at auction and eventually converted into a large ranch. It's the same ranch where, in 1881, Sheriff Pat Garrett gunned down Billy the Kid, who's buried in a cemetery just off nearby NM 212. Adjacent is the Billy the Kid museum. *Fort Sumner State Monument, 2 mi east and 2 mi south of the town of Fort Sumner on NM 212, tel. 505/355–2573. I–40 east from Albuquerque to Santa Rosa, then NM 84 south for 45 mi and look for signs. Total distance from Albuquerque: about 180 mi. Admission: $2 adults, $1 children 6–16. Open May 1–Sept. 15, daily 9–6, Sept. 16–Apr. 30, daily 8–5. Closed all state holidays except July 4, Memorial Day, and Labor Day.*

Fort Selden State Monument Established in 1865 to protect settlers of the Mesilla Valley and pioneers who were traveling through, this fort was typical of frontier posts in the Southwest, consisting of flat-roofed adobe brick buildings arranged around a drill field. In the early 1880s, Captain Arthur MacArthur was appointed post commander. With him was his young son Douglas, who spent several years on the post. He grew up to become World War II hero General Douglas MacArthur. A permanent exhibit called "Fort Selden: An Adobe Post on the Rio Grande" depicts the roles of officers, enlisted men, and women on the American frontier during the Indian Wars. Food and gas are available locally, and there are camping facilities at the adjacent Leasburg State Park. *Fort Selden State Monument, 13 miles north of Las Cruces at the Radium Springs exit, off I–25, tel. 505/526–8911. I–25 south from Albuquerque to Exit 19, about 225 mi. Admission: $2 adults, $1 children 6–16. Open May 1–Sept. 15, daily 9–6, Sept. 16–Apr. 30, daily 8–5. Closed all state holidays except July 4, Memorial Day, and Labor Day.*

Petroglyph National Monument Located 8 miles west of Albuquerque in the West Mesa area, at the site of five extinct volcanoes, the Petroglyph National Monument contains nearly 15,000 ancient Native American rock drawings (petroglyphs) inscribed on the 17-mile-long West Mesa escarpment. Native American hunting parties camped at the base of the lava flows for thousands of years, chipping and scribbling away. Archaeologists believe the petroglyphs were carved on the lava formations between AD 1100 and 1600. Viewers can see many of the drawings—there are four walking trails—at this former state park. *Petroglyph National Monument, 6900 Unser Blvd. NW, Albuquerque 87120, tel. 505/897–8814 or 505/823–4016. Admission free; parking $1 weekdays, $2 weekends. Open Memorial Day–Labor Day, daily 9–6; rest of the year, daily 8–5.*

Rio Grande Nature Center State Park On the east bank of the Rio Grande in a cottonwood forest known as the "bosque," the Rio Grande Nature Center State Park is home to all manner of birds and migratory fowl that can be viewed year-round. Its unique visitor center is constructed half above and half below ground; viewing windows provide a look at what's going on at both levels as birds, frogs, ducks, and turtles do their thing. *2901 Candelaria Rd. NW, Albuquerque 87107, tel. 505/344–7240. Admission: adults $1, children 50¢; under 6 free. Open daily 10–5, closed major holidays.*

Shopping

Shopping anywhere in northern New Mexico brings on a feeling of *déjà vu:* After a while, one shop looks like the next. Still the prowl, shopping bag in hand, is well worth the effort. The tourist trail in New Mexico is paved with Native American arts and crafts (handsome turquoise and silver jewelry, baskets, blankets, pottery, etc.), Spanish Colonial handmade furniture, leather goods, textiles, colorful items from south of the border, trendy Taos and Santa Fe designs in interior furnishings, and antique mementos of the early West, everything from Billy the Kid's gunbelt (of dubious authenticity) to Kit Carson's hat (well, maybe). Tourist demand has forced prices up, but if you diligently stalk the fairs and powwows, the back-street shops, flea markets, and secondhand stores, you'll surely come away with a treasure or two.

When it comes to art, buy what you like and let the experts hiss and howl. But unless you're really knowledgeable, beware of those high-priced, once-in-a-lifetime purchases. You'll also find some funky, good-natured souvenir art and merchandise that's always worth a few dollars, if only as a keepsake of happy days spent visiting dusty pueblos or flea markets in the sun.

As with most large, sprawling Western cities, Albuquerque's main shopping areas are malls and shopping centers

scattered throughout the community. Hours are generally
10 AM–9 PM weekdays, Saturdays 10–6, and Sundays noon–6.

Shopping Malls

Among the major shopping centers are **Coronado Center**
(Louisiana Blvd. and Menaul Blvd., tel. 505/881–2700),
New Mexico's largest shopping center, with over 160 stores
including Broadway, Sears, and J.C. Penney; **Fashion
Square** (San Mateo Blvd. and Lomas Blvd., tel. 505/265–
6931), anchored by Kistler Collister department store, but
mostly filled with boutiques selling jewelry, shoes, home
furnishings, children's clothes, and beauty products; **First
Plaza Galeria** (20 First Plaza, tel. 505/242–3446), with a variety of small shops and restaurants; and **Winrock Center**
(Louisiana Blvd. exit off I–40, tel. 505/883–6132), with 120
stores, including Dillard's, Montgomery Ward, and Mar-
shall's, and 17 restaurants, from fast-food to upscale fare.

Specialty Stores

Antiques   The **Antique Specialty Mall** (4516 Central Ave. SE, tel. 505/
268–8080, and 330 Washington St. SE, tel. 505/256–9653) is
Albuquerque's most prestigious center for collectibles and
fine antiques, with special emphasis on memorabilia from
the early 1880s to the 1950s. When the set designers for the
hit television miniseries *Lonesome Dove* needed special
props to establish authenticity, they came here. At the
mall's two locations, collectors will find Art Deco and Art
Nouveau items, Depression glass, pottery, Native American arts and crafts, quilts and linens, vintage clothes,
cherrywood furniture, antique jewelry, and Western memorabilia.

Books   **Book Fare** (56901 Wyoming Blvd. NE, tel. 505/821–6758)
handles books on such subjects as horses, children, travel,
cooking, the Southwest, and nature and hiking guides. Also
available are large-print books, gift books, and books by local authors. The store also features a wide selection of domestic and foreign maps.
Page One (11200 Montgomery Blvd. NE, tel. 505/294–
2026), voted the best bookstore in Albuquerque by *Albuquerque Monthly Magazine*, is certainly one of the biggest,
claiming the largest selection of titles in New Mexico. It
also handles computer software, technical and professional
books, maps, globes, racing forms, and 150 out-of-state and
foreign newspapers.

Home   **Mariposa Gallery** (113 Romero St. NW, tel. 505/842–9658)
Furnishings   is a six-room Old Town space handling contemporary American crafts, including jewelry, sculptural art glass, mixed
media, clay works, and painted wooden coyotes in the tradition of New Mexican folk art.
Ortega's de Chimayo (324-C San Filipe Ave. NW, tel. 505/
842–5624) is the Old Town showcase of the Ortega family's

famous weaving and arts-and-crafts shop in Chimayo, the tiny village located on the High Road between Santa Fe and Taos (*see* Excursion 3 in Chapter 3). One of the original families to settle Chimayo, the Ortegas have been weavers for eight generations, from Gabriel de Ortega in the early 1700s to 13-year-old Katherine Ortega, the youngest weaver in the family today. Also featured are Southwestern paintings, *santos* (saints) and other wood carvings, kachina dolls, and Navajo and contemporary rugs and blankets.

Native American Arts and Crafts

Adobe Gallery (413 Romero St. NW, tel. 505/243–8485) specializes in historic and contemporary art of the Southwestern Native Americans: Pueblo pottery, Hopi kachinas, Navajo rugs, blankets, and paintings. Founded in 1978, the shop is housed in a historic *terrones adobe* (bricks are cut from the ground rather than formed from mud and dried) homestead that dates from 1878; it is owned and managed by Alexander E. Anthony, Jr. The shop also has an extensive stock of books about Southwestern Native Americans.

Andrews Pueblo Pottery (Suite 8, 400 San Felipe Ave. NW, tel. 505/243–0414) handles Pueblo pottery, fetishes, kachina dolls, and Southwestern graphics.

Penfield Gallery of Indian Arts (2043 S. Plaza Ave. NW, tel. 505/242–9696) is owned by Julia Reidy, who specializes in Pueblo pottery, storytellers, Hopi jewelry, kachina dolls, Zuni fetishes, and sand paintings.

Sam English Gallery (400 San Felipe Ave. NW, tel. 505/843–9332), a half block north off the Plaza in Old Town, features traditional and contemporary Native American works, plus oils, watercolors, prints, and lithographs by Sam English and his son, Sam Jr.

Tanner Channey Gallery (410 Romero St. NW, tel. 505/247–2242) is housed in a beautiful old pre–Civil War adobe hacienda in Old Town. On display in several showrooms is an extensive collection of jewelry, sculpture, contemporary and historic pottery, and weaving by Native Americans. Huge hand-carved wooden doors lead from the showrooms to a flagstone patio, shaded by old *latillas* (strips of wood laid in a herringbone pattern); bougainvilleas and hibiscus tumble this way and that; and the famous Angel of Old Town fountain bubbles forth. It's one of the prettiest courtyards in town. The main showroom, the Great Gallery, is filled with Navajo rugs (some dating from the early 1800s), pottery, baskets, and an extensive selection of books on the Southwest. The shop also has a branch at the Hyatt Regency.

Weyrich Gallery (2935D Louisiana Blvd. E, tel. 505/883–7410) features contemporary and traditional fine crafts, jewelry, sculpture, etchings, clay, paintings, and clothing.

Wright's Collection of Indian Arts (6600 Indian School Rd., tel. 505/883–6122), one block north of the Marriott in Park Square, was founded as a trading post in 1907. Considerably more upscale these days, Wright's offers authentic Native American arts and crafts, from the traditional to the contemporary. Shoppers may also visit the unique museum on the premises, with its impressive display of Southwestern art and pottery.

Art Galleries **Amapola Gallery** (2045 S. Plaza St. NW, tel. 505/242–4311), just west of the Plaza near Rio Grande Boulevard, has a lovely cobbled courtyard and an indoor space, both of which are overflowing with pottery, paintings, textiles, carvings, baskets, jewelry, and more. It's worth a visit just to see the handsome displays. Amapola is one of the largest co-op galleries in New Mexico.

Concetta D. Gallery (Suite 29, 20 First Plaza NW, tel. 505/ 243–5066) features multimedia, traditional, and contemporary art by Southwestern artists.

Dartmouth Street Gallery (3011 Monte Vista Blvd. NE, tel. 505/266–7751) is owned by John Cacciatore, who handles paintings and tapestries by regional artists.

Navajo Gallery (323 Romero St. NW, tel. 505/843–7666) is the Albuquerque branch of famed Navajo artist R. C. Gorman's trend-setting Taos space. The first Native American painter to open his own fine-arts gallery, Gorman now has outlets in Hawaii, New York, and Tokyo that represent his work exclusively.

Russell's Gallery (7720 Central Ave. SE, tel. 505/255–1918) features works from several area painters and a select group of signed and numbered prints by internationally acclaimed Southwestern artists, including Bill Rabbit and Robert Redbird. Also featured are the paintings and ceramics of co-owner Vera Russell. The latter are hand-cast pottery pieces accented with Native American figures and scenes of Southwestern landscapes.

Weems Gallery (2801-M Eubank Blvd. NE, tel. 505/293–6133) represents over 150 artists, with emphasis on originality and quality. Featured are paintings, pottery, sculpture, jewelry, weaving, stained glass, and original-design clothes. Gift items and a framing service are also available.

Sports and the Outdoors

Participant Sports

The **Albuquerque Parks and Recreation Department** (Box 1293, Albuquerque 87103, tel. 505/768–3490) maintains a widely diversified network of parks and recreational programs, encompassing over 20,000 acres of open space, four golf courses, 200 parks, six paved tracks for biking and jogging, as well as numerous recreational facilities, such as swimming pools, tennis courts, ball fields, playgrounds, and even a shooting range.

Ballooning Known for its Kodak International Balloon Fiesta (*see* Spectator Sports, *below*), Albuquerque also offers myriad opportunities for those who want to take to the skies themselves. If you'd like to give it a try, contact any of the following:

A & R Sky Voyages (2901 Oak Hills St., tel. 505/891–9529).
Ad Venture Balloons (31232 San Mateo NE, tel. 505/298–8887).
Aerco Balloon Port (523 Rankin Rd., tel. 505/344–5844).
Balloon Fiesta (8309 Washington Pl. NE, tel. 505/821–1000).
Cameron Balloons New Mexico (2950 San Joaquin Ave. SE, tel. 505/265–4007).
Duke City Balloonport (12100 Anaheim Ave. NE, tel. 505/299–5481).
Rainbow Riders (430 Montclaire Dr. SE, tel. 505/268–3401).
World Balloon Corporation (4800 Eubank Blvd. NE, tel. 505/293–6800).

Bicycling   Albuquerque is big on biking, both as a recreational sport and as a means of cutting down on automobile traffic and its resulting emissions. In 1973, the city established a network of bikeways, recommending existing streets and roadways as bike routes, lanes, and trails. Since then, many new ones have been added, and the program continues to expand. On designated bike routes, bicycles share lanes of traffic with automobiles, with no separation between car and bicycle; the bicyclist has the same right to use the street as does the motorist and must obey the same traffic laws and signals. Bike lanes, on the other hand, are designated exclusively for bike riders. Designated Recreational Trails are shared with pedestrians and provide the safest off-road area for both (*see* Jogging, *below*, for a list of these routes). An elaborately detailed **Metropolitan Albuquerque Bicycle Map** can be obtained free of charge by calling 505/768–3550. The foldout map also includes rules and regulations concerning biking in the city, as well as safety tips. For information about mountain biking in the adjacent national forest, call the Sandia Ranger Station (tel. 505/281–3304).

Golf   The Albuquerque Parks and Recreation Department maintains four public golf courses. Greens fees range from $7.35 for nine holes to $11.55 for 18 holes, with special discount rates for Early Bird and Sundown play. (The courses are open from sunup to sundown.) Each has a clubhouse and pro shop, where clubs and equipment can be rented. Weekday play is on a first-come basis, but reservations are advised for weekend use. The city's **Golf Management Office** (6401 Osuna Rd. NE, tel. 505/888–8115) can provide more information.

Arroyo del Oso (7001 Osuna Rd. NE, tel. 505/884–7505) has an 18- and a 9-hole regulation course and practice facilities. Selected as one of the top 50 27-hole public golf courses in the country by *Golf Digest*, **Puerto del Sol** offers a driving range, a full-service restaurant, and an up-to-the-hour information line for tee-off status (tel. 505/889–3699).

At **Ladera** (3401 Ladera Dr. NW, tel. 505/836–4449), 10 miles west of downtown, there are an 18-hole regulation course, practice facilities, a 9-hole executive course, a large driving range, a restaurant, and a full-service pro shop.

Los Altos (9717 Cooper Ave. NE, tel. 505/298–1897) includes an 18-hole regulation course, a short 9-hole course, and practice facilities. One of the Southwest's most popular facilities, Los Altos has a driving range, grass tees, a restaurant (mainly Mexican food), instructors for individuals or groups, and a large selection of rental equipment.

Located near the Albuquerque airport, **Puerto del Sol** (1800 Girard Blvd. SE, tel. 505/265–5636) has a 9-hole regulation course, a lighted driving range, and a full-service pro shop. There are no reservations for tee times.

The University of New Mexico also maintains two public golf courses. One, **UNM North** (on Yale Blvd., tel. 505/277–4149), is a first-class 9-hole course on campus; the other, **UNM South** (on Rio Bravo, tel. 505/277–4546), is an 18-hole championship course, including an excellent beginners' 3-hole regulation course. Both are open daily (except Christmas) and have full-service pro shops, instruction, and snack bars offering New Mexican favorites.

Health Clubs Most of the large hotel health clubs are reserved for guests' use only. However, keeping fit in Albuquerque is easy, with numerous health clubs, gyms, and fitness centers from which to choose in virtually every neighborhood.

Albuquerque Rock Gym (3300 Princeton Dr. NE, tel. 505/881–3073) has a complete indoor climbing facility, with a pro shop and equipment rentals. It's one block east of I–25, one block north of Candelaria Road.

Body Elite (640 Coors Blvd. NW, No. 15, tel. 505/831–2934) offers complete body management, with free weights, specialized machines, aerobics, personalized training programs, sauna, whirlpool, karate lessons, tanning, and daycare facilities. The walk-in fee for nonmembers is $5.

Downtown Athletic Club (40 First Plaza, tel. 505/242–1500) has free weights, handball/racquetball courts, a heated swimming pool, rowing machines, treadmills, aerobicycles, Nautilus equipment, sauna, whirlpools, massages, tanning—and a fine downtown location. Nonmembers pay $10.50 per day.

Gold's Gym (5001 Montgomery NE, Suite 147, tel. 505/881–8500) is a state-of-the-art fitness complex, part of the national chain. It offers free weights, a cardiovascular deck, aerobics, sportswear, and Pro-line supplements. Nonmembers pay $8 per day.

The facilities at **Liberty Gym** (2401 Jefferson St. NE, tel. 505/884–8012), one of the largest body-building and fitness centers in the Southwest, include specialized machines (such as Stairmasters), free weights, personalized instruction, and nutritional counseling. The nonmembers' walk-in fee is $5.

Jogging The **Albuquerque Parks and Recreation Department** maintains an extensive network of Designated Recreational Trails that joggers share with bicyclists, as follows:

Bear Canyon, a 1-mile trail along the Bear Arroyo, extends east from Eubank Boulevard to Juan Tabo Boulevard, going through El Oso Grande Park.

Embudo, a 1½-mile trail, connects with the Las Montanas trail at Morris Street NE, then runs east along the Embudo Channel to Tramway Boulevard. A bicycle-pedestrian bridge at Tramway Boulevard links this with the Tramway Trail.

Jefferson-Osuna, a 4-mile trail, runs along the Bear Arroyo between Jefferson Street and Osuna Road NE.

Paseo del Bosque, a 5-mile trail, is parallel to the irrigation ditch on the east side of the Rio Grande. Trail users may enter at Candelaria, Campbell, and Mountain roads or at Central Avenue SW.

Paseo de las Montanas, a 4.2-mile trail, goes from east of Winrock at Pennsylvania Street to Tramway Boulevard NE.

Paseo de Nordeste, a 6.13-mile asphalt trail, begins at Tucker Avenue (University of New Mexico campus) and ends at Sandia High School, Pennsylvania Street NE.

Pino, a 1.5-mile trail, starts at Wyoming Boulevard near Harper Road at the Albuquerque Academy and proceeds west along the South Pino Channel to San Pedro Drive NE.

Tramway, a 4-mile trail, runs along the east side of Tramway Road from Montgomery Boulevard to I–40.

Swimming The City of Albuquerque has a number of year-round pools that are open to both lap and recreational swimming. (Admission: children 6 and under 35¢, children 7–12 $1, children 13–19 $1.50, adults $1.75, and senior citizens 25¢. Special monthly and yearly rates are available. A number of pools have swim-for-25¢ Friday-night specials.)

Highland Pool (400 Jackson St. SE, tel. 505/256–2096) is open for lap swimming 6–8 AM and 11:45 AM–12:30 PM for adults only on weekdays, and for recreational swimming at all other times.

Los Altos Pool (10100 Lomas Blvd. NE, tel. 505/291–6290) has lap-swim hours for adults only 6–9 AM weekdays, and recreational-swimming hours at all other times.

Sandia Pool (7801 Candelaria Rd. NE, tel. 505/291–6279) is open for lap swimming 6–8 AM and 4:30–6 PM for adults weekdays only and for recreational swimming at all other times.

Valley Pool (1505 Candelaria Rd. NW, tel. 505/761–4086) is reserved for lap swimming for adults only 6–8 AM and 4:30–6 PM weekdays, and for recreational swimming at all other times.

A number of public swimming pools are open only from June 1 to August 18:

East San José (2015 Galena St. SE, tel. 505/848–1396), weekdays noon–4 and weekends noon–5.

Eisenhower (11001 Cino Cuatro NE, tel. 505/291–6292), weekdays 12:30–5 and weekends noon–5.

Montgomery (5301 Palo Duro Ave. NE, tel. 505/888–8123), weekdays 12:30–5 and weekends noon–5.

Rio Grande (1410 Iron Ave. SW, tel. 505/848–1397), weekdays 12:30–5 and weekends noon–5; lap swimming only weekdays noon–1.

Sierra Vista (1410 Iron Ave. SW, tel. 505/897–8819), weekdays 12:30–5 and weekends noon–5; reserved for lap swimming weekdays 5:15–6:15.

Sunport (5301 Palo Duro Ave. NE, tel. 505/848–1398), weekdays 12:30–5 and weekends noon–5.

West Mesa (5301 Palo Duro Ave. NW, tel. 505/836–8718), weekdays 12:30–5 and weekends noon–5.

Wilson (6000 Anderson Ave. SE, tel. 505/256–2095), weekdays 12:30–5 and weekends noon–5.

Tennis Albuquerque's wide-ranging network of public parks contains nearly three dozen public tennis facilities that generally have one to six courts. Lessons are available at some; others are lighted for night play (until 10 PM). For information call the Albuquerque Parks and Recreation Department (tel. 505/848–1381). In addition, the city maintains three tennis complexes.

Albuquerque Tennis Complex (1903 Stadium Blvd. SE, tel. 505/848–1381) consists of 16 Laykold tennis courts and 4 racquetball/handball courts, which may be reserved by phone or in person; reservations are taken two days in advance at 10 AM. The rate is $2 per hour.

The **Jerry Cline Tennis Complex** (Louisiana Blvd. and Constitution Ave., tel. 505/256–2032) has 12 Laykold courts, 3 of which are lighted. There is no charge, and no reservations are needed to play here.

Sierra Vista Tennis Complex (5001 Montano Rd. NW, tel. 505/848–1381) consists of 10 tennis courts (2 Omni courts), 2 platform tennis courts, and a swimming-pool area. The reservation policy and charge for courts are the same as at the Albuquerque Tennis Complex. No racquetball facilities are available.

Along with the numerous tennis courts located in the city's various hotels and resorts (*see* Lodging, *below*), a number of private clubs have excellent facilities and generally allow guest privileges at a member's invitation or honor memberships from out-of-town clubs with reciprocal arrangements or equal status. Among these are the **Highpoint Racquet and Swim Club** (43001 Landau Dr. NE, tel. 505/293–5820), **Tanoan Country Club** (10801 Academy Rd. NE, tel. 505/822–0455), and the **Tennis Club of Albuquerque** (2901 Indian School Rd. NE, tel. 505/262–1691).

Spectator Sports

The **Albuquerque Dukes** are the Triple-A farm team of the Los Angeles Dodgers and members of the Pacific Coast League; Orel Hershiser is a Dukes alumnus. Exciting professional baseball can be seen from April through September at the city-owned Albuquerque Sports Stadium, located at Stadium and University boulevards, the only stadium anywhere with a drive-in spectator area. Admission varies from $1 to $4. Call or write the Albuquerque Dukes (1601 Stadium Blvd. SE, Albuquerque 87125, tel. 505/243–1791) for schedules and information.

The **University of New Mexico's** Lobo football and basketball games are also a major draw. The University Arena has a 17,000-seat capacity to accommodate the city's intensely loyal UNM basketball fans. Across the street is the 30,000-seat Lobo football stadium. For schedules and ticket information, call 505/277–3901 (basketball) and 505/277–2116 (football).

Downs at Albuquerque is a glass-enclosed, climate-controlled racing facility located in the center of Albuquerque at the State Fairgrounds. Quarter-horse and Thoroughbred racing begins in January and runs through June 10. General admission, including parking, is $2, with preferred seating tickets from $4 to $6. Afternoon racing takes place on Friday, Saturday, Sunday, and holidays. Call 505/262–1188 for post times.

Ballooning Mention hot-air ballooning to an enthusiast, and Albuquerque automatically comes to mind. The city's high altitude, few obstructions, and steady but manageable winds make it especially suitable. Albuquerque's long history of ballooning dates from 1882, when Professor Park A. Van Tassel, a saloon keeper, made the first balloon ascent at the Territorial Fair. Van Tassel's craft was destroyed during a subsequent flight, but that didn't dampen his enthusiasm. He bought another balloon; went on a world flight; and, during the trip, fell into the Pacific Ocean, where, it was rumored, he was eaten by sharks.

Since those colorful early beginnings, Albuquerque has become the hot-air-balloon capital of the world, partly because of the success of the annual **Kodak Albuquerque**

International Balloon Fiesta, the first one of which took place in 1972, when 16 balloons participated. Today the nine-day event, held in early October, is the largest hot-air-balloon gathering in the world, attracting more than 500 registered hot-air balloons and entrants from as far away as Australia and Japan.

A special feature of the annual gathering is the "balloon glow," when hundreds of balloons are inflated after the sun sets. Propane burners send heat into the colorful envelopes, the balloons light up like giant light bulbs, and the magical glow can be seen for miles. The balloons remain grounded, or tethered; ballooning at night, when balloonists can't see telephone wires or other obstacles, is forbidden.

An estimated 1.5 million people attend the nine-day program, and thousands more glimpse the balloons as they float over Albuquerque's backyards, setting off a serenade of barking dogs. Most spectacular are the Saturday- and Sunday-morning ascensions on the opening and closing weekends of the fiesta. In the early hours of dawn 500 massive, candy-colored balloons are inflated and, shortly after, lift off, silently caressing the sky with fantasy and brilliance. It is one of New Mexico's biggest draws for out-of-state visitors and a delight for those who live here. For additional information, contact Kodak Albuquerque International Balloon Fiesta (8309 Washington Pl. NE, 87113, tel. 505/821–1000).

Dining

Albuquerque, like many cities in the West, loves to eat out. Many of the city's favorite dining spots specialize in northern New Mexican–style cooking, with flavorful Spanish recipes that have been handed down for generations. (*See* Dining in Chapter 1 for an explanation of Mexican food terms.) French, Continental, Mediterranean, and Italian fare are also readily available, as are standard American favorites of seafood, steaks, and burgers. The clientele is folksy for the most part. You can dress as casually as you like and order wine by color instead of label. Restaurants in the major business hotels tend to be a bit more formal, of course, but as the evening wears down, so do the restrictions.

Highly recommended restaurants in each price category are indicated by a star ★.

Category	Cost*
Expensive	over $20
Moderate	$16–$20
Inexpensive	under $16

per person, excluding drinks, service, and sales tax (5.75%)

Expensive **High Noon Restaurant and Saloon.** Located in one of Old Town's original 200-year-old adobe buildings, this restaurant was once a woodworking shop. It now offers fine dining in a Territorial setting, with viga ceilings, brick floors, and handmade Southwestern tables and chairs. A skylight offers cool, defused lighting during the day and a glimpse of the sky at night. Native American rugs and New Mexican art decorate the walls, and antique pots rest on ledges and sills. White tablecloths and well-appointed table settings offer an upscale accent. A flamenco guitarist plays here on weekends. Topping the menu offerings are pepper steak, steak Diane, seafood specials, and Southwestern dishes, along with veal, chicken, and beef entrées. *425 San Felipe Ave. NW, tel. 505/765–1455. Reservations suggested. Jacket and tie advised. AE, D, DC, MC, V.*

Monte Vista Firestation. This spacious, airy restaurant on Central Avenue was once an actual working fire station—it even has a brass pole. The adobe-style building, built in 1936, was used as a fire station until 1972; it's listed on Albuquerque's National Register of Historic Places. The new American menu includes a wide variety of seafood, beef, and pasta dishes; wild mushroom cakes and crab cakes highlight the menu. Chef Rosa Rajkovic was recently nominated for a James Beard Award. *3201 Central Ave. NE, tel. 505/255–2424. Reservations suggested. Dress: casual. AE, DC, MC, V. No lunch weekends.*

Rio Grande Yacht Club. This restaurant, located two blocks north of the airport, offers fresh seafood and traditional American entrées—baby-back ribs, smoked pork loin, steaks, and chicken—in a nautical atmosphere. The dining room has lots of wood and brass, accented with hanging greenery; vintage prints and paintings of clipper ships, fish, and foaming seas hang on the walls. Other yachty touches include an ornate steering wheel looking fresh from the South Pacific and a colored sailcloth hanging from one section of the dining room, which is built in levels. The floors are carpeted; the tables are of wood with black inlay designs; and the chairs are captain's, of course. The full-service bar is nautical as well. There is also background music, patio dining in warmer weather, and a fireplace for cooler evenings. *2500 Yale Blvd. SE, tel. 505/243–6111. Reservations required. Jacket and tie advised. AE, D, DC, MC, V.*

Moderate **Antiquity Restaurant.** This secluded restaurant is in the heart of Old Town, with adobe walls as old as time (thus the name). Two separate dining areas face an open kitchen with

Antiquity
Restaurant, **13**
Artichoke Cafe, **10**
Bella Vista, **3**
Casa Vieja, **1**
Classic Grille, **5**
Cooperage Restaurant
and Lounge, **6**
El Pinto, **2**
High Noon Restaurant
and Saloon, **15**
La Hacienda
Cantina, **11**
La Placita, **14**
Maria Teresa, **12**
Monte Vista
Firestation, **7**
Rio Grande Yacht
Club, **8**
Seagull Street, **4**
66 Diner, **9**

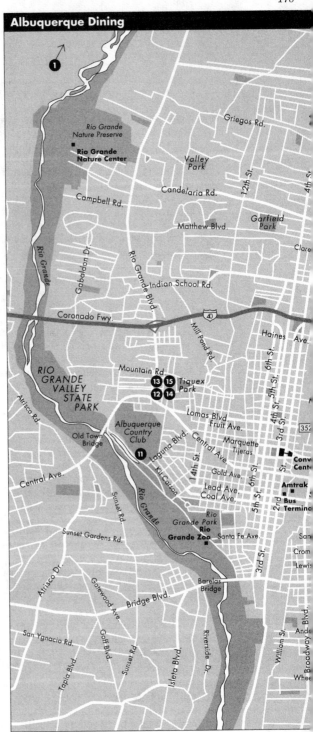

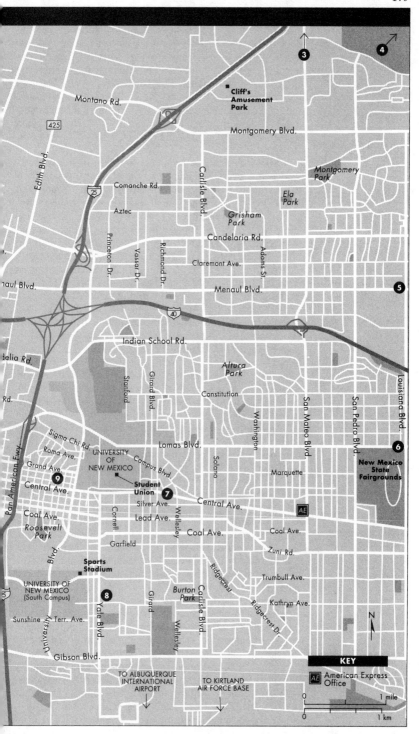

Montano Rd.

Cliff's
Amusement
Park

Montgomery Blvd.

Edith Blvd.

425

Comanche Rd.

Montgomery
Park

Aztec

Ela
Park

Grisham
Park

Candelaria Rd.

Claremont Ave.

Carlisle Blvd.

Princeton Dr.

Vassar Dr.

Richmond Dr.

Adams St.

Menaul Blvd.

naul Blvd.

Indian School Rd.

delia Rd.

Altura
Park

Rd.

Constitution

Stanford

Girard Blvd.

Washington

San Mateo Blvd.

San Pedro Blvd.

Louisiana Blvd.

New Mexico
State
Fairgrounds

Sigma Chi Rd.

Roma Ave.

Grand Ave.

UNIVERSITY
OF
NEW MEXICO

Campus Blvd.

Lomas Blvd.

Solano

Central Ave.

Coal Ave.

Roosevelt
Park

Student
Union

Silver Ave.

Lead Ave.

Coal Ave.

Marquette

Central Ave.

AE

Coal Ave.

Cornell

Wellesley

Garfield

Zuni Rd.

Sports
Stadium

UNIVERSITY OF
NEW MEXICO
(South Campus)

Pan American Fwy

Blvd.

Yale Blvd.

Girard

Burton
Park

Carlisle Blvd.

Wellesley

Ridgecrest

Ridgecrest Dr.

Trumbull Ave.

Kathryn Ave.

Sunshine Terr. Ave.

University

Gibson Blvd.

N

TO ALBUQUERQUE
INTERNATIONAL
AIRPORT

TO KIRTLAND
AIR FORCE BASE

KEY

AE American Express
Office

0   1 mile

0   1 km

a charcoal grill, where the chef performs his wonders for all to see. The floors are brick, and local art is featured on the walls, along with framed posters touting the glories of Albuquerque, its balloon rallies and art festivals. The restaurant was originally built as a honeymoon cottage, and the aura of romance remains. This Old Town favorite features chateaubriand and charcoal-grilled steaks, fresh seafood, veal, and excellent homemade desserts in an intimate setting. *1112 Romero St. NW, tel. 505/247–3545. Reservations suggested. Dress: casual. AE, D, DC, MC, V. No lunch. Closed Sun.*

★ **Artichoke Cafe.** This outstanding café, located in a turn-of-the-century brick building just east of downtown on Central Avenue, offers a variety of cuisines—new American, Italian, and some French—and specializes in broiled salmon, veal, and lamb. Founded in 1989 by Terry Keene (his wife, Patricia, is the chef), the restaurant, which does all its own baking, has gotten high local acclaim. The building is old, but the decor is uptown modern—soft muted colors, a few plants, lots of art. Its one large dining room on three broad levels spills onto a small courtyard, where there are seven tables. Exhibited on the dining-room walls, and replaced every two months, are the works of local artists, some established, others up-and-coming. All the paintings are for sale. *424 Central Ave. SE, tel. 505/243–0200. Reservations suggested. Dress: casual. AE, D, DC, MC, V. Closed Sun.*

Bella Vista. Set on a tree-covered hill in Cedar Crest, about 20 miles east of town, this restaurant specializes in steaks and seafood; lobster tails are particularly popular. Preparations are Italian, American, and Mexican style, but the red tablecloths and taped background music will bring you quickly back to Sorrento. The restaurant is in a huge, rambling building with 12 dining rooms, six of which have gaslog fireplaces. The Bella Vista has a seating capacity of 1,200, making it one of the few restaurants anywhere where any number of people could turn up without reservations and barely fluster the maître d'. The full bar holds almost as many people as does the restaurant itself. Founded in 1961 as an "all-you-can-eat" restaurant, one of the first anywhere to establish this policy, it still offers all-you-can-eat chicken, fish, spaghetti, and Mexican dishes, but draws the line on lobster and steak. Bella Vista also has a packaged liquor store, deli, and seafood mart. *N. Hwy. 14, Cedar Crest, tel. 505/281–3370 or 505/281–3914. Reservations suggested. Dress: casual. AE, MC, V.*

★ **Casa Vieja.** Casa Vieja, in Corrales about 13 miles northwest of Albuquerque, offers Continental dining in a charming 280-year-old adobe that has a history almost as long as its menu. The oldest building in Corrales, it was originally a homestead, then became a church, the territorial governor's home, and a military outpost; it became a restaurant in 1970. There are two large dining rooms, a smaller one, and a patio for outdoor dining in the summer. With beamed viga ceilings, regional paintings, Native American rugs on the walls, and handsome tinwork on the hand-carved doors, it has a rich frontier flavor without straining to achieve it. Owner-chef Jean Pierre Gozard specializes in French and northern Italian cuisine, with wild game, quail, duck, and pheasant offered in season. *4541 Corrales Rd., tel. 505/ 898-7489. Reservations suggested. Jacket and tie required. AE, D, DC, MC, V. Dinner only. Closed Mon.*

Classic Grille. The elegant and formal Chardonnay's restaurant recently underwent a drastic concept change; the result is The Classic Grille, a comfortable and casual spot with an emphasis on mesquite-grilled meats and seafood. The menu lists everything from steaks and ribs to shrimp and yellow fin tuna, all cooked and flavored on a mesquite-wood-burning grill and served with your choice of a variety of sauces; nongrilled items, such as pasta dishes and salads, are also available. A broad selection of reasonably priced California wines is featured on the wine list. The dining room has cozy alcoves, walnut paneling, and lots of leafy plants. A chrome antique car grill (1941 Mercedes) on the host station is a whimsical decorative touch. *Ramada Hotel Classic, 6815 Menaul Blvd., tel. 505/881-0000. Reservations suggested. Dress: casual. AE, D, DC, MC, V. No lunch Sat. Closed Sun.*

Cooperage Restaurant and Lounge. As the name suggests—cooperage means barrel making—the one-story restaurant is built to resemble an enormous barrel. The top of the barrel is a skylight, offering atrium dining below. The main dining room is dominated by a huge lightning-shaped salad bar, surrounded by circular rooms with intimate nooks and booths. The decor is bright and cheerful, with light tan walls, green carpeting, and bay windows that afford diners a good view of the world outside. Featured on the menu are prime rib, lobster, and steaks. On weekends there's dancing in the lounge to blues and jazz (*see* Nightlife, *below*). *7220 Lomas Blvd. NE, tel. 505/255-1657. Reservations suggested. Dress: casual. AE, D, DC, MC, V.*

El Pinto. This family-owned Mexican restaurant has been in business since 1962. It is located in an adobe-style hacienda, with shade trees and a year-round heated dining patio (the largest in New Mexico). Specialties include chiles rellenos, hot or mild Hatch (a breed apart in the world of chili), *sopa de pollo* (chicken soup), fajitas, tamales, and frijoles. There's a full bar and soft Mexican background music. *10500 Fourth St. NW, tel. 505/898-1771. Reservations suggested. Dress: casual. AE, MC, V.*

★ **La Hacienda Cantina.** Ted Garcia, chef-owner of this restaurant, also owns and operates La Hacienda restaurant in Old Town (only blocks away), and seems to manage to be in both places at once, meeting and greeting customers and dashing into the kitchen to see what's cooking. The menu here features a wide range of Mexican specialties—fajitas, enchiladas New Mexico, sopaipillas, chiles rellenos, and chimichangas—as well as a number of fine northern Italian dishes to placate longtime customers of the site's former occupant, Al Monte's, whose owner and namesake died in 1990 after more than 40 years in business. The decor of the new restaurant is bright and colorfully Mexican throughout, while retaining some of the furnishings from the previous establishment, including the handsome wooden tables with copper tops and the five fireplaces that glow cozily in wintertime. In the full bar the margaritas flow and happy hour reigns from 5 to 7 on weekdays and from 8 to 10 on Saturday. Sunday brunch lasts from 11 to 4. Weather permitting, there's dining alfresco on the patio. *1306 Rio Grande Blvd., tel. 505/243-3709. Reservations suggested. Dress: casual. AE, DC, MC, V.*

La Placita. Housed in a historic hacienda on Old Town Plaza, La Placita offers traditional New Mexican dishes, such as chiles rellenos, enchiladas, tacos, and sopaipillas, plus a wide selection of American entrées. The building dates from 1706. For years it housed Ambrosio Armijo's mercantile store, where ladies' lace gloves sold for 10¢ a pair and gents' linen underdrawers could be purchased for $1. The adobe walls are 3 feet thick in places. La Placita has six dining rooms, and since it's an art gallery as well, patrons dine surrounded by outstanding examples of Native American and Southwestern painting. *302 San Felipe Ave. NW, tel. 505/247-2204. Reservations suggested. Dress: casual. AE, D, DC, MC, V.*

Maria Teresa. This nationally preserved landmark in historic Old Town, next to the Sheraton, offers aged beef, seafood, poultry, and New Mexican specialties; recommended entrées include chicken Acapulco (breast of chicken stuffed with avocado and crab, topped with a delicate lemon-lime sauce) and *carne adovada* (cubed, marinated pork, rolled in a flour tortilla and covered with red chiles and cheese). The restored 1840s adobe, its 32-inch-thick brick adobe walls plastered with straw and more adobe, is entered through an attractive courtyard, a cool oasis even during the hottest days of summer. Maria Teresa's has early Spanish American furnishings—chests, carvings, and tables—Southwestern paintings, fireplaces, and walled gardens. In the summer, everyone wants to eat in the Plum Tree Courtyard. *618 Rio Grande Blvd. NW, tel. 505/242-3900. Reservations suggested. Jacket and tie advised. AE, D, DC, MC, V.*

Seagull Street. Seagull Street is a little bit of Cape Cod, clapboard shingles and all, set down in Albuquerque, where fresh fish is grilled over mesquite fires. The restaurant features an average of 20 seafood entrées flown in daily from Pacific, Atlantic, and Gulf waters. Choice cuts of steak are also offered. Tables set up on the dock outside (a little bit of Cape Cod, remember?) are the perfect place to enjoy cocktails and oysters on the half shell. The decor is nautical, outside and in, with starfish, fish nets, and pictures of boats and sea captains on the walls. *5410 Academy Rd. NE, tel.*

505/821–0020. Reservations suggested. Dress: casual. AE, DC, MC, V. No lunch Sat.

Inexpensive **66 Diner.** Once a transmission shop on old Route 66, the 66
★ Diner is now a glitzy art deco establishment with neon
lights outside, black-and-white tile floors and turquoise-
and-pink vinyl seats (rarely an empty one) inside. Burgers,
blue-plate specials—spaghetti and meatballs, pot roast,
chicken-fried steak, grilled liver and onions, and beef
stew—and a separate soda fountain all add to the pervasive
tone of 1950s nostalgia, as do the framed photos of old
Route 66 on the wall. The soda fountain's milkshakes were
voted the best in town by a local publication, but you might
want to try the 95¢ hot fudge sundae (small but yummy).
*1405 Central Ave. NE, tel. 505/247–1421. No reservations.
Dress: casual. AE, MC, V.*

Lodging

As is typical of many large cities in the Southwest today,
Albuquerque's hotels offer a comfortable mix of modern
conveniences and technology and Old West flavor. The
city's accommodations range from budget motels to bed-
and-breakfast inns to soaring hotel skyscrapers. All are
uniformly friendly and folksy, and include much of the
Southwest heritage in their decor and design. A waitress
sitting down to chat with customers having dinner in a restaurant may be the stuff of TV sitcoms, but in the West—
and cities come no more "Western" than Albuquerque—it
really happens. This informality rubs off on guests as well.
Ties come off, boots come on, and the streets outside are lit-
tered with briefcases.

Highly recommended lodgings in each price category are
indicated by a star ★.

Category	Cost*
Expensive	over $100
Moderate	$65–$100
Inexpensive	under $65

**All prices are for a standard double room, excluding 5% room
tax, 5.75% sales tax, and service charges.*

Hotels

Expensive **Albuquerque Hilton.** The charm and decor of the colorful
Southwest—Native American rugs, arched doorways, and
high ceilings—are blended with the sophistication and elegance of a contemporary hotel at the Albuquerque Hilton,
located just 2 miles from downtown. The guest rooms are
done in Southwestern pastels, with Santa Fe–style wooden
furniture and bleached wood bedsteads; many have balco-

Albuquerque Hilton, **8**

Albuquerque
Marriott, **9**

American Inn, **12**

Barcelona Court
All-Suite Hotel, **10**

Best Western Fred
Harvey Hotel, **14**

Casa del Granjero, **6**

Casas de Suenos, **18**

Casita Chamisa, **20**

Corrales Inn, **1**

DeAnza Motor
Lodge, **13**

Elaine's, A Bed and
Breakfast, **2**

Howard Johnson
Plaza Hotel, **4**

Hyatt Regency
Albuquerque, **17**

La Posada de
Albuquerque, **16**

Le Pommier, **3**

Radisson, **15**

Ramada Hotel
Classic, **7**

Sheraton Old Town, **19**

Turquoise Inn Bed and
Breakfast, **5**

William E. Mauger
Estate, **11**

Windmill Ranch Bed
and Breakfast, **21**

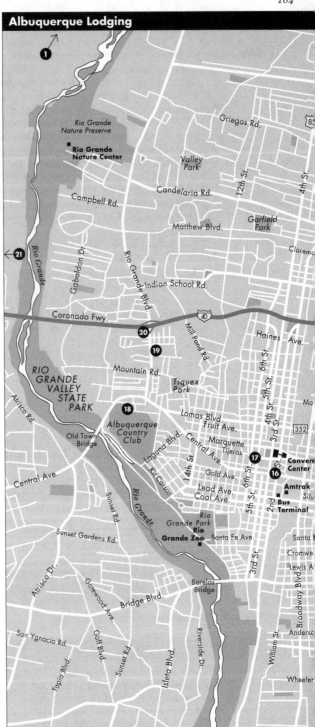

Albuquerque Lodging

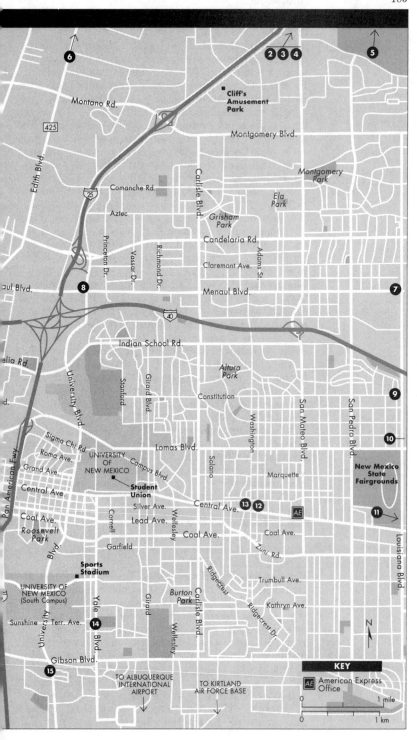

Cliff's Amusement Park

Montano Rd.

425

Edith Blvd.

I-25

Montgomery Blvd.

Montgomery Park

Comanche Rd.

Aztec

Carlisle Blvd.

Ela Park

Grisham Park

Candelaria Rd.

Claremont Ave.

Adams St.

Princeton Dr.

Vassar Dr.

Richmond Dr.

aul Blvd.

Menaul Blvd.

I-40

Indian School Rd.

alia Rd

d.

University Blvd.

Stanford

Girard Blvd.

Altura Park

Constitution

San Mateo Blvd.

San Pedro Blvd.

Pan American Fwy.

Sigma Chi Rd.
Roma Ave.
Grand Ave.

UNIVERSITY OF NEW MEXICO

Campus Blvd.

Lomas Blvd.

Solano

Washington

Marquette

New Mexico State Fairgrounds

Central Ave.

Student Union

Silver Ave.

Cornell

Wellesley

Central Ave.

AE

Coal Ave.
Roosevelt Park

Lead Ave.

Coal Ave.

Coal Ave.

Louisiana Blvd.

Garfield

Zuni Rd.

Ridgecrest

Sports Stadium

UNIVERSITY OF NEW MEXICO (South Campus)

Girard

Burton Park

Carlisle Blvd.

Trumbull Ave.

Ridgecrest Dr.

Kathryn Ave.

Sunshine Terr. Ave.

University

Yale Blvd.

Wellesley

N

Gibson Blvd.

TO ALBUQUERQUE INTERNATIONAL AIRPORT

TO KIRTLAND AIR FORCE BASE

KEY

AE American Express Office

0   1 mile
0   1 km

nies. Original Native American and Western art is featured throughout, including numerous works by famed Taos painter R. C. Gorman. The elegant Ranchers Club restaurant has high beamed ceilings and a roaring fireplace over which a mounted buffalo head stares down benevolently. Its authentic grill room—you almost expect to find J. R. Ewing here—features prime meats and fresh seafood prepared over a selection of aromatic woods (patrons select the flavor—piñon, mesquite, and so on—themselves). The Casa Chaco, the hotel's other restaurant, serves typical coffee-shop breakfast and lunch fare but is transformed at night, when nouvelle Southwestern cuisine is served in considerably more elegant style: candlelit tables, waiters in tuxedos, crisp linens, and sparkling crystal. *1901 University Blvd. N.E., Box 25525, Albuquerque 87102, tel. 505/884–2500 or 800/HILTONS; fax 505/889–9118. 428 rooms. Facilities: indoor pool, outdoor pool, whirlpool, sauna, free transportation to and from the airport and bus and train stations, 2 "Luxury Level" floors, bar, lounge, café, dining room. AE, D, DC, MC, V.*

Albuquerque Marriott. This luxury property is located uptown at the junction of I–40 and Louisiana Boulevard, near some of the city's best shopping areas (Winrock and Coronado malls). Geared to the executive traveler with its special 28-room Concierge Level, complete with faxes and computer hookups, it also has the vacationer in mind. The 17-story hotel with its elegantly decorated lobby (the glowing hues of the furnishings reflect the region's natural colors) has Southwestern touches throughout—kachina dolls, Native American art, and native pottery. It recently completed a $3.2 million renovation. Nicole's Restaurant is the hotel's upscale dining room, with soft lighting, pink napkins and tablecloths, and tableside service; Herbs & Roses, open for breakfast, lunch, and dinner, is more informal. Guest rooms feature walk-in closets, in-room movies, and modern furnishings, all in those pleasing Southwestern tones. *2101 Louisiana Blvd. NE, Albuquerque 87110, tel. 505/881–6800 or 800/228–9290; fax 505/888–2982. 412 rooms. Facilities: 2 restaurants, lounge, gift shop, health club, indoor-outdoor pool, exclusive concierge level with 28 rooms, free limousine service to and from Albuquerque Airport. AE, D, DC, MC, V.*

Best Western Fred Harvey Hotel. This 14-story hotel, the former Amfac, has completed a $2.5 million remodeling program and changed its name. Located at the Albuquerque Airport, 3 minutes from the freeway, its modern decor is embellished with a Southwestern flair. The spacious guest rooms feature cool earth tones, with large framed abstract and impressionistic watercolors on the walls. Bathrooms have a separate vanity. The upscale family-style restaurant, Lil's, serves Continental cuisine in a Southwestern setting—Mexican tiles on the floors, and viga ceilings. With its airport location, it's not surprising that the hotel is geared toward the traveling businessperson. *2910 Yale*

Blvd. NE, Albuquerque 87119, tel. 505/843–7000 or 800/ 227–1117; fax 505/843–6307. 266 rooms. Facilities: heated pool, lighted tennis courts, fitness center, nearby golf. AE, DC, MC, V.

★ **Hyatt Regency Albuquerque.** Adjacent to the Convention Center in the heart of downtown is the city's newest major hotel addition, and a beauty it is, with two soaring desert-colored towers climbing high above the city skyline. A private forest and a splashing fountain outside, a shopping promenade inside—it's all totally modern and luxurious. The spacious guest rooms are finished in contemporary Southwestern style with a mauve, burgundy, and tan color scheme and all the standard Hyatt amenities. The Presidential Suite has a canopy bed, as though Abe Lincoln himself might stop by. McGrath's, the hotel's award-winning restaurant, offers steaks, chops, chicken, and seafood in an intimate atmosphere of levels and alcoves, with rich-colored wood furnishing. It's open for breakfast, lunch, and dinner. *330 Tijeras Ave., Albuquerque 87102, tel. 505/842–1234 or 800/233–1234; fax 505/766–6710. 395 rooms, 14 suites. Facilities: restaurant, 2 lounges, health club, spa, outdoor pool, special Regency Club accommodations. AE, D, DC, MC, V.*

Radisson. This two- and three-story motor hotel at the Albuquerque Airport has a Southwestern Spanish flavor throughout, with arched balconies, tan desert colors, a year-round courtyard pool, and indoor and outdoor dining. The guest rooms are comfortable enough, but not outstanding. Diamondback's Café and Coyote's Cantina offer a Western setting and regional northern New Mexican cuisine. This property also caters to traveling business executives. *1901 University Blvd., Albuquerque 87106, tel. 505/ 247–0512 or 800/333–3333; fax 505/843–7148. 148 rooms. Facilities: restaurant, lounge, year-round outdoor pool and spa, and complimentary airport and train and bus-station transfers. AE, D, DC, MC, V.*

Ramada Hotel Classic. Set in the heart of Albuquerque's uptown business and financial district, across from the Coronado Shopping Mall, the city's largest, this modern, eight-story hotel has convention facilities and enough bars, restaurants, and space to keep all the delegates happy. Each of the hotel's recently refurbished, oversize guest rooms and suites is equipped with a refrigerator and boasts a grand view of the majestic Sandia Mountains or the desert West Mesa and the downtown skyline. Southwestern colors (mauve and light green) predominate in the rooms, complementing the Southwestern-style bedspreads and curtains. The bed lamps have pottery bases, and the ceiling lamps are brass. (One wonders why the featured artworks are primarily bland florals and European landscapes when so much good local art is available.) The Café Fennel is open for breakfast, lunch, and dinner, and The Classic Grille (*see* Dining, *above*) features grilled meat and seafood in a casual setting. *6815 Menaul Blvd. NE, Albuquerque 87110, tel.*

*505/881–0000 or 800/228–2828; fax 505/881–3736. 287
rooms. Facilities: heated indoor pool, whirlpool and sauna, American Airlines ticket counter in lobby, 2 restaurants, 2 lounges, courtesy transportation to and from the
airport. AE, D, DC, MC, V.*

Sheraton Old Town. In the heart of Albuquerque's historical district, the Sheraton Old Town is a modern, 11-story
structure that gracefully sits amid the region's 400 years of
culture and history with no overly jarring effects. The
guest rooms are large and modern, with tan desert-colored
appointments and hand-wrought furnishings. The large
bathrooms have vanities with lighted makeup mirrors. The
Rio Grande Customs House Restaurant offers prime rib,
steaks, seafood, and poultry specialties, while the casual
Café del Sol has a varied menu, with lots of Southwestern
favorites for breakfast, lunch, and dinner. *800 Rio Grande
Blvd. NW, Albuquerque 87104, tel. 505/843–6300 or 800/
325–3535; fax 505/842–9863. 190 rooms. Facilities: 2 restaurants, 2 lounges, heated pool, whirlpool, shopping arcade, free airport and train and bus-depot pickups. AE, D,
DC, MC, V.*

Moderate   **Barcelona Court All-Suite Hotel.** This colorful, three-story
hotel just off I–40 offers a touch of old Mexico with tile and
wrought-iron decor. On the second floor is a large atrium
fountain around which guests sip cocktails at sundown and
enjoy complimentary breakfast. Each two-room suite has a
galley kitchen with a wet bar and a microwave oven. Furnishings are contemporary, with Southwest flourishes and
regional prints and posters—by Georgia O'Keeffe, R. C.
Gorman, and company—on the walls. *900 Louisiana Blvd.
NE, Albuquerque 87110, tel. 505/255–5566; fax 505/255–
5566, ext. 6116. 164 suites. Facilities: complimentary
breakfast and cocktails, 2 pools, sauna, whirlpool, gift
shop, free airport pickups, underground parking. AE, D,
DC, MC, V.*

Howard Johnson Plaza Hotel. This happy Ho Jo off I–25 has
a five-story atrium flooding its large lobby with sunlight.
The rooms, some with refrigerators, are cheery as well,
done in traditional Southwest styling with bright colors
and contemporary regional art. *6000 Pan American Freeway NE, Albuquerque 87109, tel. and fax 505/821–9451.
150 rooms. Facilities: bar, café, indoor/outdoor swim-
through pool, coin laundry, free pickups from airport and
train and bus stations. AE, D, DC, MC, V.*

★   **La Posada de Albuquerque.** This historic, highly lauded hotel in the heart of downtown Albuquerque oozes Southwestern charm, with its tiled lobby fountain, massive vigas,
encircling balcony, fixtures of etched glass and tin, and Native American war-dance murals behind the reception
desk. The guest rooms, many with fireplaces, are large and
decorated throughout with Southwestern and Native
American themes, from the designs on couches, slipcovers,
and drapes to incidental pieces of Hopi pottery and R. C.

Gorman prints on the walls. In 1939, Conrad Hilton opened the hotel, then called the Albuquerque Hilton, as his first lodging venture outside Texas; it was also the first air-conditioned building in New Mexico, Hilton's native state. The hotel mogul honeymooned here with his bride, Zsa Zsa Gabor. La Posada has been carefully restored and is listed in the National Register of Historic Places. Its dining room, the popular Eulalia's Restaurant, features waiters and waitresses singing snippets from the latest Broadway hits. The cuisine is Continental, with veal, duck, and salmon topping the list of specialties. There's live jazz and a good happy-hour buffet in the Lobby Lounge (*see* Nightlife, *below*). *125 Second St. NW, Albuquerque 87102, tel. 505/242–9090 or 800/777–5732; fax 505/242–8664. 114 rooms. Facilities: bar, restaurant, gift shop, exercise room, free airport pickups by limousine. AE, D, DC, MC, V.*

Inexpensive **American Inn.** This stately, two-story, red brick hotel is a find for budget watchers. It's small in price and large in service, and is centrally located—one mile east of the University of New Mexico. Rooms are done in modern style with mostly browns, greens, and other earth tones. Room rates include breakfast. *4501 Central Ave. NE, Albuquerque 87108, tel. 505/262–1681 or (in NM) 800/343–2597. 130 rooms. Facilities: 24-hour restaurant, swimming pool, free shuttle service. AE, D, DC, MC, V.*

DeAnza Motor Lodge. It's not in the best section of town, but this one- and two-story pueblo-style motel (the sign out front is shaped like a tepee) is easy on the wallet. Free Continental breakfast is served in the lobby, and small refrigerators are furnished upon request. Decor and furnishings are in modern Santa Fe style. *4301 Central Ave. NE, Albuquerque 87108, tel. 505/255–1654. 81 rooms. Facilities: café, gift shop. AE, D, DC, MC, V.*

Bed-and-Breakfasts

Moderate **Casa del Granjero.** Casa del Granjero (The Farmer's House), 10 miles from the airport, is a sprawling old Territorial adobe with a land grant that goes back to 1740. The 5,000-square-foot dwelling is decorated throughout with Southwestern and Mexican furnishings. Even the dishes are Mexican—"Old, old Mexican"—says owner Victoria Farmer, who also runs a catering service. Full breakfasts feature Mexican, French, or American specialties and are served in the guest rooms or in the living room in front of the two-story-high adobe fireplace. There's also a garden room with a sunken hot tub and miles of nature trails outside. Casa del Granjero shares its grounds with horses, goats, and other ranch animals. Experienced riders are occasionally permitted to saddle up. *9213 4th Ce De Baca La. NW, Albuquerque 87114, tel. 505/897–4144. 3 rooms, all with private baths and sitting area. No credit cards.*

★ **Casas de Suenos.** Long a historic gathering spot for artists, Casas de Suenos—Houses of Dreams—provides a uniquely New Mexican setting. The 2-acre garden compound, adjacent to Old Town on Rio Grande Boulevard SW (not NW), is made up of 10 attractively decorated casitas that have beehive fireplaces, pigskin furniture, bleached cattle skulls on the wall, regional paintings, and Native American rugs. Breakfasts start with decadent French toast or savory eggs, a fruit platter, and a selection of fresh breads and muffins. *310 Rio Grande Blvd. SW, Albuquerque 87104, tel. 505/247–4560. 9 suites, 3 rooms, all with private bath. AE, MC, V.*

Casita Chamisa. Set in a cottonwood-shaded valley in Los Ranchos, this guest house is only about 15 minutes north of Old Town and 12 miles from the Albuquerque Airport. With just two bedrooms, the house sleeps one to six and is rented to one party at a time. The furnishings are Southwestern, with Native American blankets, pottery, and artifacts adding authenticity. Owners Kit and Arnold Sargeant opened their guest house in 1974, the first bed-and-breakfast in Albuquerque. The property is also an archaeological site, with remnants of a prehistoric Native American dwelling still visible. Kit Sargeant, an archaeologist, supervised the dig herself. Also for guests use, even at 2 AM if the urge strikes, is an enclosed 15- by 33-foot swimming pool. The solar-heated pool house has a hot tub and full bath. Breakfast is Country Continental, which translates into waffles, pancakes, and lots of seasonal fruits (14 of Casita Chamisa's more than 200 trees are fruit bearing). Arnold Sargeant is famous for his sourdough bread, "with a starter," he says, "that's 110 years old." *850 Chamisal Rd. NW, Albuquerque 87107, tel. 505/897–4644. 2-bedroom guest house sleeps 1–6. Facilities: enclosed pool, hot tub. AE, MC, V.*

Corrales Inn. This Territorial adobe–style, solar-heated home located 14 miles north of Albuquerque in picturesque Corrales, was built to serve as a bed-and-breakfast in 1987. Each of the guest rooms is theme decorated—Oriental, Native American, Victorian, Corrales (Southwestern), and Balloon (in honor of the hot-air-balloon festivals held nearby). Each room has an individual temperature control, as well as a sitting and dressing area. Full gourmet French country breakfasts—quiche, soufflés, omelets, crêpes, croissants—are served in the guest rooms or in the inn's common room. Outside is a courtyard with a hot tub. *Plaza San Ysidro, Box 1361, Corrales 87048, tel. 505/897–4422. 6 rooms, all with full private baths. Facilities: hot tub. MC, V.*

★ **Elaine's, A Bed and Breakfast.** This beautiful three-story log home, located in the evergreen folds of the Sandia Peaks, is tastefully furnished throughout with European antiques and a sprinkling of early regional pieces. The top two floors are for guest rooms, with balconies and big picture windows bringing the lush mountain views indoors. The third-floor room has cathedral ceilings and a brass bed, while the second-floor accommodations share a massive stone fireplace, as well as a bath. A well-stocked library and big fireplaces invite cerebral pursuits while 4 acres of wooded grounds beckon just outside the back door. Full ham-and-egg–style breakfasts are served, with all the accompaniments. *72 Snowline Rd., Snowline Estate, Box 444, Cedar Crest 87008, tel. 505/281–2467. 3 rooms, 2 with shared bath. No credit cards.*

Le Pommier. Formerly the Apple Tree Bed and Breakfast, this inn in Cedar Crest is 15 miles and a world away from downtown Albuquerque. Nestled in the Sandia Mountains, at 7,000 feet, where hummingbirds feed outside the guestroom windows, the Apple Tree offers two large units, accommodating one to four people. "The Casita" is a rustic adobe room with white walls, red brick floors, a viga ceiling, and a kiva fireplace. It's filled with country antiques, a Victorian desk and bookcase, and a deluxe king-size bed. The bright and sunny "Hummingbird Suite" has antique furnishings, with comfortable chairs and sofa, and a gas-log stove. Blue corn waffles, apple pancakes, and honey-glazed whole-wheat cinnamon rolls are typical of the breakfasts that are served in the guest rooms. *12050 Hwy. 14 N, Box 287, Cedar Crest 87008, tel. 505/281–3597 or 800/648–4262. 1 casita and 1 suite, both with private bath. No credit cards.*

Turquoise Inn Bed and Breakfast. Nestled on 2¼ acres adjacent to Cibola National Forest (25 mi northeast of the Albuquerque Airport on the road to Sandia Crest), the Turquoise Inn Bed and Breakfast is surrounded by cedars, and ponderosa and piñon pines. The house was originally a four-bedroom private home that was remodeled and modified to become a bed-and-breakfast. One guest room, formerly the master bedroom, is furnished in Colonial antiques, with Southwestern touches. The large upstairs suite, with a private outside entrance, fireplace, and wet bar, showcases modern Scandinavian furnishings. A Continental breakfast served in the rooms helps guests get a good start on the day. *142 Sandia Crest Rd., Sandia Park 87047, tel. 505/281–4745. 1 room and 1 suite, both with private bath. D, MC, V.*

William E. Mauger Estate. Centrally located downtown, 12 blocks from historic Old Town, this elegant 1897 Queen Anne residence offers comfortable accommodations. Four of the guest rooms are Victorian style, with either a brass bed, a cherry-wood sleigh bed, an iron bed, or a standard Victorian bed with a large, ornate headboard. The other two rooms are Art Deco in design, with tinted mirrors and fluted vases. Full breakfasts—egg dishes, home-baked pastries, juice, and coffee—are served in the guest rooms or in the downstairs parlor or common room. *701 Roma Ave. NW, Albuquerque 87102, tel. 505/242–8755. 5 rooms and 1 suite, all with private bath. AE, D, DC, MC, V.*

Windmill Ranch Bed and Breakfast. Located on the west side in the heart of the bosque (4 mi west of I–40, Exit 155), this bed-and-breakfast offers a spectacular view of the

Sandia Mountains. Guest rooms and public areas are furnished with antiques, including a player piano (with often-played tunes such as "Red River Valley"), a roller-type Edison, and a Victrola. (For the benefit of guests who are trying to sleep, not all of them get cranked up at the same time.) There's also a large-screen VCR with a film library of over 200 titles. The Windmill is only 100 yards from the Rio Grande, where ancient elms and cottonwoods grow in profusion. Paths along the river are ideal for biking, jogging, or walking. The 5,000-acre spread is a working ranch, so there are horses, ducks, and chickens about. Freshly laid eggs are served for breakfast, with all the country trimmings. From the Windmill's balcony, visitors can overdose on scenery, watch the hot-air balloons glide by during seasonal balloon rallies, or just breathe the good air. *6400 Coors Blvd. NW, Albuquerque 87120, tel. 505/898–6864. 4 rooms, each with private bath, 2 with fireplaces. MC, V.*

Camping

Isleta Lakes and Recreation Area. This property, 15 minutes south of Albuquerque on I–25 (take Exit 215 to NM 47), has complete campground facilities and tent sites, and three fishing lakes. *Box 383, Isleta 87022, tel. 505/877–0370. Over 100 tent sites. 40 RV hookups (water and electricity). Tent site $9 per night, RV site $12 per night. Showers and flush toilets in central bathhouse. MC, V.*

KOA Albuquerque Central. This campground has full hookups, Kamping Kabins, a swimming pool and spa, hot showers, flush toilets, LP gas refills, and laundry facilities. There is also a shuttle between the campground, which is located within the city limits (Exit 166 off I–40), and Old Town. *12400 Skyline Rd., Albuquerque 87123, tel. 505/296–2729. 200 sites, 101 full hookups. Water and electric hookup $21.95 per night, full hookup $23.95 per night. D, MC, V.*

KOA has another property in Albuquerque with similar services, the **Albuquerque North KOA** (1021 Hill Rd. in Bernalillo, tel. 505/867–5227).

Turquoise Trail Campgrounds. This campground is in the Sandia Mountains, 15 minutes east of Albuquerque (east on I–40, Exit 175, 4 mi north on I–14). It has full hookups, hot showers, laundry, and a wooded tent area. *22 Calvary Rd., Cedar Crest 87008, tel. 505/281–2005. Camping space for 2 is $10.50; a full hookup is $15.*

The Arts and Nightlife

To find out what's on in town, check the *Albuquerque Journal* on Friday and Sunday, and the *Albuquerque Tribune* on Thursday.

The Arts

Dance   **The Southwest Ballet** (tel. 505/294–1423), under the direction of Edward Androse and now in its 15th season, is in the forefront of regional ballet companies and presents a wide variety of classical and contemporary performances.

Music   The conductor of the **New Mexico Symphony Orchestra** (220 Gold Ave. SW, tel. 505/842–8565), now in its 62nd year, swings a wide baton, with presentations of pops, Beethoven, and Handel's *Messiah* at Christmas. Performances are frequently scheduled under the stars at the Rio Grande Zoo Bandshell and at Popejoy Hall on the University of New Mexico campus.

Opera   **Albuquerque Civic Light Opera Association** is one of the largest community-based producers of musical theater in the country. Its five annual productions are seen by a total audience of 75,000. Performances are held in the 2,000-seat Popejoy Hall at the University of New Mexico campus. For information or tickets, call the box office, tel. 505/345–6577.

Theater   **The KiMo Theater** (419 Central Ave. NW; box office, tel. 505/764–1700; business office, tel. 505/848–1370), an old movie palace on Central Avenue restored to its original design—Pueblo Deco–style architecture painted in bright colors—offers a varied program, everything from traveling road shows to local song-and-dance acts. The KiMo is also where the **New Mexico Repertory Theatre** (tel. 505/764–1700), the state's only resident professional theater group, stages its seasonal offerings of comedies, dramas, musicals, and mysteries. The Rep's season runs from October through May, alternating two-week productions in Albuquerque and Santa Fe. The **Albuquerque Little Theater** (224 San Pasquale Ave. SW, tel. 505/242–4750), a nonprofit community troupe, combines local volunteer talent with a staff of professionals to present an annual series of comedies, dramas, musicals, and mysteries of the highest caliber. The company theater, located across the street from historic Old Town, was built in 1936 and was designed by famed Southwestern architect John Gaw Meen. It contains an art gallery; a large, comfortable lobby; and a cocktail lounge. **La Compania de Teatro de Albuquerque** (518 First St. NW, tel. 505/242–7929), New Mexico's largest bilingual theater, performs classic and contemporary plays in English and Spanish during April, June, October, and December.

Nightlife

Bars and Lounges   You'll find live entertainment of the jazz, blues, folk, and rock variety in the lounge of the **Cooperage Restaurant and Lounge** (*see* Dining, *above*). **Fat Chance Bar and Grill** (2216 Central Ave. SE, tel. 505/265–7531), across the street from the University of New Mexico, is a hangout for boisterous college students. It's got booths, a bar, tables, a dance floor, and live entertainment, from rock to reggae, Wednesday through Sunday nights.

Comedy Clubs **Laff's** (3100 Juan Tabo Blvd. NE, tel. 505/296–5653) is the place to go for live comedy in Albuquerque.

Country-and-Western Clubs **Caravan East** (7605 Central Ave. NE, tel. 505/265–7877) is a country-and-Western nightclub offering free dance lessons and partners galore. Two live bands play nightly. There is a free buffet and half-price drinks during the 4:30–7 happy hour. **Midnight Rodeo** (4901 McLeod Rd. NE, tel. 505/888–0100) is an enormous country-and-Western complex, with a huge race-track-style dance floor, several bars, and even boutiques. The happy-hour buffet spread is incredible. The **Sundance Saloon** (12000 Candelaria Rd. NE, tel. 505/296–6761) is another C&W favorite in Albuquerque.

Jazz Clubs **La Posada Lobby Lounge** (La Posada de Albuquerque Hotel, tel. 505/242–9090) offers live jazz performances and a happy-hour buffet that's very popular among the locals.

6 Carlsbad and Southern New Mexico

Carlsbad Caverns National Park, in the southeastern part of the state, contains one of the largest and most spectacular cave systems in the world. As such, it is the area's main lure, but the town of Carlsbad and such nearby attractions as Living Desert State Park are also well worth visiting. About 3½ hours northwest of Carlsbad are the historic towns of Lincoln County and the striking White Sands National Monument, which make an interesting one- to two-day excursion from Carlsbad.

Essential Information

Important Addresses and Numbers

Tourist Information

Carlsbad Caverns National Park (3225 National Parks Hwy., Carlsbad 88220, tel. 505/785–2232 or 505/885–CAVE for 24-hour recorded information).

Carlsbad Chamber of Commerce (302 S. Canal St., Carlsbad 88220, tel. 505/887–6516 or 800/221–1224).

Living Desert State Park (Box 100, Carlsbad 88220, tel. 505/887–5516).

Arriving and Departing

By Car

Driving south from Albuquerque on I–25 for about 77 miles, exit on U.S. 380 East and continue for 165 miles to Roswell. There switch to U.S. 285 and continue directly to Carlsbad, about 75 miles from Roswell (a total of 320 miles from Albuquerque). The drive is a bit monotonous, with dry rolling hills and nothing to see but brown wooden road signs heralding "Carlsbad Caverns" along the way. From El Paso, Texas, going east on U.S. 180, the distance to Carlsbad is 167 miles. From Pecos, Carlsbad can be reached via U.S. 285 (off I–10 at Van Horn).

By Plane

The **Albuquerque International Airport,** 380 miles north of Carlsbad, is the gateway to New Mexico and is served by most major airlines (*see* Essential Information in Chapter 1). Air-shuttle service via **Mesa Airlines** (tel. 800/637–2247 or, in Carlsbad, 505/885–0245) connects four times daily to and from Cavern City Air Terminal in Carlsbad. Flying time aboard the nine-passenger Cessna Caravan is about 90 minutes. The fare ranges from $101 (for a 21-day advance purchase) to $204 round-trip, and half that one-way, depending on time of year and advance purchase discounts. Interline buses at Albuquerque International Airport connect Mesa Airlines with all Albuquerque connections.

Carlsbad car-rental agencies include **Hertz Car Rental** (tel. 505/887–1500) at Cavern City Air Terminal and **Independent Auto Rental** (tel. 505/887–1469) at Park Inn International. Taxi transfers from the Carlsbad airport are also available via **Cavern City Cab Company** (tel. 505/887–0994).

By Bus **TNM&O Greyhound** (tel. 505/887–1108) provides transcontinental bus service and connects Carlsbad and White's City. **Sun-Country Tours** (tel. 505/785–2291) offers van service between Carlsbad Caverns National Park and White's City. The buses leave from the gift shop at White's City (where you can purchase tickets, tel. 505/785–2291) and from the visitor center at the caverns. The round-trip fare is $15 for one to three people, $5 per additional person.

Festivals and Seasonal Events

The **Bat Breakfast** is not exactly the swallows returning to Capistrano, but on the second Thursday of August each year, early risers—would you believe 5 AM?—gather for a sit-down breakfast at the entrance to Carlsbad Cavern. Last year over 600 bat fanciers showed up to watch tens of thousands of bats, which had just been out for the night feeding on insects, fly back into a black hole descending steeply into the ground. Park rangers are on hand to lecture and answer questions. The bats' departure can be viewed at sunset each evening mid-May through October, but the early morning homecoming breakfast is a once-a-year affair. For additional information, contact Carlsbad Caverns National Park (3225 National Parks Hwy., Carlsbad 88220, tel. 505/785–2232).

Guided Tours

While explorations of the main cavern are designed to be self-guided, park rangers frequently conduct guided tours during the low-visitation winter months when the crowds are more manageable.

Pets

Not even leashed pets are allowed into the cavern, and park rangers advise that animals not be left in parked cars, even with the windows open. Suffocating heat can build up quickly in the desert. Clean, air-conditioned kennels are available at the visitor center. Inquire at the gift shop. The cost is $3.50 for the duration of the tour, usually four hours.

A Note of Caution

Be aware that motor homes and RVs are frequently the target of thieves in national parks and forests. Don't leave vehicle doors unlocked or windows open. And don't leave behind valuables, such as cameras and traveler's checks, whether hidden under seats or in blankets or towels; they're the first places thieves will look. The visitor center has safe coin-operated lockers. If you are the victim of a crime or see someone tampering with a car, call the park rangers (tel. 505/785–2232) or the Eddy County sheriff (tel. 505/887–7551).

Exploring Carlsbad

Carlsbad Caverns National Park

The huge, subterranean chambers, fantastic rock formations, and delicate mineral sculptures of Carlsbad Caverns
National Park draw about three quarters of a million people
each year to a remote corner of southeast New Mexico. Although the park is in the Chihauhuan Desert, near the rugged canyons and peaks of the Guadalupe mountain range
and the piñon and ponderosa pines of Lincoln National Forest, the most spectacular sights here are all below the
earth's surface, with such evocative names as the Green
Lake Room, the King's Palace, the Devil's Den, the Sequoia
Room, the Hooded Klansman, the China Wall, and Iceberg
Rock.

This cave system, hundreds of million years in the making,
is one of the largest and most impressive in the world, but it
was discovered relatively recently. Pictographs near the
cave entrance tell us that prehistoric Native Americans
took shelter in Carlsbad Caverns more than 1,000 years
ago, but archaeologists doubt that they ventured in very
far; access to the depths was limited and the tribe may have
believed that the dwellings of the dead lay below.

It wasn't until the 19th century that nearby settlers, curious about the huge groups of bats they saw in the area, rediscovered the caves. They were mined for bat guano
(dung), which was used as fertilizer, for a number of years,
but no one was interested in the caves for any other reason
until the early 20th century, when one of the guano miners,
Jim White, began exploring and told people about this
amazing underground universe.

White brought a photographer, Ray Davis, to bear witness
to his extravagant claims for the place. Displayed in the
nearby town of Carlsbad in 1915, Davis's black-and-white
pictures astounded people and started a rush of interest in
the caverns. White turned tour operator, taking people
down 170 feet in a bucket left over from the days of mining
bat guano and lighting their way with kerosene lamps.

Washington got wind of this natural wonder in the early
1920s, and in 1923 inspector Robert Holley was dispatched
by the U.S. Department of Interior to investigate. His report was instrumental in getting Carlsbad Caverns declared a national monument later that year by President
Calvin Coolidge. The area was designated a national park
in 1930.

Carlsbad Caverns National Park was much in the news early in 1991 when Emily Davis Mobley, an expert caver,
broke her left leg some 1,000 feet underground while map-
ping one of the system's rugged caves. It took rescuers four

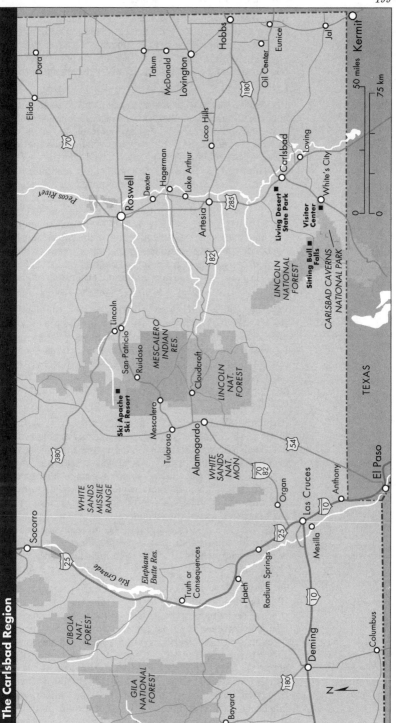

The Carlsbad Region

Kermit

Hobbs

Oil Center
Eunice

Jal

50 miles

75 km

Dora
Elida
Tatum
McDonald
Lovington

180

Loco Hills

Carlsbad
Loving

Roswell
Dexter
Hagerman
Lake Arthur

Artesia

285

White's City

Living Desert State Park

Visitor Center

Sitting Bull Falls

LINCOLN NATIONAL FOREST

CARLSBAD CAVERNS NATIONAL PARK

Pecos River

70

Lincoln
San Patricio
Ruidoso
MESCALERO INDIAN RES.

Cloudcroft

LINCOLN NAT. FOREST

Ski Apache Ski Resort

Mescalero

Tularosa

Alamogordo

WHITE SANDS NAT. MON.

70
82

54

Organ

Las Cruces

Anthony

El Paso

TEXAS

380

WHITE SANDS MISSILE RANGE

Socorro

25

Elephant Butte Res.

Rio Grande

Truth or Consequences

Hatch

Radium Springs

Mesilla

10

10

Deming

Columbus

Bayard

GILA NATIONAL FOREST

CIBOLA NAT. FOREST

180

N

days to carry, lift, and pull her over gaping pits and narrow
passageways to safety. Of course, unless you're an expert,
you won't be allowed to go exploring the same route or even
anything like it. Of the 77 caves in the park, only two, Carlsbad Cavern and Slaughter Canyon Cave, are open to the
public.

Carlsbad Caverns owes its existence as much to slow drips
and accretions as to cataclysmic events. Its origins go back
some 250 million years, when Capitan Reef, 400 miles long,
formed around the edge of the warm, shallow sea that once
covered this region. The sea evaporated and the reef was
buried until a few million years ago, when a combination of
erosion and convulsions that also created the Guadalupe
Mountains brought parts of it back above ground. Rainwa-
ter seeping down through the reef's cracks gradually enlarged them into cavities, which eventually collapsed,
forming huge rooms. Over millennia, evaporated limestone
deposited on the ceilings grew into great hanging
stalactites, which in turn dripped the crystals that over
time rose into massive stalagmites and other, more delicate
formations—cave pearls, draperies, popcorn, and lily pads.

Whether you take the long route or the elevator shortcut,
the trek through Carlsbad Cavern is long and you may find
yourself getting a bit disoriented. The sheer vastness of the
interior is overwhelming, and the proportions seem to
change as one goes along. In places where pools of water
have formed beside the walkway, reflections and reality
merge; you may have to pause for a moment to regain your
equilibrium.

Although you may be tempted to touch the cave's walls and
jutting rock formations, heed the ranger's warning against
doing so. Oil from the human hand forms a type of water-
proofing that inhibits the natural water seepage. One or
two people pawing at the rocks wouldn't make much of a difference, but thousands tour the cavern daily. Visitors are
also warned not to leave the guided pathways. They're not
told, however, that if they wander astray, silent alarms will
quickly summon park rangers. The interior of Carlsbad
Cavern is well lighted, but many people seem more concerned about where they're stepping than with what's
ahead and make most of the trip looking down at their feet.

The two routes into Carlsbad Cavern are designated the
Blue Tour and the Red Tour. If you take the former, you'll
proceed on foot along the paved walkway that winds down
into the caverns' depths for about 1¾ miles, passing
through a series of underground rooms and descending
slowly to a depth of about 830 feet. The trek takes about two
hours; the trail can be slick in parts and the grades are fair-
ly steep. The other way is to take a high-speed elevator
from the visitor center down 750 feet to an underground
lunchroom, and then begin your exploration from there; it
should take another hour. (The elevator makes a portion of

the main cavern accessible to visitors in wheelchairs.) In both cases you'll visit the Big Room, so called because it's large enough to hold 14 Houston Astrodomes; one corner could contain the White House. The highest ceiling reaches 256 feet.

The temperature inside Carlsbad Cavern remains at a constant 56°F, and it's damp, so a sweater or warm clothes are recommended. So are comfortable shoes with rubber soles—because of the moisture, the underground walkways are slippery. But the cavern is well lighted and numerous park rangers are stationed about to offer assistance and information. Radio-tour guides are also available; small radio receivers can be rented for 50¢ each. Hold them to your ear as you walk through the cavern and you'll be enlightened.

Apart from the cave itself, one of the great attractions at Carlsbad Cavern is the **nightly bat flights.** Each evening between late May and mid-October at about sunset, bats by the tens of thousands exit from the natural entrance of the cavern and go flying about the countryside scouting for flying insects. They consume the insects in flight, collectively more than three tons of yummy bugs per night. (No scientist has yet figured out how a bat hanging upside down in a dark cave knows when the sun has set outside.) Because bats, albeit less lovable than furry kittens, are among the most maligned and misunderstood creatures, park rangers give informative talks about them each evening prior to the exodus, at about 7 PM. The time of the bat flights varies over the course of the season, so ranger lectures are flexible as well; the time is usually posted, but if not, check at the visitor center. Lectures are suspended during the winter months, when the bats leave for Mexico.

Slaughter Canyon Cave, 25 miles from the main cavern, is much less accessible. You'll have to provide your own transportation to get there, and reservations (tel. 505/785–2232) are required at least a day in advance; during the busy summer months, two weeks in advance are recommended. The last few miles of the roadway there is gravel, and the mouth of the cave is a half-mile climb up a 500-foot rise. Millions of years old, Slaughter Canyon Cave was discovered by Tom Tucker, a local goatherd, in 1937. Guided tours have been available only during the past few years. The cave consists primarily of a single corridor, 1,140 feet long, with numerous side passages. The total extent of the surveyed passage is 1¾ miles, and the lowest point is 250 feet below the surface. Outstanding formations are the Christmas Tree, the Monarch, the Hooded Klansman, the Tear Drop, and the China Wall. Rangers lead groups of 25 on a two-hour lantern tour. Children under 6 aren't permitted. The cave temperature is a constant 62°F, and the humidity is a clammy 90%. You'll need to bring along your own flashlight, hiking boots or good walking shoes (sneakers aren't recommended), and drinking water. Photographs are permitted, but no tripod setups are allowed, since the group moves along at a relatively brisk pace and you *really* wouldn't want to be left behind. Unless you're in great physical shape, with a long attention span, New Cave may be more cave peeping than you bargained for.

While you're exploring Carlsbad Cavern, you can pretty much set your own pace, either walking, which takes about three hours, or using the elevators up and down, for a total of perhaps 1½ hours. Add another hour or two if you have lunch at the cavern and peruse the museum exhibits and the gift and book shops. That means a half day would certainly cover all the highlights. Then you can relax and enjoy the natural wonders of the park itself. Box lunches are available at the caverns' underground lunchroom, so you may want to have lunch at **Rattlesnake Springs.** (Don't let the name scare you. No one's seen a rattlesnake there in years.) A pleasant picnic area, with shade trees, grass, picnic tables, water, grills, and toilets, it's also a favorite spot for bird-watchers. Located near the Black River, Rattlesnake Springs was a source of water for Native Americans hundreds of years ago. Army troops exploring the area used it as well, and today it's the main source of water for all the park facilities.

Another option is to take the scenic 9½-mile **Walnut Canyon Drive.** This loop begins a half mile from the visitor center and travels along the top of the ridge to the edge of Rattlesnake Canyon and back down through upper Walnut Canyon to the main entrance road. It's a one-way gravel road, and the backcountry scenery is stunning; go late in the afternoon or early in the morning to enjoy the full spectrum of changing light and dancing colors. There's also a self-guided **Desert Nature Walk,** about a half-mile long, which begins near the cavern's entrance. Experienced hikers might enjoy taking advantage of more than 50 miles of primitive trails that meander through the backcountry. On the other hand, if all or any of that sounds like a bit more of the Great Outdoors than you care to experience in one day, you could head into the town of Carlsbad and enjoy any number of the attractions there. *Carlsbad Caverns National Park, 3225 National Parks Hwy., Carlsbad 88220, tel. 505/785–2232. Cavern admission: $5 adults, $3 children 6–15, children 5 and under free for entry into the cavern; Slaughter Canyon Cave admission: $6 adults, $3 children 6–15, children 5 and under not permitted; fees for periodic, special guided trips into other undeveloped caves cost $10 a person; holders of Golden Access Passports get a 50% discount on all admission fees. Open June–Aug., daily 8–7; Sept.–May, daily 8–5:30. Facilities include a kennel, bookstore, gift shop, and 2 restaurants, 1 above ground and 1 750 feet below.*

Carlsbad and Environs

With the world-famous caverns nearby, the town of Carlsbad is among the most popular tourist destinations in New Mexico. Originally named Eddy after pioneer cattleman Charles B. Eddy, the town's name was changed to Carlsbad in 1889 because its spring-water mineral content was discovered to be similar to that found in Karlsbad, Bohemia, a famous health spa. Situated along the Pecos River, which affords it 27 miles of beaches and picturesque pathways, Carlsbad is an attractive town of 30,000 that seems pleasantly suspended between the past and the present. Only a block from the river, its Territorial town square encircles a pueblo-style country courthouse designed by the famed New Mexican architect John Gaw Meed, who also designed many of the buildings on the University of New Mexico campus in Albuquerque. Surprisingly for a city its size, Carlsbad has 30 parks, more than any other city in New Mexico. It also has more than its share of hokey attractions—miniature train rides, riverboat paddlewheelers, an amusement village with carnival thrill rides—but somehow it all seems to work.

Carlsbad Museum and Arts Center, on the town square, contains the bones of prehistoric animals that once roamed the region—mammoths, camels, and ancient horses. It also has pioneer Apache relics, Pueblo pottery, Native American art, early cowboy memorabilia, and remains of meteorites. The prize, however, is the McAdoo Collection, with its excellent sculptures by Frederic Remington and Charles Russell's paintings of the Old West, as well as works by painters of the Taos Society of Artists. *Fox St., Carlsbad, tel. 505/887-0276. Admission free. Open Mon.–Sat. 10–6; closed Sun. and major holidays.*

Living Desert State Park, atop Ocotillo Hills, about 1½ miles northwest of Carlsbad (off U.S. 285; look for the signs), contains an impressive collection of plants and animals native to the Chihuahuan Desert, which extends north from Mexico into southwestern Texas and southeastern New Mexico. Like many deserts, it's surprisingly rich in animal and plant life, as the park reveals. The Desert Arboretum has hundreds of exotic cacti and succulents. The Living Desert Zoo, more a reserve than a traditional zoo, is home to mountain lions, deer, elk, wolves, buffalo, rattlesnakes, and other indigenous species. Creatures of the night can be viewed below ground through special glass panels. The park has numerous shaded rest areas, rest rooms, and water fountains. *Living Desert State Park, Carlsbad, tel. 505/887-5516. Admission: $3, children 6 and under free. Open May 15–Labor Day, daily 8–8; 9–5 the rest of the year. Last tour takes place 1 hour before closing.*

Million Dollar Museum, 20 miles southeast of Carlsbad in the desert resort town of White's City (take U.S. 62/180 to

White's City, then head west on NM 7), has 11 big rooms on
two levels filled with Early American memorabilia and artifacts—antique dolls and dollhouses, guns and rifles, music
boxes, old cars, and a 6,000-year-old mummified Native
American. There's an arcade and shooting gallery next
door. *1 Carlsbad Caverns Hwy., White's City, tel. 505/785–
2291. Admission: $2.50 adults, $2 senior citizens, $1.50
children 6–12, children under 6 free. Open daily 9–5.*

Sports and the Outdoors

Bird-watching

From turkey vultures to golden eagles, more than 200 species of birds have been identified in Carlsbad Caverns National Park. The best place to go birding in the park, if not
the entire state, is Rattlesnake Springs, a desert oasis (*see*
Carlsbad Caverns National Park in Exploring Carlsbad,
above). Ask for a checklist at the visitor center, and then
start checking: red-tailed hawk, red-winged blackbird,
white-throated swift, northern flicker, pygmy nuthatches,
yellow-billed cuckoo, roadrunner, mallard, American coot,
green-winged and blue-winged teal—over 200 in all.

Hiking

More than 50 miles of trails provide access to the 46,000
acres of scenic desert, plunging canyons, steep rocky
ridges, and mountain wilderness of Carlsbad Caverns National Park. An hour's drive to the southwest is the rugged
76,293-acre Guadalupe Mountains National Park, containing eight of Texas's highest peaks.

Black walnut, oak, desert willow, and hackberry prolifer-
ate along the canyons' bottoms. The ridges and walls of the
canyons contain a variety of desert plants—yucca, agave,
sotol, sticklike branches of ocotillo, and clusters of sparse
desert grass. Higher up, piñon pine, juniper, ponderosa,
pine, and Douglas fir dominate. Animals that scamper
about or roam the area at a more leisurely pace include rac-
coon, skunk, rabbits, fox, gopher, woodrat, mice, porcu-
pine, mule deer, coyote, and the ever-elusive badger,
bobcat, and mountain lion. There are plenty of snakes in the
area, but because they're both nocturnal and shy, visitors
rarely see them.

Backcountry hiking in Carlsbad Caverns National Park can
be exhilarating—the desert terrain is stark and awesome—but few trails are marked as in other national parks,
and there is no water. A topographical map, available at the
visitor center, will be helpful in defining some of the old
ranch trails. Permits aren't required, except for overnight
backpacking expeditions, but all hikers are requested to
register at the information desk at the visitor center. Bring

plenty of water. No pets or guns are permitted. The following is a sampling of some of the most interesting and accessible trails.

Guadalupe Ridge Trail, also known as the Jeep Road, starts at Walnut Canyon Loop Road and covers 13 miles, mostly along ridge tops, to Putnam Cabin. The 2,000-foot ascent is a gradual climb to the highest point in the park.

The Guano Trail, a little more than 3½ miles, was originally the truck and wagon route that miners used to transport guano from Carlsbad Caverns to White's City. The trail starts from the Bat Flight Amphitheater and affords good views on what is mostly flat terrain.

Take the short (¼ mi) **Rattlesnake Canyon Overlook Trail** to get superlative views of Rattlesnake Canyon. You can pick it up along the Walnut Canyon Drive (*see* Carlsbad Caverns National Park in Exploring Carlsbad, *above*), a few hundred yards north of the Rattlesnake Canyon Trailhead.

Rattlesnake Canyon Trail covers close to 3 miles and descends from 4,570 to 3,900 feet as it goes down into the canyon. This trail, which is well defined and marked with rock cairns, starts from the Walnut Canyon Drive.

Yucca Canyon Trail, about 6 miles long, begins at the mouth of Yucca Canyon and climbs up to the junction of Double Canyon Trail (the elevation ranges from 4,300 to 6,150 ft); at the top of the ridge, a level, well-marked route offers wonderful views of the Guadalupe escarpment. Much of the trail leads through a lovely forested area.

Dining

Lunches can be purchased at the Carlsbad Caverns National Park's unique restaurant, located 750 feet underground, or at the full-service restaurant on the surface. There are numerous eating places in White's City and Carlsbad as well.

Category	Cost*
Expensive	over $25
Moderate	$10–25
Inexpensive	under $10

per person, excluding drinks, service, and tax (5.8%)

Carlsbad **Lucy's.** This is another family-owned (Lucy and Justo Yanez) oasis of great Mexican food. It was recently remodeled in Southwestern decor. Alas, a large-screen TV blares accompaniment to meals, which are served in the restaurant and, when it gets crowded, the adjoining lounge. But the food is fresh and fabulous. When the waitress asks you "smoking or nonsmoking?" she's not referring to your nicotine habit but to the degree of fire you want in your food. All the New Mexican standards are available, along with some not-so-standard items such as chapa chicken chacos (chicken tacos with guacamole) and Tucson-style chimichangas (chicken, beef, or brisket with chile, cheeses, and special seasonings). *701 S. Canal St., tel. 505/887–7714. No reservations. Dress: casual. MC, V. Moderate.*

Cortez Cafe. This charming family-owned Mexican restaurant, with an all-brick interior and photo murals of Old Mexico, has been in business for more than half a century. Most people choose the all-you-can-eat option: For $7 you can fill up on almost anything on the menu. Try the combination plate, fajitas (tortillas stuffed with sizzling chunks of beef or pork), or sour-cream enchiladas. *506 S. Canal St., tel. 505/885–4747. Reservations accepted. Dress: casual. No credit cards. Inexpensive.*

White's City   **The Velvet Garter Restaurant and Saloon.** Come here for steak, chicken, catfish, shrimp, and Mexican food in a whoopee Wild West atmosphere, with bawdy paintings on the wall, the Carlsbad Caverns in stained glass, and rinky-dink background music. Food prices are old style, too—a 12-ounce rib-eye steak costs $9.95—but a shot of tequila in the saloon will set you back $3. *26 Carlsbad Caverns Hwy., White's City, tel. 505/785–2291. No reservations. Dress: casual. D, DC, MC, V. Moderate.*

Fast Jack's. This fast-food favorite shares an adobe-style building with the Velvet Garter Restaurant and Saloon. Seated at one of the booths or at the counter, you can order great burgers; 32 flavors of homemade ice cream; and freshly baked pies, along with standard breakfast, lunch, and dinner fare, including Mexican specialties and some seafood selections. This is a good spot to chow down a hearty breakfast before heading off into the caverns. Owner Jack White, whose grandfather founded White's City, graduated from Stanford with a degree in electrical engineering. He makes sure the bank of video games and souvenir token slot machine are all in good working order. *26 Carlsbad Caverns Hwy., White's City, tel. 505/785–2291. No reservations. Dress: casual. D, DC, MC, V. Inexpensive.*

Lodging

Since tourism is a major industry in Carlsbad, the area offers a wide choice of motels and other services. Most of them are strung out along the highway going to the caverns, appropriately called National Parks Highway. At the turnoff from the highway to the caverns, White's City is a honky-tonk tourist complex, with three motels, a tent and RV campground, restaurants, a post office, souvenir shops, a small amusement park and museum, a miniature golf course, and a saloon.

The most highly recommended establishments are indicated by a star ★.

Category	Cost*
Expensive	$100–$150
Moderate	$65–$100
Inexpensive	under $65

All prices are for a standard double room, excluding 5.8% tax.

Carlsbad
Hotels and Motels
★

Holiday Inn Carlsbad Downtown. The city's newest hotel is the old Carlsbad Inn, the two-story structure at the corner of Canal and Lea streets, totally revamped and renamed. The rugs, the paintings, and the soft desert colors in the guest rooms all harmonize with the Territorial New Mexican decor, a combination of regional and European styles. The hotel's Phenix (*sic*) restaurant, seating 70, is a grill room and pub; Vantanos ("windows"), its gourmet restaurant, seats 65. Kids under 12 eat free, stay free, and play free. *601 S. Canal St., Carlsbad 88220, tel. 505/885–8500. 100 rooms. Facilities: 2 restaurants, bar, swimming pool, Jacuzzi, playground, free guest laundry. AE, D, DC, MC, V. Moderate.*

Best Western Stevens Motel. An old favorite, both locally and with tour groups, this is a reliable, well-operated place. The guest rooms have recently been redone, featuring bright desert colors, mirrored vanities, and modern furnishings; some have kitchenettes, some have private patios, and some have both. Buildings are scattered over a landscaped area covering more than a city block. The motel's Flume Room, an elegant local favorite dining spot, features steaks, prime rib, and table-side service. There's also a coffee shop offering regional and Mexican specialties. The hotel is owned by Carlsbad's mayor, Bob Forrest, but even knowing him won't get you a table at its Silver Spur bar and lounge on Saturday night when the Chaparrals are playing. *1829 S. Canal St., Box 580, Carlsbad 88220, tel. 505/887–2851 or 800/528–1234 for reservations. 202 rooms. Facilities: restaurant, café, lounge, pool, wading pool, playground. AE, D, DC, MC, V. Inexpensive.*

Carlsbad Travelodge South. This three-story motel, located 1 mile from the airport and one block from the Convention Center in Carlsbad, has rooms decorated in cheerful Southwestern tones, although the furnishings are generic. There is no restaurant on the premises, but Jerry's, in the immediate vicinity, serves Denny's-style fare 24 hours a day. *3817 National Parks Hwy., Carlsbad 88220, tel. 505/887–8888 or 800/255–3050 for reservations. 64 rooms. Facilities: pool, Jacuzzi, free airport transfers, complimentary full breakfast for each paying adult. AE, D, DC, MC, V. Inexpensive.*

Continental Inn. South of Carlsbad, on National Parks

Highway, the Continental Inn is about 30 minutes from Carlsbad Caverns. It has simple rooms with matching curtains and bedspreads in colorful Southwestern patterns. The small grounds are pretty and well kept. *3820 National Parks Hwy., Carlsbad 88220, tel. 505/887–0341. 60 rooms. Facilities: heated pool in season, available airport pickups, truck parking. AE, D, DC, MC, V. Inexpensive.*

Park Inn International. This two-story, stone-facaded property encloses a landscaped patio with a pool and a sun deck about as large as an aircraft hangar. Rooms are comfortable, with undistinguished modern furnishings and king-size or two double beds with bright Native American-design bedspreads. The Cafe in the Park serves breakfast and lunch, and the Chaparral Grill Room, a more formal dining room, is open for dinner. Scott's Archery Range is next door. *3706 National Parks Hwy., Carlsbad 88220, tel. 505/887–2861 or 800/437–PARK for reservations. 124 rooms. Facilities: hot tub, pool, 2 restaurants, bar, game room, guest laundry, gift shop, free airport and bus-terminal transfers. AE, D, DC, MC, V. Inexpensive.*

Stagecoach Inn. This family-style motor inn is close to many of the major Carlsbad attractions and offers basic, household-variety rooms at affordable rates. *1819 S. Canal St., Carlsbad 88220, tel. 505/887–1148. 57 rooms. Facilities: restaurant, pool, wading pool, tree-shaded park with playground and picnic area, guest laundry, truck parking. AE, D, MC, V. Inexpensive.*

White's City **Best Western Cavern Inn.** This two-story motor inn with Southwestern-style rooms is run in conjunction with the neighboring Best Western Guadalupe Inn, sharing the same pools and restaurants. The hotel offers the closest accommodations to Carlsbad Caverns and is an immediate neighbor of the popular Velvet Garter Restaurant (*see* Dining, *above*). It's a pleasant, friendly place, determined to make you have a good time. Lots of tour groups are booked here, as well as families. *17 Carlsbad Caverns Hwy., White's City 88266, tel. 505/785–2291. 62 rooms. (Guadalupe Inn has 44 newly decorated rooms.) Facilities: 2 pools, spa, in-room whirlpool tubs, café, playground. AE, DC, MC, V. Moderate.*

Camping

Backcountry camping is by permit only in Carlsbad Caverns National Park; free permits can be obtained at the visitor center, where you can also pick up a map of areas closed to camping. You'll need to hike to campsites, which may not be seen from established roadways. There are no vehicle or RV camping areas in the park.

Nearby Brantley Lake State Park, the newest state park in New Mexico, and Lincoln National Forest both have camping facilities. In addition, a number of commercial sites are available at White's City, 7 miles northeast of the Caverns, and in Carlsbad, 27 miles northeast.

Brantley Lake State Park. Twelve miles north of Carlsbad via Highway 285, this facility has a playground, boat ramps, picnic areas, grills, bathhouse with running water and flush toilets, overnight camping spaces, and a visitor center. Fishing (bass, trout, and crappie), boating, and other water sports are offered. *Box 2288, Carlsbad 88221, tel. 505/457–2384. 49 water and electric hookups, dump station. Primitive-area camping (no immediate facilities) $6 per night, developed-area camping (with facilities) $7 per night, hookup sites $11 per night. No reservations. No credit cards.*

Carlsbad Kampgrounds. This shaded, full-service campground has level gravel sites and canopied tables, trees, year-round grass for tenters, a swimming pool, laundry, public phone and phone hookups, hot showers, flush toilets, a grocery store, grills, and sewage disposal. A professional RV service is located next door. *4301 National Parks Hwy., Star Rte. 1, Box 34, Carlsbad 88220, tel. 505/885–6333. 170 sites, 46 full hookups, 68 water and electric. $8.50–$11.50 for 2 persons. Reservations recommended during the summer months. D, MC, V.*

Park Entrance RV Park. In the heart of White's City, 7 miles from Carlsbad Caverns, this popular RV park offers natural desert sites with canopied shaded tables. Included are flush toilets, hot showers, sewage disposal, gasoline, grocery store, grills, parking control gates, and nearby recreational facilities (recreation hall, arcade, playground, tennis court, and two heated swimming pools). *17 Carlsbad Caverns Hwy. (Box 128), White's City 88268, tel. 505/785–2291 or 800/CAVERNS for reservations. 150 sites. 60 full hookups, 48 pull-throughs. $14 per vehicle. Reservations suggested during the summer. AE, D, MC, V.*

Windmill RV Park. Facilities for swimming, boating, and fishing, as well as laundry, hot showers, and flush toilets, are available at this RV park located on National Parks Highway (accessed by NM 180/62 South). *3624 National Parks Hwy., Carlsbad 88220, tel. 505/885–9761. 61 RV sites, water, flush toilets, hot showers. $6 for tent sites, $11 full hookup (cable TV $1 extra). AE, D, MC, V.*

Nightlife

Carlsbad Caverns closes at 7 PM during the summer, 5:30 PM during the winter; between late May and mid-October you can hang around until sunset to watch thousands of bats leave the caves en masse to forage for food (*see* Carlsbad Caverns National Park in Exploring Carlsbad, *above*). For more conventional types of nighttime activities, you're pretty much limited to the Carlsbad lounge circuit. You can dance to country-and-Western music at the **Silver Spur Lounge** in the Best Western Stevens Motel (tel. 505/887–2851), where live bands play Monday–Saturday 9 PM–1:30 AM. (If you want to start early, happy hour is 4–7 PM.) The **Park Inn International's lounge** (tel. 505/887–2861) has a big-screen TV and a jukebox and live country-and-Western bands on Friday and Saturday nights. It's open Monday–Saturday from 4 PM until around 2 AM. Also operating during those hours is **My Way Lounge** (203 S. Central St., tel. 505/887–0212), a popular place for shooting pool, playing video games, and (you guessed it) dancing to live country-and-Western music; bands play from around 9 PM until 2 AM on Fridays and Saturdays only. For foot-stomping Western music, nightly shootouts, and a chuckwagon dinner, there's also the **Rocking M Ranch** (tel. 505/885–0195) on the Old Cavern Highway.

Excursion to Lincoln County and White Sands National Monument

This tour takes you through pine-covered mountains to four of southern New Mexico's most interesting spots. It's possible to see them all in one day, but getting to them from Carlsbad takes about four hours by car. It is probably a good idea to plan on spending a night in the area (*see* Lodging, *below*) so that you can avoid driving the eight-hour round-trip in one day. We've arranged the tour to start in Ruidoso, which makes a good base from which to explore the region.

Tourist Information

Ruidoso Valley Chamber of Commerce/Convention and Visitors Bureau (720 Sudderth Dr., Box 698, Ruidoso 88345, tel. 800/253–2255 or 505/257–7395) has free brochures, maps, booklets, and other information, and is the main source of information about San Patricio.

To find out about Lincoln, contact **Lincoln Hospitality Group,** Box 27, Lincoln 88338, tel. 505/653–4676; **Lincoln County Heritage Trust,** Box 98, Lincoln 88338, tel. 505/653–4025; **Lincoln County Historical Society,** Box 91, Lincoln 88338, tel. 505/653–4529; and **Lincoln State Monument,** Box 36, Lincoln 88338, tel. 505/653–4372.

The information desk at the **Visitor Center** of the White Sands National Monument (Box 458, Alamogordo 88310, tel. 505/479–6124) provides general information and free maps and pamphlets.

Getting There

Ruidoso, the starting point of this excursion, is 170 miles north of Carlsbad Caverns via U.S. 285 to Roswell, and then U.S. 70 to Ruidoso.

Exploring Lincoln County

Ruidoso Sprawled at the base of the Sierra Blanca Peak on the eastern slopes of the pine-covered Sacramento Mountains, midway between Alamogordo and Roswell, Ruidoso is a sophisticated year-round resort that retains, at least for the time being, its rustic small-town charm. Summer visitors arrive from all over the Southwest to fill the cabins and hotels and to fish and swim in swift-moving streams and deep blue lakes. In winter, the Mescalero Apache–run ski area, Ski Apache (*see below*), makes Ruidoso a major area ski resort. A convention center has just opened, and there's talk of building a resort hotel and performing-arts center there amid the snowy peaks, mountain streams, colorful village shops, and pine-shaded trails. At first glance, the town itself isn't much to look at. But though its business district is little longer than a shoestring, it supports a surfeit of interesting shops, antiques stores, bars, and restaurants.

Ruidoso (which means "noisy" in Spanish) has an official population of only 4,800, but it's no one-horse town. Not by a long shot. Each summer, it becomes the epicenter of American quarter-horse racing, thanks to the fabulous **Ruidoso Downs,** self-proclaimed Home of the World's Richest Horse Races and the first stop on this tour, right on Highway 70 East. On Labor Day, it is the site of the All-American Quarter Horse Futurity, with a total purse of as much as $2.5 million, more than $1 million of it going to the winner alone. Purses for other quarter-horse and Thoroughbred events throughout the season (May through Labor Day) are almost as spectacular.

Ruidoso's role as a big-money racing center came about quite naturally. The breeding and racing of horses is one of New Mexico's oldest enterprises. Among the Spanish who explored the region, horsemen were the aristocrats. In the more recent past, Ruidoso attracted freewheeling Texans, Oklahomans, and New Mexicans willing to bet on anything. While spending their summers in the cool New Mexico mountains, they were entertained by ranchers who would race their most spirited horses in the cornfields and meadows. The visitors wagered, often cleaning out their bank accounts to bet on horses. The purses got bigger and bigger, and Ruidoso Downs emerged.

In operation since 1947, the track has changed ownership numerous times. Current owner R. D. Hubbard purchased it in 1988 and immediately began a $3 million renovation;

betting windows, concession stands, and rest rooms, as well as barns and the stable area, were remodeled. Chairman and chief executive of AFG Industries, the second-largest glass manufacturer in the United States, Hubbard has infused considerable money in Ruidoso. Another of his investments is the new state-of-the-art **Ruidoso Downs Sports Theater,** a half mile east of the track, just off Highway 70 (look for the signs), which features year-round pari-mutuel racing plus other sports events on large-screen TV sets. *Hwy. 70, Box 449, Ruidoso Downs, 88346, tel. 505/ 378–4431. Admission: open seating free, reserved seating $2.50, grandstand $3.50–$5. Theater admission: free. Parking: $3. Racing May 9–July 1, Thurs.–Sun.; July 1– Labor Day, Thurs.–Mon. Post time is 1 PM (earlier on Labor Day).*

Ruidoso's newest showcase, opened in May 1992 in a newly renovated 40,000-square-foot building about a half mile east of the track, is the **Museum of the Horse,** built to house the Anne C. Stradling Museum of the Horse Collection, consisting of over 10,000 pieces related to the horse—paintings, drawings, and bronzes by master artists; saddles from Mexico and China and those used by the Pony Express; carriages and wagons; a 400-year-old oxcart; and memorabilia from Teddy Roosevelt, Frederic Remington, and the DuPont family. Some items date from Roman times, and there's a chariot bit from ancient Greece. This museum is also a Hubbard undertaking. Long a fixture of Patagonia, Arizona, the massive collection was given to Hubbard when its founder, Anne Stradling, became too ill to care for it properly (she died in 1992 at age 78). Hubbard promised to keep the collection intact and to display it under Stradling's name. *Hwy. 70, Box 1679, Ruidoso Downs 88346; tel. 505/378–4142. Admission: $4 adults, $3 senior citizens, $2.50 children 5–18, children under 5 free. Open daily 8:30–5:30.*

Bordering Ruidoso to the west, about a 15-minute drive from the racetrack, is the **Mescalero Apache Indian Reservation,** home to more than 2,500 Mescalero Apaches, most of whom work in the lumber and fishing industries. The famous **Inn of the Mountain Gods** (*see* Lodging, *below*), the most elegant resort in the state, is Apache-owned and -operated. Other sights on the reservation include a **general store,** a **trading post,** and a **museum,** which has clothing and crafts displays, a 12-minute video about life on the reservation, and regular talks about the history and culture of the Mescalero Apaches. There are also campsites (with hookups at Silver and Eagle lakes only) and picnic areas. Ritual dances are occasionally performed for the public, the most colorful during the annual Fourth of July celebrations. The reservation's **Ski Apache** area on nearby Sierra Blanca (11,400 ft) has fine powder skiing from Thanksgiving until mid-April, or longer if the snows persist. *Tribal Office, Hwy. 70, Box 176, Mescalero 88340, tel. 505/671–4494; for*

Ski Apache, tel. 505/336-4357. Admission: free. Open weekdays 8-4:30.

San Patricio Twenty miles east of Ruidoso on U.S. 70 is San Patricio. Caught in the right light at the right time of day, the tiny village, nestled in the Hondo Valley where the Ruidoso River glistens silver in the sun, is hauntingly beautiful. The all-white **church of San Patricio,** with its meager bell tower hardly scraping the sky, is the first thing to catch your eye. The peaceful valley is filled with horse ranches, orchards, and herds of sheep. In the fall, roadside fruit stands offer apples, jugs of sweet cider, and strings of bright red chiles. Small wonder that the area has long appealed to artists.

The **Hurd-La Riconada Gallery,** on the Sentinel Ranch, is part of the sprawling art compound belonging to one of America's leading art dynasties. Showcased in the unique adobe gallery is the work of the late Peter Hurd, who gained world recognition as a regional landscape painter and portraitist—and won perhaps even more fame for a portrait commissioned by President Lyndon B. Johnson who, unhappy with the results, refused to hang it in the White House. Also on display are the works of Hurd's elderly widow, Henriette Wyeth Hurd (Andrew Wyeth's eldest daughter), and their son, artist Michael Hurd. Paintings by Andrew Wyeth and his father, N. C. Wyeth, round out the impressive presentation. Signed reproductions as well as some original paintings are for sale. Bring your checkbook. *U.S. 70, mile marker 281, tel. 505/653-4331. Admission free. Open weekdays 9-4, Sat. 10-4.*

Adjacent to the Hurds' Sentinel Ranch—just turn right at the polo field and keep going—is **Fort Meigs Gallery,** designer John Meigs's lifetime collection of just about everything collectible. Meigs was a longtime friend of the Hurds as well as of other notable artists, such as Georgia O'Keeffe. Displayed in his 22-room mansion are paintings, graphics, antiques, photographs, Oriental scrolls, Chinese ceramics, a Ferris wheel made of toothpicks, furniture, coffins, an embroidery by D. H. Lawrence, a bedspread from a Juárez bordello, religious carvings, and an entire library of 40,000 books. In frail health, Meigs has decided to put his collection up for sale, piece by piece, but he appears to be in no particular hurry to part with anything. (He is currently in negotiation with the Museum of New Mexico, which has made overtures toward acquiring the gallery.) *U.S. 70, mile marker 281; tel. 505/653-4320. Open daily 10-6.*

Lincoln It may not be as well known as Tombstone, Arizona, or Deadwood, South Dakota, but Lincoln, 10 miles east of San Patricio on U.S. 70, ranks right up there with the toughest of the tough old towns of the Old West. It was just over a century ago that the violent Lincoln County Wars took place, as two opposing factions clashed over lucrative government contracts to feed the army and the Native Americans on reservations in the area. The bloody confrontation lasted six months. One of the more infamous figures to emerge from it was a short, slight, sallow young man with buckteeth, startling blue eyes, and curly reddish-brown hair. His name was Billy the Kid.

The role of Billy—born William H. Bonney—in the Lincoln County Wars is not quite clear. He was a ranch hand for cattle baron John Chisom and already enjoyed a modest reputation as a gunman when he surfaced in Lincoln County in the mid-1870s. But apparently during the last four years of his life, spent mostly in and around Lincoln, his guns hardly had time to cool. He is said to have killed 21 men, including Lincoln's sheriff Matthew Brady; it was for Brady's murder that he was convicted in 1881 and sentenced to hang. But Billy managed to elude the gallows.

On April 28 of that year, though manacled and shackled, Billy made a daring escape from the Old Lincoln County Courthouse (*see below*), killing two guards. The first, James W. Bell, was shot on the courthouse steps and managed to stumble into the backyard before he died. The other, Robert W. Ollinger, came running from the dining room of the nearby Wortley Hotel (*see* Dining and Lodging, *below*) when he heard the shots. Billy gunned him down from the second-floor window. Today, stone markers designate the places where they fell. Three months later, a posse led by Sheriff Pat Garrett tracked Billy down at the home of a friend in Old Fort Sumner, surprised him in the dark, and finished him off with two clean shots. One of the West's most notorious gunmen, and ultimately one of its best-known folk legends, was dead at 21.

Surprisingly little has changed since the Lincoln County War. The town's only street (Hwy. 380) is lined with adobe homes and buildings dating from its historic, tumultuous past. After undergoing extensive restoration in recent years, Lincoln has emerged as one of New Mexico's premier tourist attractions. Settled in the early 1850s, the town was originally called La Placita ("village square" in Spanish); today it is a National Historic Landmark and still a living, if small, community with a population of 68. Several historic structures, including the Tunstall Store Museum and the Lincoln County Courthouse Museum (*see below*), are operated by New Mexico State Monuments, part of the Museum of New Mexico.

A visit might best begin at the **Historical Center,** at the eastern end of town, where a 10-minute slide show introduces Lincoln's attractions. Exhibits here are devoted to Billy the Kid, the Lincoln County Wars, cowboys, Apaches, and Buffalo Soldiers (black horse troops of the 9th and 10th Cavalry), with guides and attendants dressed in period costumes. The center and a well-stocked museum store are operated by the Lincoln County Heritage Trust (tel. 505/653–4025).

Just west of the Historical Center are the **Tunstall Store Museum** (505/653–4372), which still contains much of its original stock dating back to the 1800s, the **Dr. Woods House** (505/653–4529), a fine example of a typical period house, and the **Lincoln County Courthouse Museum** (505/653–4372), housed in the two-story building from which Billy the Kid made his daring escape.

All sites open May 1–Sept. 30, daily 9–6; all except the Dr. Woods House open Oct. 1–Jan 1 and Mar. 1–Apr. 1, Tues–Sun 9–5. General admission pass to all sites: May 1–Sept. 30, $4.50; Oct. 1–April 30, $4; children under 17 free.

White Sands National Monument Heading back south on U.S. 70 past Ruidoso, 15 miles southwest of Alamogordo, you come to **White Sands National Monument,** a scene out of the *Arabian Nights*, with shifting sand dunes 60 feet high. White Sands encompasses 145,344 acres, the largest deposit of gypsum sand in the world (the sand on most beaches is silica; gypsum is used for making plaster of Paris); it is one of the few landforms that is recognizable from space. The **Visitor Center** here has a museum display relating to the dunes and how they were formed. There's also an information desk, a bookstore, and a snack bar. From here, a 16-mile round-trip takes you into the eerie wonderland of gleaming white sand. Who can resist climbing to the top of the dunes for a photograph, then tumbling down, wading knee-deep in the gypsum crystals? Visitors are cautioned, however, not to tunnel into the sand dunes; in loose sand, tunnels can easily collapse and cause suffocation. When you want to explore on foot, follow the **Big Dune Trail,** a mile-long, self-guided nature trail; a sign in the parking lot marks the beginning of the trail. Written information about the plants and animals you may encounter is available free at the visitor center. A picnic area has shaded tables and grills. Backcountry campsites are available by permit, obtainable at the visitor center; camping is free, but facilities are primitive—there aren't any.

Not surprisingly, White Sands has been used for many TV commercials and numerous Hollywood films, the most recent being *White Sands,* an espionage thriller starring Willem DaFoe and Mickey Rourke. Surrounded on three sides by the White Sands Missile Range and on the fourth by Holloman Air Force Base, the park occasionally delays its early morning openings as a safety precaution when missile tests are being conducted overhead. *Box 458, Alamogordo, tel. 505/479–6124. Open daily 7 AM to 30 minutes past sunset. Admission: $4 per vehicle, $2 per bus passenger.*

Dining and Lodging

Ruidoso Dining **La Lorraine.** Classic French cuisine, such as chateaubriand, beef Bourguignon, and sausage-stuffed quail, is served amid elegant Colonial French surroundings. In summer, you can dine outdoors on the patio amid cages of exotic Amazonian birds. *2523 Sudderth Dr., tel. 505/257–2954. Reservations required. Dress: formal. AE, MC, V. No lunch Sun. Expensive.*

Dan-Li-Ka. This is the dining room at the popular Inn of the Mountain Gods resort on the Mescalero Apache Reservation, just southwest of Ruidoso. Dan-Li-Ka, which means "good food" in Apache, occupies one large room with wooden chairs and tables, and knockout views of Mescalero Lake and mountains cloaked in ponderosa pine. The extensive menu includes Spanish, Native American, and regional New Mexican specialties: Texas chicken strips, mountain trout, burgers topped with green chiles and jalapeño jack cheese, Apache fry bread, and classic Reuben sandwiches for lunch; fresh game, sautéed red trout, sirloin steaks, and prime rib for dinner. *Inn of the Mountain Gods, Mescalero Apache Reservation, tel. 505/257–5315. Reservations suggested for dinner. Dress: casual. AE, D, DC, MC, V. Moderate–Expensive.*

Incredible Restaurant and Saloon. This rustic Western spot has been a local favorite for 30 years for lobster dinners, prime rib, and filet mignon. There's a lounge and an atrium for dining under the stars. *Hwy. 48 N. at Alto Village, tel. 505/336–4312. Reservations suggested for dinner. Dress: casual. DC, MC, V. Moderate–Expensive.*

Cattle Baron Steak House. This cozy lounge and steak house offers daily cut steaks, prime rib, and seafood in three separate dining rooms filled with tables and booths. Fireplaces add Western warmth, and large picture windows provide stunning mountain views. A skylit lounge at one end is bright and airy. On Sundays, there are all-you-can-eat ribs and "peel your own shrimp" specials in addition to the always-colossal salad bar. *657 Sudderth Dr., tel. 505/257–9355. Reservations suggested. Dress: casual. AE, D, DC, MC, V. Inexpensive–Moderate.*

Lodging **Inn of the Mountain Gods.** The Mescalero Apaches own and
★ operate this spectacular year-round resort on the banks of the Mescalero Lake, about 3 miles southwest of Ruidoso. The rooms are large and handsomely furnished with Western and Native American flourishes; each has a balcony. The inn has its own minicasino with poker and lotto machines, and part of the front reception desk has been given over to the sale of pull-tab gambling tickets, which seems to draw a steady line of players all day long. The resort's 18-hole golf course was designed by Ted Robinson, who also created the famous courses at the Acapulco Princess and at California's Tamarisk. *Carrizon Canyon Rd., Box 269, Mescalero 28340, tel. 505/257–5141 or 800/545–9011. 230 rooms with bath. Facilities: restaurant, lounge, casino, golf, stables, tennis, heated pool, whirlpool, fishing lake, hunting, trap, archery, skeet. AE, D, DC, MC, V. Expensive.*

Best Western Swiss Chalet. The closest hotel to Ski Apache, this two-story hilltop chalet fills up quickly in winter but is popular in the summer as well. The hotel sprawls out along the contours of the hill, with its restaurant and lounge at one end and meeting facilities at the other. The rooms are what you'd expect in a chain hotel—large, nondescript, and furnished in contemporary style. *1451 Mechem Dr. (Hwy. 48), Box 459, Ruidoso 88345, tel. 505/258–3333 or 800/47– SWISS. 82 rooms with bath. Facilities: indoor pool, spa, Jacuzzi, in-room steam saunas, restaurant, and lounge. AE, D, DC, MC, V. Moderate.*

The Lodge in Cloudcroft. This burly Victorian lodge some 40 miles south of Ruidoso was built in 1899 by the Alamagordo and Sacramento Mountain Railway to house its workers. A stuffed bear stands snarling in the mammoth lobby, and a long-horned eland stares down from above a copper-sheathed fireplace. The rooms are decorated with chenille bedspreads, period antiques, flocked wallpaper in pastel shades, ceiling fans, and, in many cases, four-poster beds. Rebeccas's, the hotel restaurant, is named after a brazen resident ghost who is given to appearing naked in guests' bathtubs. (Breakfast at Rebecca's is included in the room rate.) The lodge complex also includes the Lodge Pavilion, a rustic 11-room B&B. *1 Corona Place, Box 497, Cloudcroft 88317, tel. 505/682–2566 or 800/395–6343. 60 rooms. Facilities: pool, golf, 2 bars, restaurant, sauna, spa. AE, D, DC, MC, V. Moderate.*

Shadow Mountain Lodge. The Ruidoso River flows by just across the street from this small L-shaped hotel in the historic Upper Canyon. Fieldstone fireplaces in each room add to the lodge's alpine ambience; rooms also come equipped with California king-size beds and kitchen facilities. A veranda runs along the front of the hotel, with grills outside for marshmallow or hot-dog toasting. *107 Main Rd., Box 1427, Ruidoso 88345, tel. 505/257–4885 or 800/441–4331. 19 rooms with bath. AE, D, DC, MC, V. Moderate.*

San Patricio
Lodging

Hurd Ranch Guest Homes. These two adobe casitas on the Sentinel Ranch, adjacent to the Hurd Gallery, opened recently—becoming the sole members of San Patricio's lodging scene. Stylishly decorated with paintings, sculptures, and Native American artifacts, and with modern and Western furnishings, the casitas are an outgrowth of guest houses that artist Michael Hurd made available to friends and portrait subjects who needed accommodations while their commissions were being completed. Both casitas have fully equipped kitchens, which come in handy since there are no restaurants nearby. The area offers plenty to do if you're adventurous and ready to do some exploring. *U.S. 70, Box 100, San Patricio 88348; tel. 505/653–4331. 2 casitas with bath. Facilities: polo field. MC, V. Expensive.*

Lincoln
Dining and Lodging

The Wortley Hotel. This historic lodging was originally built as the Lincoln Hotel in 1872 to house judges, lawmen, cowboys, and others drawn to this flourishing ranching area. Burned in 1935, later rebuilt, and recently renovated, it's now in great shape, with antique dressers, marbletop tables, lace curtains, and brass four-poster beds. Drifting off to sleep at night, with your head on a cool pillow, you can almost hear the hoofbeats and gunshots down the street. At present, the dining room serves Lincoln's only sit-down meals—Western specialties, such as chicken-fried steak, enchiladas, and sautéed dishes, along with soups, salads, and sandwiches. *Hwy. 380, Lincoln 88338, tel. 505/653–4500. 8 rooms with bath. Facilities: dining room (reservations not required, casual dress). MC, V. Open May 1–Oct. 31. Moderate.*

Lodging **Casa de Patron.** This attractive bed-and-breakfast on Lincoln's main street is in a historic adobe—once the home of Juan Patron, an early settler and father of three who was gunned down at age 29 in the violence that swept Lincoln County. The main house has high viga ceilings and all new Mexican tile baths. Owners Jeremy and Cleis Jordan also offer two small adobe casitas decorated with traditional New Mexican flavor, cathedral ceilings, vigas, and portals. All rooms are furnished with antiques and collectibles. Full country breakfasts are served in the main house, Continental breakfasts in the casitas. *Hwy. 380, Box 27, Lincoln 88338, tel. 505/653–4676; fax 505/653–4671. 3 rooms in the main house, 2 casitas (1 with a 2-bedroom suite), all with private bath. MC, V. Moderate.*

7 Pueblos of the Rio Grande

Traveling across country, one is immediately impressed with the many recently built forts, Native American villages, and trading posts that dot the landscape everywhere from New Jersey to Cleveland. In some places, Indians in jeans and sports jackets sign in for work in the morning, change into tribal regalia, and then spend the rest of the day making pots and baskets and performing dances and other ancient rituals for the entertainment of tourists. Such places may be sincere in their efforts to portray Native American life and culture, but they often come across as inane and theatrical. But not so in the West, where reservations are perhaps the only places left where traditional Native American culture and skills are retained with a sense of dignity and pride. Descendants of the highly civilized Anasazi, the Pueblo peoples of northern New Mexico in particular, continue to preserve their customs amid a changing world. Each pueblo has its own personality, history, and specialties in art and design.

Before venturing off to visit the pueblos, you'd do well to visit the striking **Indian Pueblo Cultural Center** in Albuquerque (*see* Important Addresses and Numbers, *below*), which exhibits and sells the best of arts and crafts from all the New Mexico pueblos; coming here will help you decide which of the pueblos to visit. Native American ceremonial dances are held during summer weekends, and photography is allowed (photographing Indian rituals is generally not allowed at any of the individual pueblos).

Fall, when the pueblos celebrate the harvest with special ceremonies, dances, and sacred rituals, is the best time to visit. The air is fragrant with curling piñon smoke. Clusters of *ristras* (red chiles) decorate many homes, with the chiles destined to add their distinct flavor to stews and sauces through the winter. Drums throb with insistent cadence. Dancers adorn themselves with some of the most beautiful turquoise and jewelry seen anywhere. The atmosphere is lighthearted, evocative of a country fair: Excited children laugh and scamper, and wives chuckle and gossip, conversing in tongues—Tewa, Keresan, Tiwa—both strange and fascinating to outsiders.

For locations of the pueblos listed below, see the map of New Mexico on pp. xii–xiii.

Pueblo Etiquette—Do's and Don'ts

Each pueblo has its own regulations for the use of still cameras, camcorders, and movie cameras, as well as for sketching and painting. Some pueblos, such as San Juan and Santo Domingo, prohibit photography altogether. Others, such as Santa Clara, prohibit photography at certain times, such as during ritual dances. Still others allow photography but require a permit, which usually costs about $5 for a still camera and up to $35 for the privilege of setting up an easel and painting all day. Be sure to ask permission before photographing anyone in the pueblos; it's also customary to give the subject a dollar or two for agreeing to be photographed. Native American law prevails on the pueblos, and violations of photography regulations could result in confiscation of cameras. Restrictions for the various pueblos are noted in the individual descriptions below.

Possessing or using drugs and/or alcohol on Native American land is forbidden.

Ritual dances often have serious religious significance and should be respected as such. Silence is mandatory. That means no questions about ceremonies or dances while they're being performed. Don't walk across the dance plaza during a performance, and don't applaud afterward.

Kiva and ceremonial rooms are restricted to pueblo members only.

Cemeteries are sacred. They're off limits to all visitors and should never be photographed.

Unless pueblo dwellings are clearly marked as shops, don't wander or peek inside. Remember, these are private homes.

Many of the pueblo buildings are hundreds of years old. Don't try to scale adobe walls or climb on top of buildings, or you may come tumbling down.

Don't litter. Nature is sacred on the pueblos and defacing of land can be a serious offense.

Important Addresses and Numbers

The **Indian Pueblo Cultural Center** (2401 12th St. NW, Albuquerque 87102, tel. 505/843–7270) is the best source of information on New Mexico's Native Americans.

The detailed *New Mexico Vacation Guide,* available free from the **New Mexico Department of Tourism** (Lamy Bldg., 491 Old Santa Fe Trail, Santa Fe 87503, tel. 800/545–2040 or 505/827–7400), includes an informative section on the state's pueblos.

Pueblos Near Santa Fe

The pueblos around Santa Fe, the Southwest's first Spanish settlement, are more infused with Spanish culture than are the pueblos in other areas. Pueblo dwellers here also have the keenest business sense when dealing with the sale of handicrafts and art and with matters touristic.

Cochiti Pueblo

The Cochiti Pueblo is known for its excellent crafts and jewelry, storyteller pottery figures, leather, beadwork, and drums. The latter play a significant role in Cochiti ceremonials on the July 14 feast day in honor of San Buenaventura. Most of the people of the pueblo work in Santa Fe or Albuquerque, but enough members of the tribe continue to farm and practice craft-making to maintain the tribal traditions and culture. The pueblo is located on the west bank of the Rio Grande near recreational facilities at Cochiti Lake (about 45 minutes from Santa Fe, west of I–25) that are administered by the U.S. Army Corps of Engineers. These include picnic tables, boat ramps and rentals, RV hookups, and a beach for swimming. *Box 70, Cochiti 87041, tel. 505/ 465–2244. Admission free. Permission to visit from the tribal governor's office is suggested. Open daily 8–5. No cameras, recorders, or sketchbooks are allowed.*

Jemez Pueblo

This pueblo, located in the red sandstone canyon of the Jemez River, west of Santa Fe (northwest of Bernalillo, off NM 44), is noted for its polychrome pottery and fine baskets made from yucca leaves. The Jemez Reservation, encompassing 88,000 acres, contains two recreational sites, Holy Ghost Springs and Dragon Fly Pond, on NM 4 near the pueblo. Fishing licenses for both areas can be acquired from the Jemez game warden for $2 to $5 per day, depending on the season. Hunting permits are also available. The village may hold little of interest for the casual visitor. The beautiful San Diego de Jemez Mission at the Jemez State Monument, 20 miles north, is a popular attraction. The great stone mission church was founded in the early 1600s by Fra Gerónimo Zárate Salmerón. The pueblo's two major feast days are November 12, in honor of St. James, and August 2, for Our Lady of the Angels. *Box 100, Jemez 87024, tel. 505/834–7359. Admission free. Photography is restricted, except for San Diego Mission.*

Nambe Pueblo

It is here at the Nambe Pueblo, 15 miles northeast of Santa Fe (via U.S. 84/285; take a right at NM 4, then look for signs), that the famous Nambe cooking pots are made of golden micaceous clay. This ceramic work, along with other outstanding pottery pieces, woven belts, silver jewelry, and beadwork, may be purchased at the pueblo's crafts center. Recreational facilities open to the public here include trout fishing, camping, hiking, and picnicking at nearby Nambe Falls and Lake. Contemporary new buildings have replaced the original pueblo and mission church, but the landscape and the stunning views of the Sangre de Cristo Mountains remain unchanged. The pueblo holds ceremonial dances on July 4 (the Nambe Falls Celebration) and on October 4, the feast day of St. Francis of Assisi. *Rte. 1, Box 117-BB, Santa Fe 87501, tel. 505/455–2036. Fishing is allowed for a fee Mar.–Nov., and permits are available for picnicking, camping, and boating. Photo permits may be purchased as well. Fees are $5 for still cameras, $15 for video recorders and movie cameras.*

Pojoaque Pueblo

Drawing visitors from nearby Santa Fe (it's 15 mi north, just off U.S. 84/285), the Pojoaque Pueblo attracts Los Alamos and Espanola residents, too. It has more than 25 businesses aimed at the tourist trade, including a visitor center, tourist information office, tribal-owned supermarket, mobile-home park, and shops offering an extensive selection of northern New Mexican pottery and other traditional arts and crafts for sale. Tribal enterprises, conducted primarily along a commercial strip fronting U.S. 84/285, have made the Pojoaque Pueblo one of the more prosperous in northern New Mexico. However, it has no definable village as such and has virtually ceased to exist as a viable community. Of the original settlement, only low mounds scattered in fields and among houses remain. A smallpox epidemic in 1890 nearly wiped out the entire tribe, but its numbers have increased considerably since then, and prospered. The pueblo celebrates its feast day on December 12 in honor of Our Lady of Guadalupe. On the first Saturday in August, Pojoaque hosts the Plaza Fiesta, a multicultural celebration that features Native American, Western, and international folk dancing, as well as food and hot-air balloon rides. *Rte. 11, Box 71, Santa Fe 87501, tel. 505/455–3460.*

San Ildefonso Pueblo

This was the home of the most famous of all pueblo potters, Maria Martinez, whose work is now on permanent display in the Millicent Rogers Museum in Taos (*see* Tour 4 in Chapter 4) as well as in other museums throughout the Southwest. She created exquisite designs in red and black pottery from the 1920s to the 1980s. The San Ildefonso Pueblo has long been known for its outstanding pottery and boasts a number of highly acclaimed potters as well as other artists and craftspeople, many of whom open their homes to prospective buyers. There are also several trading posts on the pueblo, a visitor center, and a museum where much of Maria Martinez's work can be seen. Fishing is permitted in a nearby pond. San Ildefonso is one of the more active pueblos in retaining its ceremonial dances and customs. Its feast day is celebrated on January 23, when an unforgettable Animal dance is performed. Buffalo, Deer, and Comanche dances continue throughout the day. *Rte. 5, Box 315-A, Santa Fe 87501, tel. 505/455–3549. Cameras are not permit-*

*ted at any of the ceremonial dances but may be used at other
times with a permit. Fees are $5 for still cameras; $15 for
video recorders, movie cameras, or sketching.*

Santa Clara Pueblo

The Santa Clara Pueblo, located just off NM 30, southwest
of Espanola, is the home of the beautiful Puye Cliff Dwellings, which rise above it, and of the Santa Clara Canyon
with its four ponds, miles of stream fishing, picnicking, and
camping facilities. Most of the traditional tribal dwellings
have been demolished and replaced by more conventional
houses. Santa Clara remains famous nonetheless for its
shiny red-and-black engraved pottery and for its myriad
well-known painters and sculptors; visitors who knock on
the doors with signs announcing pottery will be invited inside to meet the artists. The population of the pueblo is
about 2,000. Self-guided and guided tours are offered to the
740-room Puye Cliff Dwellings, Santa Clara's ancestral
home. The feast day of St. Clare is celebrated on August 12.
*Box 580, Espanola 87532, tel. 505/753-7326. Open daily
8-5. Permits for the use of trails, camping, and picnic areas, as well as for fishing in trout ponds, are available at the
sites. Cameras are allowed without special permits, but
photography fees may have to be negotiated with individuals photographed.*

Tesuque Pueblo

The Tesuque Pueblo, 10 miles north of Santa Fe along U.S.
84/285, is the home of one of the smallest Tiwa-speaking
tribes. Because of its proximity to Santa Fe, it was one of
the first pueblos to establish contact with the Spanish and
eventually became one of their most vicious foes. Built
around the year 1250, it has maintained its identity well and
is today one of the oldest and most traditional of the pueblos—listed on the National Register of Historic Places—
but unfortunately it's perhaps better known for its bingo
parlor than for its arts and crafts. The pueblo has no crafts
shops or trading posts, and most sales are made from private homes. The tribe operates an RV park and general
store, among other businesses. Tesuque Farms grows food
without the use of pesticides. The pueblo's lands are some
of the most beautiful for horseback riding, camping, and
fishing, with the majestic Sangre de Cristo Mountains rising in the distance. Wind-eroded sandstone formations,
such as nearby Camel Rock, form the "badlands" north of
the pueblo. Tesuque celebrates its feast day on November
12 in honor of Santo Domingo with ceremonial dances. It's
the one time of the year during which the pueblo seems to
open its arms and its doors to visitors (bingo players don't
have access to most of Tesuque). For directions and information, stop by the administrative office. *Rte. 11, Box 1,
Santa Fe 87501, tel. 505/983-2667. Cameras, recorders,*

and sketch pads not allowed during ceremonial dances (and there's not much to photograph otherwise). Tesuque Pueblo bingo begins at 5 nightly, with the early-bird special at 6:30 and the main series beginning at 7. For bingo information, call 505/984-8418.

Pueblos Near Taos

The famous Taos Pueblo, unchanged over the centuries, is the personification of classic Pueblo Native American culture. It and the other northern pueblos near Taos offer first-rate recreational facilities as well as a glimpse into the past.

Picuris Pueblo

The Picuris Native Americans once lived in large six- and seven-story dwellings similar to those still standing at the Taos Pueblo, but they were abandoned in the wake of 18th-century Pueblo uprisings. Relatively isolated—off NM 68, between Espanola and Taos, surrounded by the timberland of the Carson National Forest—and a bit run-down, Picuris now seems the most economically depressed of all the New Mexico pueblos. A multipurpose building on the grounds contains the Hidden Valley Restaurant (American and Native American food) and a convenience store, the Picuris Market. There's also a museum where samples of mica-flecked pottery and other crafts can be seen and purchased. Guided tours are conducted to recently excavated areas of the pueblo. Fishing, picnicking, and camping are permitted at nearby trout-stocked Pu-Na and Tu-Tah lakes. (Fishing and overnight camping permits can be obtained at the Picuris Market.) The 270-member, Tiwa-speaking Picuris tribe governs itself as a separate tribal nation and has no treaties with any foreign country, including the United States. The tribe also owns controlling interest in the Hotel Santa Fe in Santa Fe. The pueblo's patron saint, San Lorenzo, is honored on August 10. *Box 127, Penasco 87553, tel. 505/587-2957. Admission to the pueblo is free, but a $1 fee is charged for guided tours to the ruins. Camera permits, available at the visitor center, are required. Fees are $5 for still cameras, $10 for video or movie cameras. Open daily 8–7; the Hidden Valley Restaurant is open 11:30–7.*

San Juan Pueblo

Site of the first regional Spanish settlement in 1598 (the first capital of *Nueva España*, New Spain), the San Juan Pueblo is situated on the confluence of the Chama River and the Rio Grande, 5 miles north of Espanola on NM 68. Headquarters of the Eight Northern Indian Pueblo Council, it has a beautiful arts center called Oke-Oweenge Arts and Crafts Cooperative where beadwork, jewelry, baskets, textiles, and the pueblo's special thick-walled red-and-black pottery can be purchased. One of the more picturesque of the pueblos along the Rio Grande, it has two handsome kivas and a French Romanesque–style church, built in the 19th century by Italian stonemasons who modeled it after the St. Francis Cathedral in Santa Fe. The pueblo also conducts public bingo games, and its Tewa Restaurant, near the center of the old village, is the only restaurant serving Native American specialties within the Eight Northern Pueblos. The pueblo has fishing ponds open in the spring and summer, with permits available on the sites. Its feast day is June 24. At Christmas, the San Juan dancers perform the Matachines dance, a colorful adaptation of a Spanish morality play based on the conquest of Mexico. *Box 1099, San Juan 87566, tel. 505/852–4400. Admission free. Open daily. No video cameras, tape recording, or sketching allowed. Still cameras are allowed by permit ($5 per camera), which can be bought weekdays from 8 to 4:30 at the San Juan Pueblo tribal office (behind the post office).*

Taos Pueblo

The Taos-Tiwa Native Americans have lived in the Taos Pueblo for almost 1,000 years. It is the largest existing multistory pueblo structure in the United States and has become Taos's number-one tourist attraction. For full coverage, *see* Exploring Taos in Chapter 4.

Pueblos Near Albuquerque

Sports enthusiasts from Albuquerque regularly escape the confines of urban life to fish in the well-stocked lakes and reservoirs of the nearby pueblos. The legendary Acoma "Sky City" Pueblo, probably the most spectacular of the pueblo communities, is a short drive from the city.

Acoma Pueblo

Situated atop a 357-foot mesa that rises abruptly from the valley floor, Acoma Pueblo deserves its name, Sky City. The pueblo was built more than a thousand years before the Spanish conquistadores discovered it while searching for the Seven Cities of Cibola. Captain Hernando de Alvarado of Coronado's Expedition of 1540, the first European to see Acoma, reported that he had "found a rock with a village on top, the strongest position ever seen in the world." However, the Acomas were defeated by a force sent by Governor Don Juan Onate in January of 1599. A smaller contingent of Spanish soldiers, led by Onate's nephew, Don Juan de Zaldívar, had been attacked by the Acomas. Only a few soldiers escaped; the rest were killed. A larger force of 70 men laid siege to the village for three days before they successfully conquered it. Then in 1629, Fray Juan Ramírez became Acoma's first permanent missionary. Father Ramírez built the incredible mission church of San Esteban del Rey at Sky City, with walls 60 feet high and 10 feet thick, between 1629 and 1641. By 1699, the Acomas had formally accepted the Spanish monks and their bearded Christ. Today, the pueblo is still inhabited, although its onetime population of 6,000 has dwindled to a mere 50 who live in the village without electricity or running water. (Acoma people from neighboring Acomita, Anzac, and McCarty return to their ancestral home during feast days and celebrations, the most important of which is on September 2.) A series of terraced adobe pueblos, dominated by the massive mission church of San Esteban del Rey, Acoma is by far the most spectacular of the pueblo communities. Although a widened road takes you there today, the pueblo was originally accessible only by a narrow path carved into the face of the rock; food and water had to be hauled up the sides of the cliffs. The Acoma Native Americans are known for their fine, thin-walled pottery, characterized by "Op Art" patterns and Mimbres (small animal and godlike figures) designs. Acoma, located 40 miles west of Albuquerque (12 mi off I–40), may be visited by guided tours only. A shuttle accommodating 16 passengers leaves every hour from the visitor center just below the mesa and drives to the top, where the tours are conducted on foot. At the visitor center there is also a museum, a restaurant, and a crafts shop. Nearby is the ubiquitous bingo hall. *Acoma Tourist Center, Box 309, Acoma 87034, tel. 505/252–1139. Admission: $6 adults, $5 senior citizens, $4 children 6–18. Open spring and summer, daily 8–7, tours daily 8–6; fall and winter, daily 8–4, tours daily 8–3:30. There is a $5 charge per camera for still photos. Movie and video cameras are prohibited.*

Isleta Pueblo

The original pueblo was abandoned during the Pueblo Revolt in 1680, when many of the Tiwa-speaking Isleta Native Americans fled to Hopi; they returned and built a new village in 1693, which stands where it did then, 13 miles south of Albuquerque off I–25. Isleta now consists of several communities spread out across the reservation, the largest of which is Shiawiba to the west of the Rio Grande. Visitors will find a bingo hall on the reservation, as well as picnicking and camping facilities and fishing at the Isleta Lakes and Recreation Area (*see* Camping in Chapter 5). Polychrome pottery with red-and-black designs on a white background is the specialty here. The pueblo celebrates with a Harvest dance on its feast day, September 4, in honor of St. Augustine. *Box 1270, Isleta 87022, tel. 505/869–3111. Open year-round. Admission free. Cameras prohibited. Camping, fishing, and picnicking permits available at Isleta Lakes.*

Laguna Pueblo

The Laguna Pueblo, 46 miles west of Albuquerque on old Route 66, consists of six scattered villages. It is one of the youngest and largest of the New Mexican pueblos, and one of the most enterprising, with such businesses as Laguna Industries (manufacturer of U.S. Army communications shelters). A large uranium field located on Laguna lands provided mining jobs for many of its members for years and is now the site of ongoing restoration through the Laguna Reclamation Project. The 1970s brought about a resurgence of interest in traditional crafts, so an abundance of fine pottery, decorated in geometric designs, is to be found in the area. The pueblo celebrates many feast days and dances (March 19, San José feast day; September 8, Virgin Mary feast day; October 17, Sts. Margaret and Mary feast day), since each of the six villages hosts its own ceremony, but all join at Old Laguna on September 19 to honor St. Joseph with Buffalo, Corn, and Eagle dances and a fair. Permits for fishing the pueblo's Paguate Reservoir can be obtained in Paguate village. *Box 194, Laguna Pueblo 87026, tel. 505/552–6654 or 505/243–7616. Open year-round. Admission free. Photography regulations vary in each village; contact the governor's office for information.*

Sandia Pueblo

The Sandia Pueblo was one of the pueblos that Francisco Coronado visited in 1540. It had been occupied since AD 1300; today, it has a population of 318 and covers 22,884 acres. The people have maintained their traditional lifestyle, their ceremonials and dances. Agriculture provides one strong source of income; others include the leasing of land for Albuquerque's aerial tramway; bingo (the tribal bingo hall is open seven nights a week); and the operation of fishing, boating, and picnicking facilities at Sandia Lakes. Although this is one of the more industrious of the Rio Grande Pueblos, its residents are not particularly well versed in traditional arts and crafts (most of the wares sold at its Bien Mur Indian Market Center on I–25 come from other pueblos and reservations). In fairness, the Sandia Pueblo does produce a variety of small, rough pottery pieces and some flat, traditional paintings. The pueblo's original Indian name was *Nafiat*, meaning "a dusty place." Coronado, the first European to visit, gave it the Spanish name *Sandía*—"watermelon"—for the bright-red watermelon hue of the surrounding mountains at sunset. The pueblo's patron saint is St. Anthony, whose feast day in June 13th—a day on which, traditionally, mothers bring their unmarried daughters to church to pray that he will find husbands for them. (It's also the day of the pueblo's major festival, the San Antonio Corn Dance.) The pueblo is off I–25, 10 miles north of Albuquerque. *Box 6008, Bernalillo 87004, tel. 505/867–9235, fax 505/867–9235. Open year-*

round. Admission free. Cameras, sketching, and recording prohibited.

San Felipe Pueblo

San Felipe is one of the most traditional and conservative of the pueblo communities. Ceremonial dances are performed several times a year; the most notable is the Green Corn dance on May 1, celebrating the feast of St. Philip, the pueblo's patron saint. Wearing symbolic costumes, hundreds of men, women, and children participate in the singing and dancing rituals that continue throughout the day. The plaza on the pueblo has been worn deep, like a rounded-out bowl, 3 feet below the surface of the surrounding ground, by years of dancing feet. San Felipe is located off I–25, between Albuquerque and Santa Fe, about 10 miles north of Bernalillo. *Box A, San Felipe Pueblo 87001, tel. 505/867–3381. Admission free. Open daily 9–6 except special feast days; closed days of religious celebrations. Cameras, sketching, and recording are prohibited.*

Santa Ana Pueblo

Except for ceremonial feast days, the Santa Ana Pueblo, located 8 miles northwest of Bernalillo on NM 44, appears to be empty most of the time because many members live in houses off the grounds. However, life returns to the pueblo with a passion on Santa Ana feast day, July 26, when the Corn dance is held. Craftspeople of the pueblo are noted for their woven belts and headbands, paintings, and pottery, all of which can be purchased through the pueblo's Cooperative Association (open Tues. and Thurs. 10–4:30). Tribal lands are currently being redeveloped, with agricultural projects and a new 27-hole golf course in the works. Since the pueblo is not always open to visitors, check with the tribal governor's office before making the trip. *Santa Ana, Star Rte., Box 37, Bernalillo 87004, tel. 505/867–3301. Admission free. Open Jan. 1 and 6, Easter Day, June 24 and 29, July 25 and 26, Dec. 25–28, and by appointment. Check with the governor's office for tribal rules regarding photography and recordings.*

Santo Domingo Pueblo

The Santo Domingo Pueblo operates a Tribal Cultural Center, where its outstanding *heishi* (shell) jewelry is sold, along with other traditional arts and crafts. Sales are also made from stands along the road, leading into the pueblo, which is located off I–25 at the Santo Domingo exit between Albuquerque and Santa Fe. Long a farming community, the Santo Domingo Pueblo is now developing commercial property along the interstate. It is the Santo Domingo Native Americans who are most often seen selling their wares beneath the portal of the Palace of the Governors on the Santa

Fe Plaza. The August 4 Corn dance is one of the most colorful and dramatic of all the pueblo ceremonial dances, often with more than 500 dancers, clowns, singers, and drummers participating. *Box 99, Santo Domingo 87052, tel. 505/465-2214 or 505/465-2645. Open daily sunrise–sunset. Admission free, but donations are encouraged. Cameras, recorders, and sketching materials prohibited.*

Zia Pueblo

The Zia Pueblo has existed at its present site, 17 miles northwest of Bernalillo on NM 44, since the early 1300s. The sun symbol appearing on the New Mexican flag was adopted from this ancient pueblo. Bird motifs, another easily recognized pueblo marking, adorn the fine polychrome ware produced by the skillful Zia potters. The tribe's painters are equally skilled, producing outstanding watercolors that are highly prized. A colorful Corn dance is held on August 15, the pueblo's annual feast day honoring St. Anthony. Permits for fishing in Zia Lake, about 2 miles west of the pueblo, may be purchased on the site. *Zia Pueblo, San Ysidro 87053, tel. 505/867-3304. Cameras, recorders, and sketching materials prohibited.*

Index

Fodor's Travel Guides

Available at bookstores everywhere, or call 1–800–533–6478, 24 hours a day.

Special Series

Fodor's Affordables

Caribbean

Europe

Florida

France

Germany

Great Britain

London

Italy

Paris

Fodor's Bed & Breakfast and Country Inns Guides

Canada's Great Country Inns

California

Cottages, B&Bs and Country Inns of England and Wales

Mid-Atlantic Region

New England

The Pacific Northwest

The South

The Southwest

The Upper Great Lakes Region

The West Coast

The Berkeley Guides

California

Central America

Eastern Europe

France

Germany

Great Britain & Ireland

Mexico

Pacific Northwest & Alaska

San Francisco

Fodor's Exploring Guides

Australia

Britain

California

The Caribbean

Florida

France

Germany

Ireland

Italy

London

New York City

Paris

Rome

Singapore & Malaysia

Spain

Thailand

Fodor's Flashmaps

New York

Washington, D.C.

Fodor's Pocket Guides

Bahamas

Barbados

Jamaica

London

New York City

Paris

Puerto Rico

San Francisco

Washington, D.C.

Fodor's Sports

Cycling

Hiking

Running

Sailing

The Insider's Guide to the Best Canadian Skiing

Skiing in the USA & Canada

Fodor's Three-In-Ones (guidebook, language cassette, and phrase book)

France

Germany

Italy

Mexico

Spain

Fodor's Special-Interest Guides

Accessible USA

Cruises and Ports of Call

Euro Disney

Halliday's New England Food Explorer

Healthy Escapes

London Companion

Shadow Traffic's New York Shortcuts and Traffic Tips

Sunday in New York

Walt Disney World and the Orlando Area

Walt Disney World for Adults

Fodor's Touring Guides

Touring Europe

Touring USA: Eastern Edition

Fodor's Vacation Planners

Great American Vacations

National Parks of the East

National Parks of the West

The Wall Street Journal Guides to Business Travel

Europe

International Cities

Pacific Rim

USA & Canada

WHEREVER YOU TRAVEL, *H*ELP IS NEVER FAR AWAY.

From planning your trip to providing travel assistance along the way, American Express® Travel Service Offices* are always there to help.

New Mexico

Albuquerque
Atlas Travel Service
1301 Wyoming, NE
(505) 291-6575

Roswell
Zink's Travel Reservation
500 North Main Street
(505) 622-3523

For the office nearest you, call
1-800-YES-AMEX

*Comprises Travel Service locations of American Express Travel Related Services Company, Inc., its affiliates and Representatives worldwide. © 1993 American Express Travel Related Services Company, Inc.

INTRODUCING

AT LAST, YOUR OWN PERSONALIZED LIST OF WHAT'S GOING ON IN THE CITIES YOU'RE VISITING.

KEYED TO THE DAYS WHEN YOU'RE THERE, CUSTOMIZED FOR YOUR INTERESTS, AND SENT TO YOU BEFORE YOU LEAVE HOME.

EXCLUSIVE FOR PURCHASERS OF FODOR'S GUIDES...

Fodor's WORLDVIEW
TRAVEL UPDATE

Introducing a revolutionary way to get customized, time-sensitive travel information just before your trip.

Now you can obtain detailed information about what's going on in each city you'll be visiting <u>before</u> you leave home—up-to-the-minute, objective information about the events and activities that interest you most.

Your Itinerary:
Customized reports available for 160 destinations

This is a special offer for purchasers of Fodor's guides – a customized Travel Update to fit your specific interests and your itinerary.

Travel Updates contain the kind of time-sensitive insider information you can get only from local contacts – or from city magazines and newspapers once you arrive. But now you can have the same information before you leave for your trip.

The choice is yours: current art exhibits, theater, music festivals and special concerts, sporting events, antiques and flower shows, shopping, fitness, and more.

The information comes from hundreds of correspondents and thousands of sources worldwide. Updated continuously, it's like having your own personal concierge or friend in the city.

You specify the cities and when you'll be there. We'll do the rest — personalizing the information for you the way no guidebook can.

It's the perfect extension to your Fodor's guide and the best way to make the most of your valuable travel time.

Re
Th
in th
doma
tion as
worthwh
the perfo
Tickets are
venue. Alte
mances are ca
given. For more
Open-Air Theatre,
NW1 4NP. Open A
Tel: 935-5756. Ends:
International Air Tattoo
Held biennially, the worl
military air display incl
demostra-
tions, militar
bands a

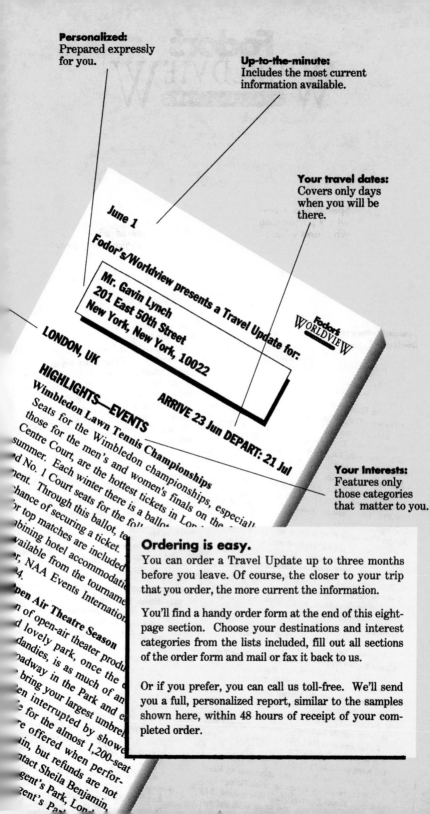

Personalized:
Prepared expressly for you.

Up-to-the-minute:
Includes the most current information available.

Your travel dates:
Covers only days when you will be there.

June 1

Fodor's/Worldview presents a Travel Update for:

Mr. Gavin Lynch
201 East 50th Street
New York, New York, 10022

Fodor's
WORLDVIEW

LONDON, UK

ARRIVE 23 Jun DEPART: 21 Jul

HIGHLIGHTS—EVENTS

Wimbledon Lawn Tennis Championships

Seats for the Wimbledon championships, especiall
those for the men's and women's finals on the
Centre Court, are the hottest tickets in Lo
summer. Each winter there is a ballo
d No. 1 Court seats for the foll
ent. Through this ballot, t
chance of securing a ticket.
r top matches are include
bining hotel accommodati
vailable from the tourname
r, NAA Events Internation
4.

pen Air Theatre Season
n of open-air theater produ
d lovely park, once the
dandies, is as much of an
oadway in the Park and e
bring your largest umbre
en interrupted by showe
e for the almost 1,200-seat
e offered when perfor-
ain, but refunds are not
ntact Sheila Benjamin,
gent's Park, Lon
gent's Pa

Your Interests:
Features only those categories that matter to you.

Ordering is easy.

You can order a Travel Update up to three months before you leave. Of course, the closer to your trip that you order, the more current the information.

You'll find a handy order form at the end of this eight-page section. Choose your destinations and interest categories from the lists included, fill out all sections of the order form and mail or fax it back to us.

Or if you prefer, you can call us toll-free. We'll send you a full, personalized report, similar to the samples shown here, within 48 hours of receipt of your completed order.

Fodor's
WORLDVIEW
TRAVEL UPDATE

**Special concerts—
who's performing
what and where**

**One-of-a-kind,
one-time-only events**

**Special interest,
in-depth listings**

Children — Events

Angel Canal Festival
The festivities include a children's funfair, entertainers, a boat rally and displays on the water. Regent's Canal. Islington. N1. Tube: Angel. Tel: 267 9100. 11:30am-5:30pm. 7/04.

Blackheath Summer Kite Festival
Stunt kite displays with parachuting teddy bears and trade stands. Free admission. SE3. BR: Blackheath. 10am. 6/27.

Megabugs
Children will delight in this infestation of giant robotic insects, including a praying mantic 60 times life size. Mon-Sat 10am-6pm; Sun 11am-6pm. Admission 4.50 pounds. Natural History Museum, Cromwell Road. SW7. Tube: South Kensington. Tel: 938 9123. Ends 10/01.

Childminders
This establishment employs only women, providing nurses and qualified nannies to

Music — Jazz & Blues

Tito Puente's Golden Men of Latin Jazz
The father of mambo and Cuban rumba king comes to town. Royal Festival Hall. South Bank. SE1. Tube: Waterloo. Tel: 928 8800. 8pm. 7/15.

Georgie Fame and The New York Band
Riding a popular tide with his latest album, the smoky-voiced Fame and his keyboard are on a tour yet again. The Grand. Clapham Junction. SW11. BR: Clapham Junction. Tel: 738 9000. 7:30pm. 7/07.

Jacques Loussier Play Bach Trio
The French jazz classicist and colleagues. Kenwood Lakeside. Hampstead Lane. Kenwood. NW3. Tube: Golders Green, then bus 210. Tel: 413 1443. 7pm. 7/10.

Tony Bennett and Ronnie Scott
Royal Festival Hall. South Bank. SE1. Tube: Waterloo. Tel: 928 8800. 8pm. 7/11.

Santana
Royal Festival Hall. South Bank. SE1. Tube: Waterloo. Tel: 928 8800. 8pm. 7/12.

Count Basie Orchestra and Nancy Wilson Trio
Royal Festival Hall. South Bank. SE1. Tube: Waterloo. Tel: 928 8800. 8pm. 7/14.

King Pleasure and the Biscuit Boys
Royal Festival Hall. South Bank. SE1. Tube: Waterloo. Tel: 928 8800. 6:30 and 9pm. 7/16.

Al Green and the London Community Gospel Choir
Royal Festival Hall. South Bank. SE1. Tube: Waterloo. Tel: 928 8800. 8pm. 7/13.

BB King and Linda Hopkins
Mother of the blues and successor to Bessie Smith, Hopkins meets up with "Blues Boy" King. Royal Festival Hall. South Bank. SE1. Tel: 928 8800. 6:30 and 9pm.

Music — Classical

Marylebone Sinfonia
Kenneth Gowen conducts music by Puccini and Rossini. Queen Elizabeth Hall. South Bank. SE1. Tube: Waterloo. Tel: 928 8800. 7:45pm. 7/16.

London Philharmonic
Franz Welser-Moest and George Benjamin conduct selections by Alexander Goehr, Messiaen, and some of Benjamin's own compositions. Queen Elizabeth Hall. South Bank. SE1. Tube: Waterloo. Tel: 928 8800. 8pm.

London Pro Arte Orchestra and Forest Choir
Murray Stewart conducts selections by Rossini, Haydn and Jonathan Willcocks. Queen Elizabeth Hall. South Bank. SE1. Tube: Waterloo. Tel: 928 8800. 7:45pm.

Kensington Symphony Orchestra
Russell Keable conducts Dvorak's Requiem. Queen Elizabeth Hall. South Bank.

Here's what you get . . .

Detailed information about what's going on — precisely when you'll be there.

Show openings during your visit

Reviews by local critics

Exhibitions & Shows—Antique & Flower

Westminster Antiques Fair

Over 50 stands with pre-1830 furniture and other Victorian and earlier items. Thu-Fri 11am-8pm; Sat-Sun 11am-6pm. Admission 4 pounds, children free. Old Royal Horticultural Hall. Vincent Square. SW1. Tel: 0444/48 25 14. 6-24 thru 6/27.

Royal Horticultural Society Flower Show

The show includes displays of carnations, summer fruit and vegetables. Tue 11am-7pm; Wed 10am-5pm. Admission Tue 4 pounds, Wed 2 pounds. Royal Horticultural Halls. Greycoat Street and Vincent Square. SW1. Tube: Victoria. 7/20 thru 7/21.

Hampton Court Palace International Flower Show

Major international garden and flower show taking place in conjunction with the British

Theater — Musical

Sunset Boulevard

In June, the four Andrew Lloyd Webber musicals which dominated London's stages in the 1980s (Cats, Starlight Express, Phantom of the Opera and Aspects of Love) are joined by the composer's latest work, a show rumored to have his best music to date. The 1950 Billy Wilder film about a helpless young writer who is drawn into the world of a possessive, aging silent screen star offers rich opportunities for Webber's evolving style. Soaring, aching melodies, lush technical effects and psychological thrills are all expected. Patti Lupone stars. Mon-Sat at 8pm; matinee Thu-Sat at 3pm. In-person sales only at the box office; credit card bookings, Tel: 344 0055. Admission 15-32.50 pounds. Adelphi Theatre. The Strand. WC2. Tube: Charing Cross. Tel: 836 7611. Starts: 6/21

Leonardo A Portrait of Love

A new musical about the great Renaissance artist and inventor comes in for a London premiere, tested by a brief run at Oxford's Old Fire Station in autumn. The work explores the relationship of Vinci and the woman

Alberquerque • Atlanta • Atlantic City • N
Baltimore • Boston • Chicago • Cincinnati
Cleveland • Dallas/Ft.Worth • Denver • De
• Houston • Kansas City • Las Vegas • Los
Angeles • Memphis • Miami • Milwaukee •
New Orleans • New York City • Orlando •
Springs • Philadelphia • Phoenix • Pittsburg
Portland • Salt Lake • San Antonio • San Di
San Franc • Seattle • St. Louis • Tamp
Oslo • Was • nlu • Island •
Hawaii • Kauai • Maui • Abacos • Bimini
Ber • Countryside • Hamilton • Islan
Antigua & B • lla
Gorda • Barbados • Dominica • Gren
ucia • St. Vincent • Trinidad &Tobago
ymans • Puerto Plata • Santo Doming
Aruba • Bonaire • Curacao • St. Mac
ec City • Montreal • Ottawa • Toron
Vancouver • Guadeloupe • Martiniqu
eleny • St. Martin • Kingston • Ixta
o Bay • Negril • Ocho Rios • Ponce
n • Grand Turk • Providenciales • S
St. John • St. Thomas • Acapulco •
& Isla Mujeres • Cozumel • Guadal
• Los Cabos • Manzanillo • Mazatl
City • Monterrey • Oaxaca • Puerto
do • Puerto Vallarta • Veracruz • Ix
dam • Athens • Barcelona • Berlin
• Budapest

Fodor's WORLDVIEW
TRAVEL UPDATE

Spectator Sports — Other Sports

Greyhound Racing: Wembley Stadium

This dog track offers good views of greyhound racing held on Mon, Wed and Fri. No credit cards. Stadium Way. Wembley. HA9. Tube: Wembley Park. Tel: 902 8833.

Benson & Hedges Cricket Cup Final

Lord's Cricket Ground. St. John's Wood Road. NW8. Tube: St. John's Wood. Tel: 289 1611. 11am. 7/10.

Press-Fax & Overnight Mail

Post Office, Trafalgar Square Branch

Offers a network of fax services, the Intelpost system, throughout the country and abroad. Mon-Sat 8am-8pm, Sun 9am-5pm. William IV Street. WC2. Tube: Charing Cross. Tel: 930 9580.

Interest Categories

For <u>your</u> personalized Travel Update, choose the categories you're most interested in from this list. Every Travel Update automatically provides you with *Event Highlights* – the best of what's happening during the dates of your trip.

1.	**Business Services**	Fax & Overnight Mail, Computer Rentals, Photocopying, Secretarial , Messenger, Translation Services
	Dining	
2.	**All Day Dining**	Breakfast & Brunch, Cafes & Tea Rooms, Late-Night Dining
3.	**Local Cuisine**	In Every Price Range—from Budget Restaurants to the Special Splurge
4.	**European Cuisine**	Continental, French, Italian
5.	**Asian Cuisine**	Chinese, Far Eastern, Japanese, Indian
6.	**Americas Cuisine**	American, Mexican & Latin
7.	**Nightlife**	Bars, Dance Clubs, Comedy Clubs, Pubs & Beer Halls
8.	**Entertainment**	Theater—Drama, Musicals, Dance, Ticket Agencies
9.	**Music**	Classical, Traditional & Ethnic, Jazz & Blues, Pop, Rock
10.	**Children's Activities**	Events, Attractions
11.	**Tours**	Local Tours, Day Trips, Overnight Excursions, Cruises
12.	**Exhibitions, Festivals & Shows**	Antiques & Flower, History & Cultural, Art Exhibitions, Fairs & Craft Shows, Music & Art Festivals
13.	**Shopping**	Districts & Malls, Markets, Regional Specialities
14.	**Fitness**	Bicycling, Health Clubs, Hiking, Jogging
15.	**Recreational Sports**	Boating/Sailing, Fishing, Ice Skating, Skiing, Snorkeling/Scuba, Swimming
16.	**Spectator Sports**	Auto Racing, Baseball, Basketball, Football, Horse Racing, Ice Hockey, Soccer

Please note that interest category content will vary by season, destination, and length of stay.

Destinations

The Fodor's/Worldview Travel Update covers more than 160 destinations worldwide. Choose the destinations that match your itinerary from this list. (Choose bulleted destinations only.)

United States (Mainland)
- Albuquerque
- Atlanta
- Atlantic City
- Baltimore
- Boston
- Chicago
- Cincinnati
- Cleveland
- Dallas/Ft. Worth
- Denver
- Detroit
- Houston
- Kansas City
- Las Vegas
- Los Angeles
- Memphis
- Miami
- Milwaukee
- Minneapolis/ St. Paul
- New Orleans
- New York City
- Orlando
- Palm Springs
- Philadelphia
- Phoenix
- Pittsburgh
- Portland
- St. Louis
- Salt Lake City
- San Antonio
- San Diego
- San Francisco
- Seattle
- Tampa
- Washington, DC

Alaska
- Anchorage/Fairbanks/Juneau

Hawaii
- Honolulu
- Island of Hawaii
- Kauai
- Maui

Canada
- Quebec City
- Montreal
- Ottawa
- Toronto
- Vancouver

Bahamas
- Abacos
- Eleuthera/ Harbour Island
- Exumas
- Freeport
- Nassau & Paradise Island

Bermuda
- Bermuda Countryside
- Hamilton

British Leeward Islands
- Anguilla
- Antigua & Barbuda
- Montserrat
- St. Kitts & Nevis

British Virgin Islands
- Tortola & Virgin Gorda

British Windward Islands
- Barbados
- Dominica
- Grenada
- St. Lucia
- St. Vincent
- Trinidad & Tobago

Cayman Islands
- The Caymans

Dominican Republic
- Puerto Plata
- Santo Domingo

Dutch Leeward Islands
- Aruba
- Bonaire
- Curacao

Dutch Windward Islands
- St. Maarten

French West Indies
- Guadeloupe
- Martinique
- St. Barthelemy
- St. Martin

Jamaica
- Kingston
- Montego Bay
- Negril
- Ocho Rios

Puerto Rico
- Ponce
- San Juan

Turks & Caicos
- Grand Turk
- Providenciales

U.S. Virgin Islands
- St. Croix
- St. John
- St. Thomas

Mexico
- Acapulco
- Cancun & Isla Mujeres
- Cozumel
- Guadalajara
- Ixtapa & Zihuatanejo
- Los Cabos
- Manzanillo
- Mazatlan
- Mexico City
- Monterrey
- Oaxaca
- Puerto Escondido
- Puerto Vallarta
- Veracruz

Europe
- Amsterdam
- Athens
- Barcelona
- Berlin
- Brussels
- Budapest
- Copenhagen
- Dublin
- Edinburgh
- Florence
- Frankfurt
- French Riviera
- Geneva
- Glasgow
- Interlaken
- Istanbul
- Lausanne
- Lisbon
- London
- Madrid
- Milan
- Moscow
- Munich
- Oslo
- Paris
- Prague
- Provence
- Rome
- Salzburg
- St. Petersburg
- Stockholm
- Venice
- Vienna
- Zurich

Pacific Rim Australia & New Zealand
- Auckland
- Melbourne
- Sydney

China
- Beijing
- Guangzhou
- Shanghai

Japan
- Kyoto
- Nagoya
- Osaka
- Tokyo
- Yokohama

Other
- Bangkok
- Hong Kong & Macau
- Manila
- Seoul
- Singapore
- Taipei

Fodor's
WORLDVIEW Order Form
TRAVEL UPDATE

THIS TRAVEL UPDATE IS FOR (Please print):

Name		
Address		
City	**State**	**ZIP**
Country	**Tel #** ( ) -	

Title of this Fodor's guide:

Store and location where guide was purchased:

INDICATE YOUR DESTINATIONS/DATES: Write in below the destinations you want to order. Then fill in your arrival and departure dates for each destination.

		Month Day		Month Day
(Sample) LONDON	From:	6 / 21	To:	6 / 30
1	From:	/	To:	/
2	From:	/	To:	/
3	From:	/	To:	/

You can order up to three destinations per Travel Update. Only destinations listed on the previous page are applicable. Maximum amount of time covered by a Travel Update cannot exceed 30 days.

CHOOSE YOUR INTERESTS: Select up to eight categories from the list of interest categories shown on the previous page and circle the numbers below:

1   2   3   4   5   6   7   8   9   10   11   12   13   14   15   16

CHOOSE HOW YOU WANT YOUR TRAVEL UPDATE DELIVERED (Check one):

❑ Please mail my Travel Update to the address above **OR**

❑ Fax it to me at **Fax #** ( ) -

DELIVERY CHARGE (Check one)

	Within U.S. & Canada	Outside U.S. & Canada
First Class Mail	❑ $2.50	❑ $5.00
Fax	❑ $5.00	❑ $10.00
Priority Delivery	❑ $15.00	❑ $27.00

All orders will be sent within 48 hours of receipt of a completed order form.

ADD UP YOUR ORDER HERE. *SPECIAL OFFER FOR FODOR'S PURCHASERS ONLY!*

	Suggested Retail Price	Your Price	This Order
First destination ordered	$13.95	$ 7.95	$ 7.95
Second destination (if applicable)	$ 9.95	$ 4.95	+
Third destination (if applicable)	$ 9.95	$ 4.95	+
Plus delivery charge from above			+
		TOTAL:	$

METHOD OF PAYMENT (Check one): ❑ AmEx   ❑ MC   ❑ Visa   ❑ Discover
❑ Personal Check   ❑ Money Order

Make check or money order payable to: Fodor's Worldview Travel Update

Credit Card # _____ **Expiration Date:** _____

Authorized Signature

SEND THIS COMPLETED FORM TO:
Fodor's Worldview Travel Update, 114 Sansome Street, Suite 700, San Francisco, CA 94104

OR CALL OR FAX US 24-HOURS A DAY
Telephone **1-800-799-9609** • Fax **1-800-799-9619** (From within the U.S. & Canada)
(Outside the U.S. & Canada: Telephone 415-616-9988 • Fax 415-616-9989)

(Please have this guide in front of you when you call so we can verify purchase.)

Offer valid until 12/31/94.